Crisis on the Danube

CRISIS ON THE DANUBE

Napoleon's Austrian Campaign of 1809

James R. Arnold

ARMS AND
ARMOUR

First published in Great Britain in 1990 by Arms and Armour
Press, Villiers House, 41-47 Strand, London WC2N 5JE.

Published in the United States by Paragon House

British Library Cataloguing in Publication Data
Arnold, James R. *1952–*
Crisis on the Danube : Napoleon's Austrian campaign of 1809.
1. Napoleonic wars.   Franco-Austrian campaign
I. Title
940.27

ISBN 1-85409-083-6

Manufactured in the United States of America

Contents

Acknowledgments

This book would never have been completed and published without the timely help of a number of people. The six-year path from inception to completion has had many detours. Professional and emotional support from others has seen the project through. I thank you all.

Mr. and Mrs. R. C. Arnold, whose early and constant encouragement of my historical pursuits included a Parisian vacation timed to coincide with Napoleon's bicentennial, gave me the background from which all else has stemmed.

Christopher Bigler read and reread the manuscript, correcting flaws, reinforcing strengths. A superb editor, he gave much of himself and the book is infinitely better for his efforts.

Professor David Chandler of the Royal Military Academy, Sandhurst, read early draft chapters and encouraged me to persevere. He graciously lent the book's title from his *Campaigns of Napoleon*. It well describes the situation Napoleon faced in 1809, and is a fine, illustrative example of David's outstanding synthetic thinking.

Richard Hasenauer lent his professional skills to many of the book's maps.

Philip Haythornthwaite provided a key link in the tortuous chain that led to publication. He also contributed excellent photographs culled from his extensive archives. Without him this book would not have seen the light of day.

Fritz Heinzen reviewed draft chapters, offered pithy comments, and most importantly recommended me to the publisher. He too was indispensible.

I also thank the people at Paragon House for having the confidence to support this project, in particular Charles Decker and Ken Stuart. My editors, Laura Greeney and Andy DeSalvo, contributed professional skill and unflagging good cheer even during moments of difficulty.

John Slonaker of the U.S. Army Military History Institute in Carlisle, Pennsylvania, helped mightily by locating obscure references and allowing me to use them.

Ralph Reinertsen urged me to press on when it seemed publication was a distant fantasy.

Dr. Gunther Rothenberg, the foremost English-language expert on Karl and his army, offered expert opinion when answering my many inquiries about the Austrian Army.

Finally, and foremost, I am deeply grateful for unswerving support from my life companion and wife, Roberta Wiener. Her map-reading skills led us true during our two trips to Bavaria, and her map-making talents came forward in the breach. She provided topnotch editing and proofreading as well as business acumen. No writer could have a better colleague.

Maps

References to towns and villages use the spelling from an 1811 Austrian map with two notable exceptions, the French names Eckmühl (Eggmühl) and Ratisbonne (Regensburg).

German spellings are used for Austrian names and ranks, although the English translation Archduke (*Erzherzog*) is used. *Kaiser* is German for Emperor. The following provides an explanation of Austrian officer rankings and designations.

Generalissimus	Commander in chief of field armies
FM (Feldmarschall)	Field Marshal
FZM (Feldzeugmeister)	Full General (Infantry)
GdK (General der Cavalerie)	Full General (Cavalry)
FML (Feldmarschall-Leutenant)	Lieutenant General
GM (General-Feldwachtmeister)	Major General
Inhaber	Regimental proprietor

Maps

Foreword

The Austrian campaign of 1809 holds many interesting features and special aspects for the student of Napoleon and his times. After Great Britain, Austria was indubitably France's most stubborn opponent—but, unlike London, Vienna was occupied by conquering armies on two occasions (1805 and 1809); and, unlike "the Nation of Shopkeepers," the Austrian people were twice forced to acquiesce to a conqueror's terms, by the treaties of Pressburg (26 December 1805) and Vienna (14 October 1809), and twice more to accept unfavorable peaces (Camp Formio, 17 October 1797, and Luneville, 9 February 1801). Small wonder that the Emperor Francis (1768–1835) looked older than his years: in 1806 he had to agree to the abolition of the Holy Roman Empire, of which he was titular head as Francis II, and accept the lesser title of Emperor of Austria and Hungary with the title of Francis I, probably the only example in history of a monarch losing a number after his name. The main cause of all these woes was, of course, one man—the dynamic, ruthless, and supremely able Napoleon Bonaparte. How Francis I took to additionally becoming his Corsican scourge's father-in-law from 1810 is tactfully not recorded (royal marriages were, after all, matters of high policy) but his attitude toward his returned daughter, Marie-Louise, and toward his infant grandson, the King of Rome (1811–1832) from their transfer to Austria in mid-1814 seems to have been correct enough, although neither was permitted any contact with the Exile of St. Helena.

But this is to diverge from the subject of this present book and to anticipate historical events. The year 1809 would see Austria re-enter the lists against the

Napoleonic empire with great determination and a retrained and reorganized army led (under the Emperor) by his able brother Feldmarschall the Archduke Charles, Duke of Teschen (1771–1847). Charles was an able reformer and a gifted commander—none from any country (save, arguably, the Duke of Wellington, who was no reformer) proving more of a match for the redoubtable Napoleon, who was to be more than a little extended during the various phases of the campaign in the Danube Valley in 1809. Indeed, the Emperor was to suffer his first major defeat at Aspern-Essling in May at the hands of the Archduke, and although he would wreak a full revenge at Wagram two months later, he had to accord the epileptic Austrian prince a large measure of respect.

James Arnold examines the first half of the Franco-Austrian War of 1809 in the present book. It covers the political and diplomatic background to the struggle; the Austrian preemptive strike of 9 April against Francophile Bavaria without any declaration of war; and the initial French wrong-footed reaction as Marshal Berthier, the model chief of staff, tried somewhat inadequately to come to terms with the extra responsibility (made all the more difficult through the faulty transmission of a vital message) of commanding the army in his emperor's continued absence in Paris ("In this position of affairs I greatly desire the arrival of your Majesty," he wrote plaintively on 16 April); Napoleon's very welcome arrival at headquarters on 17 April leads straight on to Napoleon's subsequent brilliant counterstroke of 20 April to 3 May—one of the finest periods of fighting in his whole career—leading to the French occupation of Vienna on the thirteenth. By any standard this is a thrilling period of military history, and the author does it full justice in what must be one of the most thorough accounts and analyses to have appeared in recent years. In addition, besides his interesting study of Napoleon and such great military figures as Marshals Davout and Masséna (not to forget poor Berthier) and of the Emperor Francis I and his brother the Archduke Charles, we are treated to fascinating insights into such devious characters as the wily Talleyrand and the ruthless Count Metternich, playing between them the cunning diplomatic game. This is an equally important aspect of the book, for as Karl von Clausewitz was to write a little later, "War is the continuation of politics by other means."

All this and much more—including details of the rival armies' organization and equipment—will be found in the chapters that follow. Given his mastery of his subject, his feeling for the period, and his intimate knowledge of the actual ground, it is to be hoped that James Arnold will continue his studies to give us a second volume on 1809, covering events on the distant but interrelated Italian front, the important battles beside the fast-flowing Danube of Aspern-Essling and then—on to the great climax of 1809 in Central Europe, and arguably Napoleon's last major victory—Wagram. It is clear from this present volume that no modern American writer could do these subjects greater justice, and the reader is bound to clamor for more, as indeed I do.

DAVID G. CHANDLER

July 6, 1989
(180th Anniversary of the second
day of the Battle of Wagram)

Head, Department of War Studies,
Royal Military Academy, Sandhurst

CHAPTER I

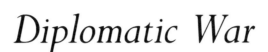

Diplomatic War

Ambassadors are, in the full meaning of the term, titled spies. [*]

Setting the Stage

The French

Napoleon Bonaparte Forty years old in 1809, Emperor of France.

Karl Talleyrand-Perigord Fifty-five, Prince of Benevent, Grand Elector, Minister of Foreign Affairs. Along with Metternich the foremost diplomat of his day. Lame, worldly, a supreme realist, a man of genius with a taste for conspiracy.

Joseph Fouché Forty-six, Duke of Otranto, Minister of Police; commands the French secret police.

The Austrians

Kaiser Franz I Forty-one, kaiser since 1792, he has unsuccessfully waged war against France throughout his reign, losing large parcels of Hapsburg territory with each defeat. A stubborn, conservative man opposed to all change and interested only in preserving the monarchy. Proceeds cautiously in his relations with France but can be swept up by the war passions of his wife and advisers.

[*] The quotations that begin each chapter are from Napoleon.

1

Clemens Metternich-Winneburg Thirty-six, Austria's ambassador to France. No man in Europe better understands Napoleon. His advice and analysis greatly influence Austria's plans.

Johann Philip Stadion Forty-six, foreign minister and leader of the war party; the power behind the throne.

The Russians

Czar Alexander I Thirty-two, emperor since 1801, the young czar is idealistic and exceedingly impressionable, a fact recognized by those who know him, including Napoleon. The likelihood of war between Austria and France hinges on his attitude toward the rival powers.

Among continental European powers no country opposed France so often as Austria. Between 1792 and 1809 Austria fought three wars against the French. The French Revolution of 1789 gave birth to a new human spirit that the conservative Hapsburg leaders of the Austrian Empire had to suppress. During the revolutionary wars from 1792–1801, Austria strove mightily to crush France and stop the spread of her revolutionary fever. Numerous large and indecisive battles occurred along the Rhine. Only in Italy did battle yield important results. A young, unknown general named Napoleon Bonaparte led the French in a dynamic campaign from the Mediterranean shores to the mountain passes leading to Vienna. Defeated and humiliated, Austria agreed to peace terms.

Propelled by martial success and public acclaim, Bonaparte became one of a triumvirate of French rulers. Austria and her allies challenged France again in 1800. Bonaparte decisively defeated the Austrians on the plains of Marengo in Italy, a victory that solidified his status as first among equals in the French government. In 1804 Bonaparte discarded revolutionary pretext and became Napoleon I, Emperor of France.

Austria entered a new coalition aimed against France in 1805. In another brilliant campaign, beginning on the Rhine, sweeping through Vienna, and ending near the small village of Austerlitz in Czechoslovakia, Napoleon once more decisively defeated the Austrians and their Russian allies. Three wars, three bitter defeats over a thirteen-year period, and Austria remained hostile. She ached for revenge.

Meanwhile, an increasingly despotic Napoleon spread French influence until it stretched from Poland through Germany south into Italy (see Map 1). The peoples of Europe greeted French hegemony in mixed fashion. Some welcomed French-inspired liberal reforms. Others chafed under the commer-

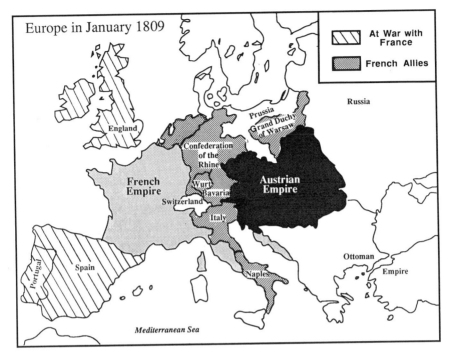

Europe in January 1809

At War with France

French Allies

Russia

Prussia

Grand Duchy of Warsaw

England

Confederation of the Rhine

French Empire

Wurt

Bavaria

Switzerland

Austrian Empire

Italy

Portugal

Spain

Naples

Ottoman

Empire

Mediterranean Sea

cial restrictions caused by France's ceaseless conflict with Britain. A small but vocal minority grew increasingly restive.

Background to Betrayal

Vienna, December 1805

Although the ink on the Treaty of Pressburg was barely dry, Count Johann Philip Stadion was thinking of war and revenge, not about peace. Indeed, few Austrians could be happy with the harsh terms of the treaty. But with one army surrendered, Vienna occupied, and their last hope erased slightly more than three weeks before in the bloody snows of Austerlitz, even the most patriotic Austrians recognized the need for a breathing spell. Stadion tolerated the peace terms embodied in the Treaty of Pressburg because they provided a necessary respite. Austria, bereft of any military leverage, had been forced to accept Napoleon's strict terms. She relinquished most Venetian territory, ceded all south German possessions, and—most humiliating of all—gave the Vorarlberg and the Tyrol (Map 2) to the detested Bavarians.

Stadion sensed one anomaly in the treaty: French financial demands were

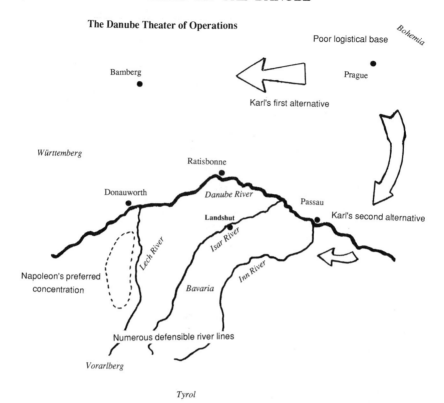

The Danube Theater of Operations

surprisingly low. Apparently his French counterpart, Talleyrand, had persuaded Napoleon to ask for far less money than Napoleon had originally intended. Stadion wondered why. In any event, to men like Stadion the treaty meant a period for reorganization and preparation, not a final judgment on the relationship between the Hapsburg empire and the upstart so-called Imperial France.

Vienna, December 1805
Schönbrunn Palace

From his residence at the Schönbrunn Palace Kaiser Franz begins the disagreeable task of writing to the Russian Czar, Alexander. He describes the Treaty of Pressburg as "a capitulation before an enemy who pressed home his advantages to the full. The sorry state of affairs has forced me to abandon part of my provinces, so that I may preserve the rest."[1] In effect, the treaty meant Franz abandoned more than just territory. He lost his preeminent position as emperor of the Holy Roman Empire and with it the dominant influence in Germany that Austria had enjoyed for centuries.[2] It was a bitter outcome to a war for which he had held such high hopes.

Berlin, January 1806

At the start of the new year the rising young star of Austrian diplomatic circles, Count Clemens Metternich, writes Stadion: "The consequences of the Treaty of Pressburg seem to me incalculable. . . . Your Excellency will be convinced that the attempts of Bonaparte to crush us . . . even at a time when we are no longer his enemy, are as active as ever."[3] With this report Metternich emerges as one of Napoleon's most implacable and dangerous enemies.

Paris, Winter 1806

Having returned to the comforts of Paris, Talleyrand also reflects on recent developments. He has just turned down a substantial Austrian bribe to mark appreciation for services rendered at Pressburg and hopes for future considerations. For now he remains, in his way, loyal to Napoleon.

Yet, examining his mail, he reads a letter from Napoleon complaining that the terms of Pressburg are greatly hampering the Emperor's plans. Talleyrand receives this with satisfaction, since hampering the Emperor's ambitions fits exactly his own plan. His vision for France rests upon a peaceful equilibrium among Europe's major powers. Napoleon's military prowess constantly threatens this vision. His victories make France supreme while creating vengeful opponents who lust for another chance to take France down. Thus Talleyrand turns to diplomatic means to try to construct a complex web of alliances and treaties to restrain the Emperor.

Vienna, Summer 1806
Schönbrunn Palace

Kaiser Franz is satisfied that his country is slowly recovering from defeat. News of the ill-advised Prussian declaration of war against France tests his peaceful resolve. Immediately hotheads in the Hapsburg entourage advocate joining ranks with their Germanic brethren. Although the Austrian army has entered a period of reform in response to the debacle of Austerlitz, the Archduke Karl, Franz's brother, fervently counsels against any action. Karl argues that the army requires a more complete overhaul. So Franz waits and watches, contenting himself with ordering an army of observation into Bohemia.

Paris, Summer 1806

Surveying his map, Talleyrand is gratified that Austria has taken his advice. Because of his foresight there is an Austrian presence in Bohemia that might check Napoleon's exploitation following the Emperor's remarkable victory at Jena–Auerstadt. With this newest victory Napoleon has conquered most of Prussia and is poised to advance into Poland. Talleyrand fears that Napoleon's ambitions are boundless.

Vienna, February 1807
Schönbrunn Palace

News of a French check (many call it a defeat) at Eylau in Poland brings renewed pressure on Franz to re-enter the lists against Napoleon. Russia has joined Prussia against Napoleon and her soldiers have fought magnificently at Eylau. So now Franz replies to Russian overtures for alliance with the admonition to beat the French twice more—and then Austria will declare war against France.

Tilsit, June–July 1807

Having triumphed on the battlefield yet again, Napoleon arranges a series of meetings with the young Czar Alexander. The French Emperor strains every nerve to make a positive impression upon the susceptible Russian. He seemingly succeeds on 7 July, when a peace treaty, agreement of alliance, and secret articles are signed. Believing that the aura he has spun around the Czar will persist once the two separate, Napoleon is convinced Russia will serve as a loyal counterweight against Austria. Accordingly, with France's boundaries in Central Europe secure, Napoleon returns to Paris to plan how to deal with the last stubborn opponent, England.

St. Petersburg, Summer 1807

German nationalists, Russian patriots, and British diplomats work to alter the Czar's favorable impression of Imperial France. With the passage of time the effect of Napoleon's personal magnetism wears off, and their efforts begin to influence Alexander's world view.

Paris, Summer 1807

Metternich arrives to become the Austrian ambassador to France. He sends his appraisal of the new strategic situation resulting from Tilsit and the subsequent establishment of the Confederation of the Rhine. The Confederation, a French-inspired union of numerous small German principalities located in central Germany, provides a buffer between France and her potential enemies (see Map 1). Although not a military man, Metternich displays brilliant intuition by predicting where war will break out two years before the event: "The Confederation of the Rhine embraces us on both sides. Any war with France would begin on the borders of the Inn. . . . Our position is infinitely worse by the Treaties of Tilsit; but the monarchy is intact and defined."[4]

Vienna, Late summer 1807
Schönbrunn Palace

Kaiser Franz reflects upon Napoleon's recent triumphs and realizes that his prevarication regarding an alliance with Russia last winter has been vindicated. At Stadion's suggestion, he concurs that the major Austrian diplomatic objective must be to determine the extent of the secret articles of the Tilsit agreement and what they portend for Austria. Stadion reports that Metternich will throw his considerable talents and energies toward solving this mystery. Meanwhile, in Austria proper, the Archduke Karl will continue with military reforms.

Paris, Summer 1807

Talleyrand, now the Prince of Benevent, unexpectedly resigns his portfolio of minister of foreign affairs.[5] Recognizing the Tilsit agreement has buoyed the Emperor's already considerable self-confidence, the Prince is frustrated that his councils go unheeded and is concerned about the fate of France. He has tried and failed to convince Napoleon that the Franco-Russian entente is ephemeral; his warnings that the stirrings of German nationalism and Napoleon's growing struggle with the Pope are making France a pariah throughout Europe are also scorned. Napoleon's apparent desire to meddle in the Iberian Peninsula convinces Talleyrand that the Emperor's designs are not in the interests of France. The prince considers what can be done to check Napoleon's swollen power and appetite. Any opposition will not escape the surveillance of Napoleon's well-informed secret police. Talleyrand therefore ponders how to approach and co-opt Fouché, head of the secret police.

Paris, Summer 1807
The Tuileries

Napoleon welcomes Talleyrand's resignation; his meddling and harassment have become increasingly annoying. Freed from Talleyrand's restraint, Napoleon instructs his new foreign minister, de Champagny, to inform the Portuguese ambassador that Portugal's ports must be closed to British trade. De

Champagny explains to the ambassador that Portugal's failure to comply would mean war. To reinforce this threat, on 2 August 1807 Napoleon directs his friend the reliable fire-eater General Andoche Junot to form a French corps of observation on the Spanish border. The fatal first steps toward the Spanish Ulcer have been taken.

Paris, August 1807

The rumple-dressed but sharp-minded Minister of Police, Joseph Fouché, considers two interrelated issues: Where is the French Empire headed and what does it portend for Joseph Fouché? He knows that all power in France rests in one man, the Emperor Napoleon. For the past several years it has become increasingly apparent that no successor will result from the Emperor's marriage to the aging Empress Josephine. From the reports of his secret police Fouché also knows that numerous plotters contemplate the assassination of Napoleon. Such threats, coupled with the hazards of the battlefield, cast an uncertain light on France's future. Without an heir, Napoleon's death would bring turmoil.

Turmoil to France would mean bad business for men like Fouché, who profit by the exercise of power. The minister pockets vast sums from his secret tax on brothels and gaming houses. This is manifestly a privilege worth protecting. Conveniently, from Fouché's viewpoint, the interests of France and its Minister of Police coincide. Both prosper in the stability offered by a secure Napoleonic dynasty. The only obstacle is the stubborn Josephine, whom— alas—Napoleon loves mightily.

Paris, Fall 1807

In pursuit of his policy of finding Napoleon and France an heir, Fouché waits for the right opportunity, then covertly approaches Josephine on the subject of divorce. He anticipates exercising great influence upon the Empress since he has earned her confidence in the past: "Urged on by an excess of zeal, I resolved to open the breach and induce Josephine to this great sacrifice which the stability of the Empire and the happiness of the Emperor demanded."[6]

Summoning his oratorical prowess, Fouché puts the proposition to the Empress: "Her color rose at first; then she paled, her lips swelled and I perceived in her being signs which made me fear a nervous attack."[7] Such coquetries fail to persuade the hardened minister of police, though they had always succeeded with Napoleon himself.

Indeed, Josephine's womanly charms work again when she tells the Emperor of her encounter with Fouché. Furious at the police chief's meddling,

Napoleon orders Fouché to refrain from interfering in his marriage. Fouché does not oblige his Emperor; he continues to speak publicly of Napoleon's impending divorce, spreading rumors in the papers and salons of Paris. But, ever a realist, he sees the need for another approach. If Napoleon cannot have an heir directly, someone else must be found to serve as Emperor in the event Napoleon dies prematurely. Fouché's search focuses on the vainglorious Marshal Joachim Murat. He enlists an important ally: Murat's wife (and the Emperor's sister), the voluptuous Caroline Bonaparte. Unknown to Fouché, Caroline is also the mistress of the Austrian ambassador, Metternich. Like a spider at the center of a tangled web, the Minister of Police sets to work weaving his plot.

Dateline to War

Paris, November 1807
The Austrian Embassy

With the secrets of Tilsit as yet unknown, Metternich engages the Russian ambassador in a long discussion. The Russian confides that appearances belie the truth. Russian and Austrian policies really have the same goal: restraining France. Encouraged, Metternich writes to Austrian Foreign Minister Stadion: "I have been for some time settled in my own mind that there was extreme exaggeration about the friendly relations between the cabinets of St. Petersburg and the Tuileries, which it is part of the French policy to encourage."[8]

In Vienna this letter, coupled with reports from the Austrian minister in St. Petersburg, begin to cut through the shroud of French propaganda disguising the true nature of Franco-Russian relations. In Paris, Napoleon seems to continue to rely upon Russian constancy. Speaking before the assembled foreign ministers, he boasts that 300,000 Russians are prepared to back up his continental blockade against England. The Emperor is wrong about Russian motives. She acts not out of sympathy with French aims but out of fear.

Paris, November 1807
The Austrian Embassy

November brings Metternich a risky opportunity. Increasingly he senses that Talleyrand is inclined to help promote Austrian interests. Although Stadion warns him to check and recheck any information from Talleyrand since no one completely understands the Frenchman's intrigues, Metternich believes much can be gained. He writes Stadion: "Such men as M. de Talleyrand are like sharp-edged instruments with which it is dangerous to play, but for great evils drastic remedies are necessary and whoever has to treat them should not be afraid to use the instrument that cuts the best."[9]

Vienna, 6 January 1808

For the third time Kaiser Franz marries. This weak, indecisive man chooses his cousin, Maria Ludovica of Austria. Twelve years earlier she had been destined to enter a convent. But in 1796 her father, the Archduke Ferdinand, captain-general of Lombardy, fled Italy with his family before the approaching French army led by a heretofore obscure general named Bonaparte. It was a humiliation the impressionable young woman never forgot. Installed as Empress, Maria Ludovica quickly allies with the war party at the inner circles of Viennese intrigue and plots revenge.

Paris, 18 January 1808

At the beginning of a new and perhaps pivotal year, Metternich meets with Talleyrand. The Austrian summarizes his view of Hapsburg policy. Open opposition and total acquiescence are equally unviable. Rather, Metternich suggests, Austria should delicately act as a check against both Russian and French ambitions. The French foreign minister responds: "That is exactly my way of looking at things."[10]

In his report to Stadion, Metternich writes: "M. de Talleyrand, who now makes profession of attachment to the court of Austria, and has latterly given me evidence of his desire to establish the closest relations between us and France, has had conversations with me on two consecutive days."[11] The shadowy figure of Talleyrand has embarked on a course of opposition, if not outright treason, to Napoleon.

Paris, 26 January 1808

Continuing his diplomatic probings, Metternich meets with Napoleon. Napoleon speaks hypothetically of English gold supporting Hapsburg rearmament. Metternich interrupts to say Austria has not received such support and has furnished undeniable proof. The Emperor hastens to say: "I have no reason but to praise the course you have followed since the peace of Pressburg . . . in the last war you maintained the strictest neutrality . . . [and, referring to the mobilization in Bohemia] you made armaments, but you did not carry them to a point dangerous for me."[12]

Napoleon then refers to the hostility shown the French minister in Vienna by the Viennese and to an incident in St. Petersburg where the Austrian ambassador's wife permitted her hand to be kissed by the English minister but declined a similar gesture from the French minister. He comments: "If there are some little pin-pricks, we return pin-pricks."[13]

Metternich apparently assuages Napoleon, for the Emperor concludes the interview by asking Metternich to emphasize French amicability in his reports to Vienna. A month later Metternich receives permission from his government to pursue contact with Talleyrand.

Vienna, Late winter 1808

While a cold wind swirls around the Schönbrunn Palace, the imperial home of the Hapsburg ruler, inside is a hothouse of intrigue. Overtly Austria has joined the continental blockade against England, but this is a front, a temporary measure. Covertly English agents declaim about the menace of France. Russian agents speak of the Czar's growing estrangement from Napoleon. Hardenberg, the king of Prussia's most trusted adviser, promises Prussian intervention should Austria declare war against France. Rome claims opposition to Napoleon in all of Catholic Italy. Patriots from the Tyrol plead for assistance in overthrowing the hated yoke of Franco-Bavarian rule. The cautious Austrian Kaiser Franz listens and waits.

Paris, 27 April 1808

Metternich writes to Stadion on the subject that has continuously been of paramount importance during his ambassadorship—relations between Austria and Russia: "It is impossible to regard a state of peace with France as a state of repose . . . an alliance, offensive and defensive, between Russia and Austria, having for its object a successful war against France, alone can arrest Napoleon in his projects."[14]

St. Petersburg, Spring–Summer 1808

Four major parties are striving to sway the impressionable Alexander. First and least important are the agents of the English government. Representing a country unalterably opposed to French domination of Europe, they seek to influence the Czar indirectly through the mercantile interests of the Russian nobility. The English point out the economic hardships Russia endures by adhering to Napoleon's continental system. These hardships are real and prevent many members of the Russian nobility from profiting from their patronage positions. Thus those with mercantile interests emphasize Russia's suffering because of the Franco-Russian alliance.

The second influence is less subtle but ultimately more powerful. Prince Karl Philipp von Schwarzenberg has ably represented Austria as the Hapsburg ambassador to St. Petersburg. Metternich will later say a better choice could not have been made. Schwarzenberg shows tact and logic in explaining to the Czar why Austria and Russia should share in the task of stopping the aggressive expansion of Imperial France. He displays diplomatic skills and a strategic competence belying his later mediocre performance in 1813–1814 as leader of the Allied armies. In 1808 Schwarzenberg contributes to the idea, growing in the idealistic Czar's mind, that it is Alexander's duty to oppose Napoleon.

The most important influence comes from the ranks of Russian patriots. Led by men like the Francophobe Count Nikolai Tolstoy, the Russian ambassador to France, patriots have been trying to capture the Czar's mind since the Treaty of Tilsit. Their efforts are eagerly seconded by the majority of the Russian military establishment, who are burning with desire for revenge for the debacles of 1805 and 1807.

The fourth influence perversely comes from the French ambassador to Russia, the Marquis Caulaincourt. His major task should have been to maintain the pro-French attitude Napoleon had imparted at Tilsit. Instead, he contributes to Alexander's decision to oppose Napoleon. In this can be seen the long arm of Talleyrand. Talleyrand's views on France's need for peace have greatly influenced the young Caulaincourt, who perhaps unwittingly serves as Talleyrand's agent in Russia. By emphasizing France's war-weariness and Napoleon's unabated lust for power, Caulaincourt supports the group seeking to direct Alexander against Napoleon. Here, as in many places, Napoleon is poorly served by his subordinates.

The combination of English, Austrian, Russian, and French influences prepare the Czar, as autumn brings the critical meeting at Erfurt, for Talleyrand's incredible betrayal of Napoleon's entire strategic aim. The four parties have mixed a clay; Talleyrand will mold it to suit his—but not Napoleon's and perhaps not France's—ambitions.

Iberian Peninsula, Midsummer 1808

On the parched plains of Andalusia in southern Spain the world has turned upside down. For the first time in recent French history a French army, heretofore victorious throughout Europe, surrenders. Near Bailen, columns of bewildered, frightened conscripts pass between rows of jeering Spaniards on the way to the misery and death of the prison hulks anchored just off Cádiz.

In Portugal a militarily minor but politically disastrous event of equal magnitude occurs shortly thereafter. On a steep ridge at Vimiero, General Junot's French are badly defeated by a British army led by a new name in Europe, Sir Arthur Wellesley. By the bumbling grace of the Convention of Cintra, Junot's men avoid the fate of their comrades at Bailen and sail back to France courtesy of the royal navy. However, in Europe news of the double French debacle causes a sensation. Patriots throughout occupied Europe are heartened. Austria accelerates her rearmament. Napoleon becomes convinced that only his personal intervention can set affairs right in the Peninsula.

Vienna, June 1808

As a result of the reduction in press censorship, Austrian newspapers begin to challenge French accounts of international events. They report extensively on the heroic resistance of the Spanish people and fan the flames of German nationalism. Such documents as the "Citizen's Catechism" are obtained from Spain and widely disseminated:

> QUESTION: Is it a sin to kill a Frenchman?
> ANSWER: Yes, excepting those who are fighting under Napoleon's standards.[15]

Paris, June–July 1808

His contacts with Talleyrand temporarily severed by the latter's departure from Paris, Metternich goes seriously astray in his appraisal of French intentions. He repeatedly writes to Vienna that France is preparing for war against Austria. In particular, he worries about the consequences should Napoleon preemptively order Austrian disarmament. Unwittingly, this alarmist information plays straight into the hands of the hawks in the Viennese councils, a result neither he nor Talleyrand desires. By August the midsummer's war scare diminishes, yet Metternich still writes to Stadion that Napoleon "does not wish for war at this moment, but he will make war upon us before very long."[16]

Vienna, July 1808

The French ambassador confers with Stadion and asks why the Austrians are making such extensive armaments. He notes that these measures require Napoleon to take countermeasures. Stadion replies ingenuously that Austrian activities are purely defensive and in response to French armaments. Meanwhile, Austrian inspectors report the completion of their count of available manpower: 316,705 regulars; 59,800 reserves; 185,714 national militia (landwehr); and about 100,000 Hungarian militia. This is a formidable host, well above the numbers needed for defense. The Austrian minister of finance reports that armaments on this scale cannot be maintained indefinitely or the empire will become insolvent. The implication, seized upon by the hawks surrounding Franz, is that the army—once created—must be used or disbanded.

Holland, August 1808

A French diplomat in Holland reports to Paris that Austria is actively raising and equipping a landwehr. He sends details of these and other Austrian armaments picked up from the editor of the Hamburg *Correspondent*, a prominent German newspaper. That editor has in his pay, to the tune of 6000 francs per year, a clerk in the Austrian war department. The clerk provides intelligence about Hapsburg war preparations to the editor, who (for a price) relays the information to the French embassy in Holland.

The French diplomat also reports that Austrian agents seem to be circulating in Hesse and Hanover. What he does not know is that a Major Dornberg of the Westphalian Guards (the personal bodyguard to Napoleon's newly installed brother, King Jerome), the Duke of Brunswick, and a Major Schill in Hanover have been particularly sympathetic to these Austrian agents.

Warsaw, August 1808

French Marshal Davout's spies report continuing Austrian armaments, particularly in the Cracow region. Alarmed, Davout writes to the Emperor: "All the measures being taken by the Austrians cause me to believe . . . they are preparing for war, either because they want war or because they fear it."[17] Napoleon, preoccupied with affairs in Spain, writes back: "The Austrians are arming, but they arm out of fear; our relations are good with this power; but nevertheless they are arming and I have begun by demanding an explanation from them. I am sure of Russia, and it is this that causes me not to fear Austria."[18]

Vienna, Summer 1808

The men in the ranks stand proudly erect. Reviewing them are the Kaiser's wife, Maria Ludovica, and the army's leader, the Archduke Karl. The sight of the Empress particularly inspires the soldiers and the watching crowd. They recognize her patriotic zeal and are beginning to hail her as a second Maria Theresa. With her own hands she presents the banners to the newly formed landwehr battalions, an act greeted with tears of emotion. An elderly archbishop blesses the men and their banners. Wild cheering replaces the tears as the Empress departs.

Paris, 15 August 1808
The Tuileries

Napoleon has visited the Spanish border and returned. His unfinished business in Spain was interrupted because of news of Austrian rearmament. This first dislocation of Napoleon's plans is in effect a major Allied victory, an unforeseen consequence of Austrian rearmament. Napoleon has been diverted and forced to leave important matters in his subordinates' hands. Thus Austria serves the Allied cause in the newest round of struggle against France.

Today the Emperor will hold a diplomatic audience, taking his usual two turns. Customarily the first turn (Napoleon's circuit of the diplomats who stand in a circle as he walks in the middle from one to the next) involves an exchange of pleasantries. The second turn carries any real message the Emperor wishes to convey, often either a display of affection or a diatribe. During his first turn Napoleon engages in his usual small talk. Pausing before the Austrian ambassador at the second turn, the Emperor dramatically inquires: "Well, and is Austria arming considerably?"[19]

Metternich, exhibiting great diplomatic cool, dissembles, saying Austria is merely carrying out the measures of the Treaty of Pressburg. Unpersuaded, Napoleon speaks of the mustering of the landwehr and other threatening gestures. Over the next hour he speaks again of the difficulties Austrian rearmament poses for both France and Austria. He stresses his desire for peace and the key role the Hapsburg empire plays in the Central European balance of power. Returning to Austria's military preparations, he brushes aside Metternich's claims about their nonthreatening nature and gives another demonstration of his still-profound military insight: "Your troops are placed in such a manner as to be able to immediately form real army corps. These are things on which military men cannot be deceived."[20]

With this observation Napoleon anticipates the actual formation of Austrian corps structures by more than five months. Yet his diplomatic wisdom lags behind his military judgment. His incomplete understanding of foreign affairs leads him to believe Austria will not risk war again. In this conclusion are the signs of a growing tendency to self-delusion; his great mind is beginning to believe only that which it desires. Since the prospects of a two-front war are unconscionable, Napoleon decides in his diplomatic mind that Austria cannot logically want war. By this process he ignores the warning signals registered by his military mind. The barometer of national mood, the Paris stock exchange, slumps dramatically following this meeting between Metternich and Napoleon. The nation's financiers greatly fear a two-front war.

Meanwhile, Metternich well comprehends Napoleon's motives, reporting to Vienna: "I am convinced that the Emperor does not think at the same time of the conquest of Spain and of war with us."[21]

Emboldened by confirmation that France does not intend a preemptive strike, Austria continues its rearmament. At the end of the month the Austrian emperor receives a letter from the Spanish Junta. In part it describes Spanish battles and victories; it ends by asking Franz not to abandon the Spanish royal family in its holy war against Napoleon. To Franz the Junta's appeal is one more sign that the moment for revenge draws near.

Shortly thereafter, faced with substantial setbacks in Spain caused largely by his own absence from the front, Napoleon recalls veteran troops from Germany, sending them down dusty roads on the long march to the Iberian Peninsula. Only a reduced army of occupation and one front-line combat corps commanded by Marshal Davout remains in Germany.

Paris, early September 1808

On the eve of the most important diplomatic encounter since Tilsit, Napoleon meets with the man of greatest diplomatic experience in France. In a critical misjudgment, he entrusts the Prince of Benevent, Talleyrand, the task of representing the Emperor and France: "My dear Talleyrand, I should like you to arrive at Erfurt a day or so before I do. You know Czar Alexander well, and you and he speak the same language."[22] Indeed they do, but their shared language is not that of Napoleon.

This discord is obvious when Napoleon reviews the draft treaty Talleyrand prepares. Napoleon's central goal at Erfurt is to define his expectations regarding Russian behavior; specifically, Russian intervention should Austria attack France. Embroiled in a difficult war in Spain, he needs Russia to serve as a counterweight against Austria so veteran French troops can be transferred from Germany to Spain. But when the Emperor receives Talleyrand's draft treaty, he is amazed at the omission of an essential clause that would force Russia to declare war against Austria should Austria attack France.

Napoleon asks Talleyrand: "How could you have left it out? You are still an Austrian?"

"Somewhat, Sire. Yet I think it would be more exact to say that I am never a Russian, but always a Frenchman."[23] Intending to frustrate Napoleon, Talleyrand departs for Erfurt.

Erfurt, 27 September 1808

From all parts of the Napoleonic empire a glittering entourage converges on Erfurt with the express purpose of dazzling the Czar Alexander. Significantly, in spite of Metternich's and Talleyrand's efforts, high-ranking Austrian envoys have not been invited. Napoleon commands the presence of all allied German royalty from the seemingly inexhaustible well of minor royal families whose squabbles and overlapping, inbred dynastic claims allow the Emperor to make and remake the map of Central Europe at will. Their presence is designed to add legitimacy to the proceedings and to impress the Czar with the extent of French might. In straining every diplomatic nerve to impress Alexander, Napoleon does not ignore the cultural amenities. By his order, actors from the Parisian theaters arrive to give command performances during the planned swirl of diplomatic gatherings. As at Tilsit, the Emperor intends to overawe the impressionable Czar, rekindling the personal bonds between the two heads of state.

After a long pull through the forests of Russia and Poland and across the plains of Central Europe, the young Czar's carriage clatters into Erfurt accompanied by his favorite, the French ambassador Caulaincourt. Napoleon will find Alexander a very different man from the one he met a year earlier.

Erfurt, 28 September 1808

In a display of public cordiality, the Czar and Napoleon meet. No business is to be transacted during this encounter, but an important message is nonetheless transmitted. As Alexander retires to his carriage he says repeatedly to Talleyrand in a low voice: "We will see each other."[24]

While Napoleon, still dissatisfied with Talleyrand's draft treaty, goes to his chambers to make corrections, Talleyrand finds at his chambers a note from the Queen of Prussia's sister, the Princess of Thurn und Taxis, that simply informs Talleyrand of the Princess' arrival. The Princess is devoid of power. However, the Queen has long been one of Napoleon's most inveterate enemies. Talleyrand departs to pay a visit.

Erfurt, 28 September 1808
The Princess of Thurn's Drawing Room

Fifteen minutes after Talleyrand's arrival, the Czar Alexander enters. Over tea the Czar suggests that the Princess host a tea each afternoon following the day's business, so a convenient means is established whereby Talleyrand and Alexander can meet. At one of the first teas Talleyrand says to the Czar: "Sire, what are you doing here? It is in your power to save Europe, but you can do so only by standing up to Napoleon."[25] Talleyrand's overt betrayal of Napoleon has begun.

Erfurt, 29 September 1808
Conference Chambers

Napoleon is frustrated with the conference's lack of progress. While on the surface all seems agreeable, the Czar is proving singularly difficult to pin down on any essentials. The Emperor resolves on a different tack. He personally drafts a new treaty, keeping its contents secret from all—including Talleyrand. Napoleon presents this new treaty to the Czar, strictly cautioning Alexander not to show it to anyone, including the Russian ministers. It is to be a secret between the two emperors.

Erfurt, 29 September 1808
The Princess' Drawing Room

That night Alexander pulls out Napoleon's handwritten treaty and shows it to Talleyrand. Thus begins the custom of meeting each night to discuss the day's "secret" negotiations. Talleyrand closely advises Alexander on negotiating strategies, arguments, and counterarguments. At times the Czar takes notes while Talleyrand dictates. Thus does the Prince use Alexander as a spy and make Napoleon a dupe.

Erfurt, early October 1808
Napoleon's Chambers

His latest ploy a failure, the French Emperor's frustrations mount. To Caulain-court he says that Alexander "has grown wary." To Talleyrand he complains: "I have been able to do nothing with the Czar Alexander . . . he is simply acting a part. If he cares so much for me, why does he not sign?"[26] Talleyrand's anxiety when Napoleon spoke of Alexander "playing a part" and his satisfaction with Napoleon's bemusement must have been considerable.

Erfurt, early October 1808

As the conference drags on, more than one violent outburst occurs between Napoleon and the Czar. At last Alexander, acting on Talleyrand's advice, agrees to a vaguely stated promise of Russian intervention should Austria provoke hostilities. Showing signs of the growing self-deception that will contribute to his downfall, Napoleon writes to Josephine: "I am satisfied with Alexander; he must be satisfied with me. If he were a woman, I think I would make him my mistress."[27] The Emperor, confident Austria has been checked by the Russian alliance, hastens away to Spain to supervise an increasingly nasty war.

While Napoleon leaves Erfurt self-satisfied with what would turn out to be a hollow achievement, Talleyrand, ever thorough, makes sure his arrangements are conveyed to the real victor of Erfurt. "The Emperor Franz," he tells the Czar, "is in great need of consolation."[28] Thus prompted, Alexander writes to the Austrian explaining Russia's true position. Then, satisfied with his role as power broker, the Russian emperor returns to St. Petersburg to plot new aggressions against Finland and Turkey.

Talleyrand alone could rest on his accomplishments at Erfurt. He had, in his words, performed "the final service that I was able to render to Europe during Napoleon's reign."[29]

Somewhat disappointed that his efforts to create a stable European balance of power were at an end, the Prince quickly found consolation when he reaped the first tangible rewards for his activities. Following a short negotiation, Alexander readily agreed to marry off a very rich Russian princess named Dorothée to Talleyrand's son. Equally satisfying to the worldly Talleyrand was the Princess' mother, whose ageless porcelain looks Talleyrand found "delightful." Whatever lofty objectives Talleyrand fulfilled through his expert manipulation of the Erfurt conference, he also met two personal goals: money and pleasure.

Paris, Fall 1808
The Austrian Embassy

Deliberately excluded from Erfurt, Metternich must focus on two problems: What arrangements have been made regarding Austria at Erfurt and what is the true role of Talleyrand in the French government? The idea that France's former foreign minister is working against his master is too fabulous to accept without great skepticism. Metternich turns his considerable energies to fathoming the behavior of the Prince.

Unknown to Metternich, one of the two new Russian ambassadors to France meets with Talleyrand. His public role is a front. "It is to you that I am really accredited,"[30] he informs Talleyrand. As proof he produces a personal letter from the Czar. Unraveling this incredible arrangement is part of Metternich's task. Persuading Vienna of his findings will also prove a difficult chore.

Vienna, Fall 1808

Amid tense audience silence the stage actor dramatically declaims "Awaken! Awaken, Germans, from the stupor of shame and ignominy! Awaken and act for the sake of German honor! There is still time! Austria's powerful forces are approaching, imbued with a spirit of courage and faithfulness. They are led by Karl. . . ."[31] In a frenzy of patriotic zeal, the audience stands and applauds, thus interrupting the performance. Such scenes are repeated in theaters and salons, in dramatic readings, and in the newspapers throughout German-speaking Austria as the people's nationalistic spirit is summoned as never before. Rich and poor alike hasten to join the landwehr, where they vie with one another to display patriotism and martial prowess. An observer writes: "Fathers left their families, while manufacturers, artists, and professionals left their calling to enlist."[32]

Bagneux, France, Fall 1808

Had the meeting at the quiet, secluded house of a minor functionary in the French Foreign Office been witnessed by the secret police, the resultant report would have stunned French officialdom. Although the minister of police, Fouché, boasted that no meeting of three or more people could occur in France without his knowledge, no secret police were present to spy on this clandestine gathering. Instead, by invitation their chief himself attended.

The house's owner, a man named Hauterive, knew Fouché from the days when both had been teachers. He had known the other participant, Talleyrand, from the time both had emigrated to America. The meeting produced a reconciliation between the two bitter rivals. Here at Bagneux they joined forces out of mutual self-interest. Fouché, worried about the fate of France should Napoleon die, required the assistance of Talleyrand to implement the plan he had in mind. Talleyrand shared some of Fouché's concern while recognizing that the cooperation of the secret police would greatly reduce the dangers of his continuous contact with Austrian and Russian diplomats. So was born an unlikely alliance.

That evening, in later meetings at the home of a royalist friend of Fouché, and again in the home of Napoleon's master of the wardrobe, details of the plot were set out. The conspirators proposed that in the event of the Emperor's death, Marshal Murat, the recently crowned King of Naples and Napoleon's brother-in-law, would rally the army to support a new government with Murat occupying the vacant throne. Fouché's preliminary advances indicated Murat and his wife were more than agreeable. Thus Talleyrand and Fouché agreed that a letter specifying the particulars of the transfer of power be sent to Murat and that a courier route from Paris to Naples be installed to quickly call the king to Paris should Napoleon die.

Paris, December 1808
Rue de Varennes (Talleyrand's residence)

One of the political facts of Europe, well known to the guests assembled this evening for one of the Prince of Benevent's brilliant soirées, was the animosity between the Prince and the Minister of Police. Consequently, the guests react with slack-jawed amazement when, late in the evening, Talleyrand's major-domo announces in a loud voice the arrival of Joseph Fouché. Stupefaction increases when Talleyrand limps across the floor to greet the new arrival: "People could scarcely believe their eyes; and they were even more astounded when in their determination to appear on good terms, these two men spent the rest of the evening walking from room to room arm-in-arm."[33] The guests could only speculate why these two enemies had united. But to Napoleonic loyalists, the meeting on the Rue de Varennes presented an unmistakable public challenge to the Emperor's rule.

Paris—Vienna, December 1808

Metternich has been recalled to Vienna for consultation and an enthusiastic Stadion quickly apprises him of Austria's readiness for war. The ambassador is surprised. He anticipates eventual conflict but had not realized plans were so far advanced. Making the rounds of conferences and interviews, he realizes that the war party, aggressively headed by Stadion and the Empress, is ascendant. Only their counsels reach Franz. Before returning to Paris, Metternich meets with the Archduke Karl, the generalissimo of all Hapsburg military forces. Here he receives a second shock. While elsewhere are excitement and confidence, Karl exhibits at best a lukewarm attitude toward impending war. He explains that the army is not ready, its reforms only partially complete. Finances remain inadequate; further preparations are required. Pondering all of this during his travels back to France, Metternich cannot help being alarmed; while the main body of Austria embraces revenge and war, its head seems curiously unwilling.

Astorga, Spain, 1 January 1809

An exhausted courier arrives at imperial headquarters in Spain where the Emperor has been directing the war, now expanded to include the presence of an active British expeditionary force. The courier brings an urgent message from the postmaster general, Lavalette, who heads the secret bureau—the *cabinet noire*—charged with intercepting and copying letters. It describes the public meeting between Fouché and Talleyrand. Napoleon has little time to digest this extraordinary news before another dispatch arrives. Sent by Eugène de Beauharnais, Napoleon's stepson and Viceroy of Italy, the dispatch includes an intercepted letter addressed to Marshal Murat. It details the plot between Fouché and Talleyrand for Murat's succession to the throne of France. Napoleon begins arrangements to return to Paris in response to the sinister news, but with his campaign against the British reaching a climax, he cannot return immediately. Instead, he moves his headquarters closer to Paris to address what seems the graver threat. Pursuit of the flying British army is completely entrusted to Marshal Soult. Lacking the Emperor's personal presence to urge the men across atrocious Spanish roads, the pursuit will fail. Lacking the Emperor's tactical direction, the French will be repulsed in their attack against the cornered British army at Corruna. Soult's failure to destroy the British army will haunt Napoleon.

Paris, 11 January 1809
The Austrian Embassy

The just-returned Austrian ambassador reports to Vienna on his journey from Vienna to Paris: "From the frontiers of Austria to the center of Paris I have found but one opinion accepted by the public—that is, that in the spring at latest Austria will take the field against France."[34] Metternich will spend his remaining time in Paris disguising the actual timing of the Austrian assault while collecting intelligence about French preparations. In this latter effort he will be assisted by the soon-to-be-discredited Talleyrand.

Valladolid, Spain, 17 January 1809

News of plots and betrayals combines with recent reports of further Austrian war preparations to persuade the Emperor to return to Paris. Characteristically, once having made a decision, he implements it with vigor. Boarding his coach, he orders it staged to France by driving night and day, with pauses only to change horses.[35]

In Paris his sudden appearance will derail Talleyrand's and Fouché's conspiracy. Metternich anticipates this more clearly than any, identifying in his report to Stadion the reason for the plot's failure. Following a long conversation with Talleyrand, Metternich writes: "I see him, and his friend Fouché, always the same—very decided in seizing an opportunity, if the occasion presents itself, but not having enough courage to make one. They are in the position of passengers who, seeing the helm in the hands of a mad pilot guiding the vessel on to rocks . . . are ready to seize the helm just at the moment when . . . the first shock of the vessel would overturn the pilot himself."[36]

Paris, 24 January 1809
The Tuileries

Excitement and anticipation sweep through the assembled diplomatic corps at the Tuileries. Napoleon has unexpectedly returned from Spain after covering the 700 miles in six days. Today he will hold a diplomatic audience, taking his usual two turns. The attending dignitaries eagerly anticipate Napoleon's expected confrontation with the Austrian ambassador. For weeks Paris has been abuzz with rumors of a deteriorating Franco-Austrian relationship. Undoubtedly the Emperor will challenge Metternich with these rumors and a titillating scene will ensue.

One diplomat doubts this scenario—the Austrian ambassador himself. Metternich's beliefs prove well founded as Napoleon merely engages in small talk during his first turn and ignores him completely on the second. The ambassador explains this behavior by noting in his diary that the Emperor did not wish to amuse the curious. Although he did not speak to Metternich, Napoleon's silence carries a message for the astute. Metternich realizes Napoleon's silence acknowledges the probability of war.

Paris, 28 January 1809
The Tuileries

Quickly re-establishing his authority, the Emperor convenes the Council, including all the Grand Dignitaries of the Empire and all the ministers. Council tongues wag over the rumor Fouché has received a severe tongue-lashing from the Emperor. Fearful of their master's displeasure, all nervously await his appearance. All except one man, the immaculately dressed Talleyrand, who leans casually against a fireplace wall. Napoleon opens the session with a lecture. All those present exist at his pleasure and are merely reflections of the one who created them, he states. To doubt the Emperor is treason. Stirred by his own preamble, Napoleon begins to pace up and down, commencing an impassioned speech directed against the principal object of his displeasure, the lounging Talleyrand.

For over thirty minutes the impassive Talleyrand listens to a catalogue of his sins. He is informed he is godless, greedy, lame, treacherous, a cuckold, and stupid. All but the last are true. Throughout Talleyrand remains silent. As

Louis Bonaparte commented: "If he got a kick in the backside while he was talking to you, his face would never give you a sign of it."[37] This reserve serves him well as Napoleon vents his Corsican temper. Finally, in complete frustration at his inability first to work with the former minister and now to insult the gifted Talleyrand, Napoleon says: "Answer me! What are your schemes? What is it that you want? Do you dare tell me?"[38] Failing to receive the satisfaction of any reply, Napoleon, Emperor of the French, informs the Prince of Benevent, Vice Grand Elector of the Empire, Grand Chamberlain of the Imperial Court, that he is "shit in a silk stocking."[39]

With that, amid stunned silence, Napoleon exits. True to form, Talleyrand has the last word. Limping from the room, he comments: "What a pity that so great a man should be so ill bred."[40] Fortunately for Talleyrand, the ill-bred Napoleon does not comprehend the extent of his betrayal.

Rome, late January 1809

The Austrian ambassador to the Pope had one overriding mission: to prepare Italy for a revolt against France. Recently he had worked with papal representatives to encourage the desertion of Italian soldiers enlisted in a French mercenary regiment. What is now required is espionage on a much vaster scale.

Arrangements are made only slowly. French and French-allied garrisons in Italy have been weakened by the demand for troops in Spain. Better yet, many areas in Italy resent Napoleon's cavalier attitude toward Catholicism. Finally, British agents report that the royal navy will cooperate. The ambassador reports to Vienna: "In a word, circumstances are favorable, but only if the plan will result in a spontaneous and general revolt."[41] He predicts that such a revolt is a certainty if Austrian or British forces land on the coast and march to liberate Rome.

Paris, 1 February 1809
The Russian Embassy

Paris is alive with talk of the approaching conflict. Metternich meets with one of the Russian ambassadors in an attempt to sound him out before the ambassador leaves for St. Petersburg. Metternich seeks one last reassurance regarding Russian intentions: "One cannot do the Emperor Alexander the injustice of believing that he could ever be found on a course hostile to us."

"That depends on the position," the Russian replies. "There might be very embarrassing anterior engagements."

Recognizing the delicacy of the conversation and the political importance attached to which country is perceived as the aggressor, Metternich says: "Embarrassing in case of the aggression of France, the question from which side the war comes should be more clear to you than to anyone else."

Responding with a historical truth, the Russian notes: "When once guns are heard, it is very difficult to decide from which side the aggression is."

Metternich concludes: "War does not date from the first shot."[42]

This was a less-than-satisfactory exchange from Austria's viewpoint. With the Hapsburg empire about to risk all in a desperate military adventure, the possibility of a hostile Russia in the rear is unconscionable. In the remaining days of the Russian embassy, Metternich seeks clarification but fails because strategic planning takes place in St. Petersburg, outside the Austria's direct sphere of contact. Russia's vacillating minister in Paris, who seems to fall under the sway of Napoleon whenever the two meet, is an observer, not a decision-maker. Metternich cannot learn about Russia's ultimate resolve from this subordinate who doesn't know himself.

In fact, another Austrian ambassador, the able Prince Schwarzenberg in St. Petersburg, has successfully buttressed the Czar's resolve to resist Napoleon—or at least to resist him in the sense of not intervening in the manner expected by the treaties and discussions between Russia and France. This vital information Schwarzenberg reconfirms in dispatches to Vienna.

Paris, February 1809
The Tuileries

Napoleon and Fouché are alone. The Emperor suddenly demands: "What would you do if I were killed by a cannonball or an accident of some other kind?"

"Sire, I should seize as much power as possible, so as to control events instead of being swept along by them."

Napoleon stands silent. Then, with the understanding of a man who came to power in the middle of revolution and anarchy, he replies: "Very well, it's the rule of the game."[43]

Paris, 1 February 1809
The Austrian Embassy

Metternich has just received the latest report from his newest and best spy. He writes to Stadion in Vienna: "X has just warned me that General Oudinot has received orders to march on Augsburg and Ingolstadt. . . . Great importance attaches to any movements on the part of Oudinot's corps as the Emperor rates its fighting value very highly."[44]

The spy X is considered very reliable. Just three days earlier Metternich had requested from Stadion a draft of 300,000 to 400,000 francs to pay him. The money is well spent. In late February Metternich will report "X reports someone in the Emperor Napoleon's confidence told him that we [the Austrians] are in a state of absolute unreadiness and that we have no troops on any front."[45] Such intelligence on French estimates of Austrian readiness is invaluable.

Even better is the information X will supply on 17 March. It will contain the latest returns on the battle formations of the French army, complete with organizational and manpower data carefully abstracted from the ministry of war.

This comprehensive intelligence on French diplomatic and military intentions is provided by Talleyrand, the Monsieur X of Metternich's reports. Whatever noble motives previously inspired his opposition to Napoleon have been abandoned by these actions. For a fee, Talleyrand has sunk to the level of a spy, trading on information that will mean the blood of French soldiers.

Metternich sends Talleyrand's intelligence to Vienna via couriers dispatched to St. Petersburg. This roundabout route has the double purpose of evading interception on the direct route to Vienna and informing the Czar exactly what Napoleon intends. Since some of the papers are lifted straight off the desks of the French foreign ministry, they contain sensitive reports describing Napoleon's anger at Russia's unwillingness to adhere to the dictates of Erfurt. Metternich intends for the Czar to see this information in order to further estrange him from Napoleon.

Vienna, 8 February 1809

The Austrian Emperor meets with his advisers. The final decision can no longer be delayed; even the conservative, vacillating Franz realizes this. The war party reiterates its three basic arguments: Whereas before the Spanish intervention France greatly outnumbered Austria, now Napoleon will field a force in Germany barely equal to the Hapsburg armies; France is war-weary, with opposition to Napoleon growing daily; Russia will not intervene.

Furthermore, England has pledged large sums to support the war and a landing force to divert French attention. Prussia has promised 40,000 muskets to arm the Austrian landwehr and perhaps its army as well. Schwarzenberg is due back from St. Petersburg any day with perhaps even greater pledges of Russian assistance. Italy is restless, the Tyrol lies seething, ready to spring into revolt. All Germany may well join their Hapsburg brethren in a crusade against France.

Franz listens intently to these arguments eloquently elaborated by Stadion. But had he possessed great foresight he would have known English gold would not arrive on the docks of Trieste until Vienna had already fallen. The promised British expeditionary force would land at Walcheren in August, after the battle of Wagram, too late to influence events. Planning for a landing in Italy began too late to reach fruition. The King of Prussia would withdraw his offer of support in March. In four days Schwarzenberg would arrive in Vienna with the Czar's advice that Austria exercise restraint and caution. While the Tyrol would engage in a bloody guerrilla war against Napoleon, Bavaria would oppose the crossing of her borders with her entire army. Stirred up by Austrian agents, the rest of occupied Germany would engage in sporadic, uncoordinated rebellion. The Duke of Brunswick would lead a revolt following news of Aspern-Essling, briefly occupying Dresden and Leipzig. But few would rally to his cause and he would eventually be evacuated from the mainland by the royal navy. Major Schill would lead a rebellion in north Germany only to be shot down in the streets of Straslund by loyal French allies. His supporters would be executed, shouting before the firing squad "Long live a free Germany."

With ineffectual support Austrian fortunes would turn solely on the valor of her armies and the ability of her generals. But Franz couldn't know this. On 8 February he opted for war.

Paris, 21 February 1809
The Tuileries

Just as Metternich tried to influence Russian policy when in fact it had already been established far away in St. Petersburg, so Napoleon tries to influence Austrian policy after it has already been formulated. The stage for this effort is the diplomatic circle called together Sunday morning in the marble halls of the Tuileries. During the first turn, Napoleon makes small talk inquiring about the health of Metternich's wife. Completing this turn, he bypasses Metternich. His message to Austria is once more no less direct for not being delivered face to face. Stopping before the Bavarian minister, who stands near Metternich, Napoleon asks in a low voice meant to be overheard if the Bavarian fortresses are in a state of defense, especially Passau (see Map 2).

This oblique warning, pinpointing the one Bavarian fortress directly in the path of the planned Austrian advance, is an attempt by the Emperor to gain time. He hopes his warning will cause the Austrians to give pause to their plans. A more prudent Hapsburg leadership might have considered the implications of Napoleon's seeming certitude regarding Hapsburg war plans, but the prudent councilors in Vienna had lost out to the war party. The Austrian decision for war is irreversible.

Thus, while the Emperor's prescient statement highlights his immense strategic military ability, as a diplomatic effort—like virtually every other such effort during the years leading up to the war of 1809—it failed. The unwanted conflict would be forced upon France, in no small part because of Napoleon's failed foreign policy. In 1797, young General Bonaparte had written to Talleyrand that "True politics . . . is merely the calculus of combinations and of chances."[46] In 1809, Napoleon's erroneous political calculations meant that the issue would be decided on the battlefield.

CHAPTER II

The Napoleonic War Machines

Of the three arms—cavalry, infantry, and artillery—none must be despised. All three are equally important.

The Tactical Mosaic

On the Napoleonic battlefield the tactical objective was to place the opposing infantry—the only arm capable of gaining and holding ground, the Queen of Battle of this period—in a terrible dilemma by attacking with a combined-arms assault. Such an assault featured a coordinated effort by the three arms: infantry, cavalry, and artillery. If confronted by all three, there was no single formation a defender could employ to resist effectively.

The technical characteristics of the period's muskets dictated small-unit tactics. Firing tests conducted under perfect conditions, using muskets supported on fixed clamps, showed that at a hundred paces three-quarters of all shots hit an infantry target. Five-sixths struck a larger cavalry target. At 200 paces the hit rate declined to three-eighths and one-half, respectively, and at 300 paces it decayed to one-third and three-eighths.[1] These data give a misleading impression of a musket's accuracy, however. Testers firing aimed shots over flat, cleared ground while resting their clean weapons on supports were not simulating combat. The natural anxiety of battle, the problems of shooting while standing in a cramped, three-ranks-deep formation, and the difficulty of even glimpsing the enemy through the thick smoke typical of the black-powder period greatly reduced test performance. After repeated firings muskets became encrusted with unburnt powder, flints became worn, and misfires became frequent, further reducing efficiency. The first shots might

29

come at fifteen-second intervals. Such a rate of fire quickly eroded to perhaps two a minute.

To compensate for the musket's inefficiencies and generate as much firepower as possible, soldiers stood close together. They maintained their formation by standing shoulder to shoulder, twenty-two inches between ranks, elbows touching. Reliance on close-order formations accounts for the horrific casualties characteristic of Napoleonic battle.

To dislodge the tightly packed defenders and capture ground required that infantry advance and charge. Charging infantry marched in shoulder-to-shoulder formation at a rate of about seventy yards a minute.[2] This meant the waiting defenders might unleash eight volleys starting at long range before the charge struck home. Under ideal conditions this was a formidable volume of fire, quite capable of shattering an unsupported frontal charge.

More typically, the issue was decided within the final fifty yards. If the defenders stood firm, their last volley at point-blank range dropped scores of attackers, discouraging all but the most intrepid from continuing. However, if the attacker's skirmishers and artillery had inflicted enough prior losses and the sight of an advancing wall of gleaming bayonets unnerved the defenders, they would waver and fire a straggling, poorly aimed last volley. In this event the attackers' momentum carried them through. Occasionally, the defender's fire would stop but not break a charge. A close-range firefight ensued, with both sides loading and squeezing trigger as fast as possible. Here training, discipline, morale, and tradition paid off. Amid a near-deafening roar of discharging weapons, officers' commands could hardly be heard. Senses numbed, wreathed in clinging smoke, soldiers mechanically shuffled inward to replace losses as their ranks thinned. Noncommissioned officers shouted and shoved, herding the men toward the center, where the battalion and regimental flags flew above the smoke to serve as a rallying point.

Eventually the stalemate would be broken by a leader throwing fresh troops into the fight. When a charge degenerated into a prolonged, static killing match, a small reserve could tilt the balance in dramatic fashion. Good officers were known to maintain their balance amid the confusing shock of combat and to commit their reserves at just the right moment. Often this required more of an instinctive feel for battle than any textbook study. It always required bravery, since they were expected to set a calming example by remaining mounted along the battle line; visible above the smoke to their own men yet more exposed to hostile fire.

Seldom did hand-to-hand infantry fighting result in open combat; instead, one side or the other would break before bayonets actually crossed. Well-trained or highly motivated infantry rallied to the urgings of famous generals who bellowed and prodded them back into the ranks. If not, they continued to stream to the rear, where their further running awaited the battle's outcome.

While infantry in line could effectively defend against attacking infantry, the line was an inappropriate formation if the second of the three arms, the cavalry, joined the assault. Charging cavalry could pass through the defender's musketry-fire zone much faster than could charging infantry. Defending infantry in line simply could not generate enough firepower to stop a determined cavalry charge, particularly if the cavalry bore in against the defender's flanks. When this happened hundreds of foot soldiers could be ridden down, sabered, or compelled to surrender in a matter of seconds. Consequently, when facing hostile cavalry the defending infantry invariably formed the square, a boxlike formation that presented four short, unassailable sides to the enemy. In so doing they reduced the number of forward-firing muskets by about three-quarters. Yet the square's combination of firepower and the physical barrier a solid wall of bayonets presented to a horse would defeat unsupported attacking cavalry.

However, once the cavalry forced the defenders into square, the attacking foot soldiers could stand in line and shoot the hapless square apart. Worse, the square was a terribly vulnerable massed target to the third element in a combined-arms assault, the artillery. Standing off at a safe distance, the artillery fired cannonballs that literally bowled over file after file of the densely packed square. At closer range the cannons fired shotgunlike canister that erased a square's entire side. Thus an attacking general using a combined-arms assault possessed a tactical trump to any defensive maneuver: If the defender stood in line, the attacking cavalry overran it; if the defender formed square, the attacker's infantry and cannon shot it into red ruin. The multiple threats a combined-arms assault posed dominated battlefield decision-making.

Tactical coordination, the interplay of the three arms, was crucial to the battle's outcome for both attacker and defender. In an era when command control extended only as far as a general's voice carried, orchestrating a combined-arms assault amid the chaos of battle was extremely difficult. Defending, which involved the placement of the three arms to prevent the attacker from bringing a coordinated assault to bear, was a somewhat easier proposition, since generals usually made defensive decisions in the relative calm before a battle began. On both sides of the battle line, much depended upon a general's experience and ability. Timely subordinate initiative, the capacity of an officer to gauge a situation correctly and seize the moment, was crucial.

The Austrian Army

The Leaders

In 1809 Archduke Karl was thirty-eight, two years younger than Napoleon. Born the third son of Leopold II, he had been a frail, nervous youth. Subject to periodic mild epileptic attacks (a condition that hampered his performance during the 1809 campaign), Karl spent a lonely childhood. At a young age an officer who had served as an adjutant to Frederick the Great took Karl under his wing. He received extensive instruction from this officer, an experience that stimulated Karl to become a very studious officer—a rarity in the Hapsburg army—and gave the impressionable youth an overfondness for outdated Frederickian methods.[3]

Handsome, slightly built, he grew to be a little over five feet tall, the same height as Napoleon. He first experienced war during the Flanders campaign at the start of the French Revolution. He exhibited bravery and some battlefield dash, but retired from the field in late 1794 after recurring nervous attacks. He devoted himself to military writing, some of which showed an original understanding of why the revolutionary French armies were successfully competing against Austrian regulars.

In 1796 Karl returned to the field, where he beat the French in several battles along the Rhine. Transferred to Italy, he received a tough assignment: to defend the mountain passes leading to Vienna with a battered, demoralized army against a veteran, triumphant French force led by a rising star in Europe, Napoleon Bonaparte. Karl established a Frederickian-style cordon defense that Bonaparte easily penetrated. At first contact Austrian soldiers routed from the field. Their poor performance overshadowed an important lesson: Karl's conventional tactics were ill-suited for combat against the dynamic Napoleon.

Returning to the Rhine front for the 1799 campaign, Karl won a sizable victory against an outnumbered French army but failed to capitalize on his success. The great commentator Karl von Clausewitz, analyzing Karl's 1799 performance, concluded that he lacked an all-consuming hunger for victory. Karl confused the value of occupying certain strategic positions with the real aim of war, the destruction of the enemy army.

The Archduke participated in murky court intrigues in the following years, a situation that formed the seeds of distrust in the suspicious mind of his brother, the Emperor. In the resultant scramble Karl lost out to the inept General Mack for command of the main army in the 1805 campaign. Instead he fought on the secondary Italian front, where he achieved some modest successes and held his own against the shrewd French commander, Marshal Masséna.

Following the 1805 war until 1809, Karl worked hard reforming the Hapsburg army. In 1806 he coauthored *The Fundamentals of the Higher Art of War for the Generals of the Austrian Army*. This manual combined old and new concepts. It mirrored eighteenth-century philosophy in asserting the existence of fundamental laws of war that should be followed with mathematical precision. As a modern student of Austrian military history, Gunther Rothenberg, observed: "Overall the manual did not break with the formal traditions of eighteenth-century close order fighting and it was far removed from the total nature, the impetuosity and improvisations of Napoleonic warfare."[4]

Many of Karl's ideas were very sound, but he contended against Vienna's entrenched reactionaries, who resisted every change. Interestingly, Karl, a deeply conservative man, was the army's foremost reformer. He managed to modernize the army's organization and humanize its treatment of the rank and file. Formerly, an Austrian infantry conscript had to serve twenty-five years, a virtual life sentence. Over the government's objections (it feared discharged soldiers as a trained nucleus for revolution) Karl reduced this to ten years, thus offering hope to a soldier beyond the former certainty of death, disfigurement, or enfeebled old age.

Karl was undoubtedly the best man available for the job in 1809. He was popular with the people and with the army, excepting certain high-ranking officers. The great Wellington felt he was the best of the Allied generals. Yet, based on his record up to 1809, he could not be called a great commander. His military reputation hung in the balance, to be measured in full in the coming campaign.

Among Karl's subordinates, the top Austrian officers received their assignments based on seniority and birth rather than ability. Karl was neither free to choose his corps commanders nor empowered to dismiss any generals for incompetence or insubordination. Consequently he was saddled with a very mixed lot. They included the commander of the Fifth Corps, General Johann Hiller, who, although talented, was Karl's bitter rival. The two heartily detested each other. Jealousy and rivalry abound in any army and particularly plagued the French marshals. Yet to have an important subordinate such as Hiller question the army commander's judgment from the beginning of a campaign made a harmony of effort impossible.

Excepting Hiller, the corps were led by members of the old high aristocracy, including Karl's twenty-five-year-old younger brother, the Archduke Louis, and three princes—Hohenzollern, Rosenberg, and Johannes Liechtenstein. They tended to be elderly warriors (the average age of all Austrian generals was sixty-three) brought up in the school of Maria Theresa. Thus they lacked the required flexibility for Napoleonic warfare. Furthermore, with some prominent exceptions, Hapsburg senior officers avoided hardship and danger, preferring the creature comforts of a well-stocked headquarters and the security of leading from the rear.

Karl's *Fundamentals of the Art of War* neither spoke about the responsibilities of senior commanders nor senior commander initiative. It emphasized careful planning, logistics, and precise battle alignments. Whether Karl's subordinates, lacking useful doctrine and practical experience, could think on their own once the inevitable friction of war upset high-command planning remained to be seen.

Austrian Organization

Although Austria had been intensively preparing for war for three-quarters of a year, Karl waited until 2 February 1809 to order a major organizational change. Henceforth the army would be organized into corps. Napoleon had subdivided the French army into large, self-contained units comprising all three arms—infantry, cavalry, artillery—in his reforms of 1802–1804. The corps system had proved a "pre-eminent executive instrument of French conquest and military success."[5] For the Austrians, organizing a corps system, particularly on the eve of war, was a radical step. The army had never maneuvered in corps-sized formations; generals had never commanded such a force; and the staff had never administered such a complex unit.

In theory, and in practice as repeatedly demonstrated by the French, corps structure conferred important advantages. By having all three arms operating together, a corps had a balanced tactical structure that allowed it to fight several times its own number of opponents until help arrived or night came. This self-reliance meant that corps could march dispersed along several avenues of advance rather than jammed together in a vast, slow-moving mass. Karl undoubtedly hoped to reap these advantages in the coming campaign, but in February 1809 it was an untested experiment.

He arranged his corps symmetrically; each of six line corps comprised two regular and one light, advance-guard division. The regular division had two or three infantry brigades, each brigade typically having two regiments of three battalions. (In all Napoleonic-period armies the battalion was the infantry's basic tactical unit.) Battalions maneuvered and changed formation within the larger framework of regiment/brigade/division/corps. The Archduke's corps had twenty-five to thirty infantry battalions, sixteen cavalry squadrons, and sixty-four to eighty-four guns.

The corps' light division was another new feature of Austrian organization. Unlike the French, who spread their light troops out among all infantry units, the Austrians concentrated theirs into these light divisions. Each light division had four to six battalions of jäger, grenzer, or volunteers—the only Austrian battalions capable of fighting in open order, skirmish style—two light cavalry regiments, and two light artillery batteries. The light divisions were intended to march in the army's vanguard, where they would perform scouting and outpost duty. On the battlefield they acted as skirmishers for the entire corps.[6] During a retreat they formed the rear guard. This centralization of light troops had many advantages before a battle began. On the battlefield, it meant the light division had to spread out all along a corps' fighting front, with resultant complete loss of command and control. Alternatively, if it remained concentrated, the regular regiments would be unshielded from enemy skirmish fire.

Direct artillery support for the infantry brigades came from eight-gun three- or six-pound batteries (the light and medium field artillery of the Hapsburg army) controlled by the brigade commander. In addition, the division commander directed a six-piece so-called position battery that fought wherever it could best be used anywhere along the divisional front. In corps reserve were either two or three powerful twelve-pound (the army's heavy field artillery) position batteries along with an extra six-pound battery. The reserve artillery gave the corps a powerful striking force. Rounding out the corps were pioneers, staff troops, and supply and maintenance units.

In addition to the line corps, Karl had two reserve corps. They comprised battalions of the elite grenadiers, picked men from each regiment wearing imposing bearskin helmets and stiff shoulder boards designed to make them appear tall and strong. The brigades of heavy cavalry also were in the reserve corps. The larger First Reserve Corps had twelve grenadier battalions with two brigade batteries and three two-regiment cavalry brigades supported by three cavalry batteries. The Second Reserve Corps had only five grenadier battalions with one battery and two cavalry brigades with two cavalry batteries.

Organizationally, all of this represented an improvement over past Hapsburg practice. Yet an army can be no better than its leaders, and here the Austrians remained gravely deficient. Their inexperience with a corps structure placed heavy demands on the staff, and the Hapsburg staff structure was quite simply not up to the test. At the top, Karl's two ranking staff officers, Grunne and Mayer, hated each other. Their quarrel nearly consumed army headquarters until Karl relieved Mayer of command after the chief of staff finally committed one too many alcohol-induced indiscretions a bare seven weeks before the war began. Beneath these worthies were an insufficient number of trained staff officers. Those who *were* trained had received instruction in mapping, mathematics, horsemanship, drawing, and penmanship, subjects hardly relevant for practical strategic and tactical battlefield maneuver. The inability of the staff to translate paper plans into combat reality was a crippling disadvantage. Staff ineptness is well illustrated by an occurrence later in the campaign, when the army maneuvered around Vienna. As it fought on a flat plain that served as the traditional army maneuver ground and thus was more familiar to the army than any other area in Europe, Karl requested a map. After considerable fumbling, the staff produced a map for an entirely different area. Finally, overcentralization, in which army headquarters sent very detailed orders to each unit, meant that the army would be slow to respond either to tactical opportunities or to emergencies.

To a certain extent the rank-and-files' and junior officers' valor made up for command deficiencies, but even here the army had a serious inherent flaw. It was a polygot army recruited from an empire having a German majority but very large Czech, Polish, Croatian, and Serbian minorities. An earlier Hapsburg commander in chief had written: "No other Army in Europe has the problem of a rank and file differing totally not only in language but also in custom from its officers."[7]

Before the war, Austria gingerly drummed up patriotic zeal by appealing to the people's nationalism. However, such was the empire's ethnic schism that the government restricted appeals to the German majority. Inspirational broadsides were not even translated into Czech. The government felt the ethnic minorities could not be trusted with the fiery spirit of nationalism; its call might be taken too far.

A minority within the military, led by Grunne, believed that Austrian success depended upon the army's morale. Given that Austria's physical resources could not match those of France, Grunne felt that the population had to be rallied to make up for the deficiency. Grunne's views were too radical for the Austrian supreme command.[8] Instead, the army tried to walk a delicate balance between stimulating patriotic zeal and suppressing nationalist-inspired revolt. In response to an appeal for additional Hungarian troops, the Palatine archduke Joseph recommended against it: "The spirit of this country is so bad that this action might precipitate real trouble, so that while our troops are engaged abroad we may face a more dangerous enemy at home."[9] Given the lack of trust the central government placed in them, it is not surprising that Hungarian nobles were less than forthcoming when asked to support the war. Unlike German-speaking Austria, Hungary declined to establish a national militia or landwehr and raised only a fraction of the reserves needed to replace war's predictable attrition.

The presence of ethnic minorities tended to weaken the army's morale. There were exceptions. A French cavalry trooper wrote about the uhlans his regiment encountered: "An hour later we learned that the lancers had all been recruited in that part of Poland which belonged to Austria. We soon recognized that they were Poles by their courage and by the way they handled their lances."[10]

Overall, the men filling the ranks of Karl's army were of uneven quality. In German-speaking Austria, the people's latent nationalism was tapped for the first time in the monarchy's history. Since midsummer 1808 a reduction in press censorship permitted the Austrian press to inspire anti-French feelings while promoting Germanic nationalism: "All the scribes, good and bad, dedicated their genius to exalting the spirits of the people and diminishing the glory of Napoleon."[11] In the newspapers and in the theater the heroic resistance of the Spanish people to French invasion received ever greater accolades. Austrians responded patriotically and filled some German regiments with an unprecedented enthusiasm for war. Other units had large numbers of poorly motivated men. A French intelligence summary identified this weakness: According to deserter interrogation "many foreigners and recruits" are in the regiments. A veteran corporal of nine years' service added that many regiments were "filled with mere peasants."[12]

The Three Arms
Austrian Infantry

In 1809 Austria fielded forty-six German and fifteen Hungarian regiments of regular infantry. During wartime each regiment had three battalions and two grenadier companies. As noted, unlike France Austria maintained the old tradition of converging grenadiers to form elite battalions. At the start of the campaign an average Austrian line battalion had a strength of 943 men. Conscripted from the lowest in Austrian society, the men were universally illiterate, as were most corporals, sergeants, and a fair number of junior officers. Karl wanted them to be able to fight in every type of terrain, but in reality their training overwhelmingly stressed close-order drill best suited for a parade ground.

In an era when camouflage was nearly unheard of, soldiers wore bright white uniforms trimmed in distinctive regimental colors. Hungarian and grenzer regiments stood out in their cornflower-blue pants and half boots; the German regiments wore white breeches with knee-length black gaiters. In 1806 cylindrical shakos had been introduced as standard headgear for the line infantry, but many units went to war in 1809 in the older, more ornamental black leather helmet.

They carried muskets designed in 1798, a weapon some authorities claim was inferior to the French musket, along with sixty rounds of ammunition.

During the course of a peacetime year they fired ten rounds at a target, hardly sufficient to make them sharpshooters. In combat, battalions tried to fire controlled company volleys, regulated by the officers' commands.

The basic battalion formation was the three-rank line, a formation spanning some 170 yards. Officers recognized that the rear rank had difficulty shooting accurately in such a formation.[13] Nonetheless, both Austrians and French felt that units needed three ranks to maintain the necessary solidarity (it was hard to run when wedged in between neighbors) to endure combat. As noted, the basic defensive formation was the line. To attack, Austrian doctrine specified a bayonet charge in line as the ideal formation. Karl's reforms stressed shock action over firepower. He wanted his battalions to cease fire when they neared the enemy and go in with cold steel.

A major problem with linear tactics was slowness. A unit had to halt frequently to dress ranks to preserve its alignment, particularly in rough terrain. Since the French Revolution the Austrians had observed French units maneuver in the more mobile column (one company behind another rather than side by side). Recognizing a good thing, Karl's reforms copied column tactics.[14] In theory, the 1809 Austrian battalion could now maneuver in column and deploy into line for combat.[15] The basic anticavalry formation remained the square, in which a unit folded up into a box so it presented a bristling wall of bayonet-tipped muskets in all four directions.

Doctrine expected the jäger and grenzer units, the light infantry of the Hapsburg war machine, to perform all of the maneuvers of the line as well as operate as skirmishers.[16] But the jägers were untried in combat. They had been recently raised around a cadre of officers and noncommissioned officers from the Tyrolean jäger corps. The grenzer units had been in decline since the turn of the century. Originally recruited from the hardy Slavic peoples who lived along the militarized eastern border of the Hapsburg empire, the receding Turkish threat had softened them.

Nonetheless, both jägers and grenzers were considerably more flexible than the line infantry. At a minimum they wore uniforms that presented a less visible target: dove-gray for the jägers, tobacco brown for most of the grenzers. While the French army rejected rifles and other armies equipped certain special units entirely with rifles, the Austrian jägers hit on an innovative compromise between accuracy and rate of fire. A third of the jägers carried short rifles—which, compared to muskets, had vastly superior accuracy and range although a much slower rate of fire. The balance had carbines, a faster-firing weapon than the musket.

Skirmish tactics called for quick-thinking individual action, something the Austrian soldier seemed to lack. Austrian officers debated why this was so. Some thought it came from a lack of official understanding of how skirmishing should be conducted. Others believed it was simply ill suited to the Germanic character or that the Austrians were overdrilled to the point of losing all creativity. Whatever the reason, Austrian skirmishers experienced great difficulty holding their own with their French counterparts.

The 1809 war saw national militia (landwehr) take the field for the first time. Service was compulsory for all males between the ages of eighteen and forty-five unless they had an exempt status. The monarchy had very mixed feelings about the wisdom of arming its populace and excluded many areas such as Galicia, where the native Poles were suspected for being pro-French, from the landwehr law. Accordingly, while the landwehr provided a sizable reserve force, the government failed fully to exploit potential manpower reserves. The reserves who were mobilized tended to be poorly equipped and trained. In the coming campaign, few landwehr units would participate in field operations in Bavaria. (Later, in the campaign around Vienna, the landwehr would display its worth.)

The Austrian Cavalry Hapsburg cavalry had a tradition of excellence that had become tainted by lackluster conduct in recent years. The heavy cavalry comprised cuirassiers and dragoons; the light included chevaulégers, hussars, and uhlans. In theory, the heavy was reserved for decisive battlefield strokes while the light performed scouting and outpost duty and operated on the flanks during a battle. To this end the heavy had larger horses and exclusively used a heavy, straight cavalry sword, the *pallasch*. In addition, the cuirassiers wore a front armored breastplate that, while not totally musketproof, deflected sword and lance thrusts. Just as the battalion was the basic tactical brick for the infantry, so the squadron served as the basic maneuver unit for the cavalry. Austrian heavy cavalry regiments had six squadrons of 135 men each.

The larger light cavalry regiments had 150 men in each of their eight squadrons. The chevaulégers—a hybrid between heavy and light—carried the pallasch but performed light cavalry duties on the battlefield. The hussars carried the traditional curved saber, while the uhlans wielded both lance and saber. Austrian cavalry carried a mix of firearms, but these were primarily for outpost duty. Cavalry carbines were considerably less efficient than muskets.[17]

In battle the emphasis was decidedly on shock action. Doctrine strictly warned the cavalry not to receive an enemy charge at the standstill. Rather, they were to countercharge. All charges utilized flank guards and retained a reserve. While some maneuvers could be conducted in column, the basic fighting formation was the line. In a regimental charge, pairs of squadrons would attack, each wave separated by twelve-pace intervals.

In sum, in organization and equipment Austrian cavalry was on a par with other continental units. Its mounts, however, according to an Austrian officer, were not of the best. Many troopers rode only partially trained horses, an enormous combat disadvantage.[18] Furthermore, Hapsburg cavalry doctrine had no precise instructions for coordinating charges by several regiments at once. Rothenberg notes: "Together with the absence of large scale exercises which might have revealed this shortcoming, this led to the use of single regiments, even divisions and squadrons, for futile attacks."[19] Since multiregiment charges were a standard feature of French tactics, all too often French masses swamped the Austrian horsemen. Some contemporary observers also felt that Austrian cavalry generals restricted their troopers because of their conservative tendency to preserve their regiments to cover retreats rather than use them with offensive dash. In any event, the Hapsburg horse was no longer a mobile, independent strike force.

Austrian Artillery The period's artillery included foot guns (the gunners walked alongside their pieces) and horse artillery (with which the gunners rode). The sheer weight of the weapons (a twelve-pounder, for example, weighed close to two tons) greatly restricted foot artillery's mobility. A twelve-pounder required twelve horses to move. Harnessed horses presented very vulnerable targets, and as they were hit mobility further declined. Once in position foot artillery tended not to move a great deal.

The types of weapons were smooth-bore guns and howitzers. Guns were line-of-sight weapons, requiring a clear path to their target. Both fired cannonballs or round shot, a solid iron ball that depended upon velocity for its effect. It frightfully mangled a human target when it struck and was capable of knocking over rank after rank of a densely packed column or square. Round shot traveled enormous distances. Depending upon terrain, a twelve-pound shot carried 1800 yards, but effective ranges were just over a thousand. At that range, about 15 percent of the balls hit their target. True effective range was between 400 and 800 yards. At 800 yards, Austrian tests revealed that guns hit a company target between 40 and 70 percent of the time.[20]

The short-barreled howitzers, which comprised about one-quarter of all artillery weapons, usually fired explosive shells instead of round shot. Firing at about a 30-degree elevation, the howitzers lobbed their shells to the target and thus were capable of firing over the heads of friendly troops. Technical inability to manufacture reliable fuses meant howitzer fire was largely a matter of guesswork. Gunners cut the fuse's length to try to make the shell burst on target, but this required great experience to do well. The relatively small powder charges carried in the shell meant that even when they exploded on target, their fragmentation effect was feeble.

At closer ranges, 400 yards and less, guns and howitzers became much more lethal. Here they switched to canister fire. Canister was a thin tin cylinder packed with iron balls. As it emerged from the barrel the cylinder disintegrated, creating a cone of death with a diameter of 32 feet at 100 yards. At 400 yards about 40 percent of the balls hit an infantry target, the remainder plowing into the ground, passing overhead, or penetrating into the spaces between ranks. An average canister-firing battery had the same effect at 400 yards as 700 infantry firing muskets at 100 yards.

Rates of fire were about two round shot or three canister per minute for eight-pound and lighter guns, three rounds in two minutes for howitzers, and one round per minute for the giant twelve-pounder. The sheer fatigue caused by hefting a gun back into place after it violently recoiled meant that rates of fire greatly declined after a battle's opening shots. In a cavalry attack starting 1500 yards away, a six-pound gun would get off nine round shot and two canister before being overrun. Against infantry the same piece would be able to fire twenty-six round shot and two canister. Such firepower meant that a correctly positioned battery could defend its front against all comers. Storming a battery, on the other hand, was an enormously costly proposition and relied on the final run-in taking the battery from the flank.[21]

Austrian artillery was unexceptional. It had "always suffered from a shortage of trained gunners and auxiliary personnel, the absence of permanent tactical formations and control over its own transport."[22] Karl's reforms emphasized the more modern concentration of firepower by eliminating battalion guns and grouping them into brigade batteries. Light three- and six-pound guns served in this role.

Each cavalry brigade of the reserve as well as the light divisions had cavalry batteries comprising four light six-pounders and two short seven-pound howitzers. The so-called cavalry batteries were the Austrian version of horse artillery. Throughout Europe by the late eighteenth century, manufacturers had begun to make lighter guns intended for a new type of weapon, the horse artillery. Special lightweight limbers and carriages and extra horses were provided so that the horse artillery could move much more rapidly than foot artillery. Whereas foot artillery tended to stay put once positioned for battle, the horse artillery could change position. It moved about 200 yards per minute on relatively level ground and thus could exploit tactical opportunities. In the Austrian service some gunners rode horses, while the remainder traveled somewhat precariously balanced on the cushioned top of the caisson or the ammunition box atop the gun's trail.

This system had an advantage in that some of the crew merely had to hop off, rather than dismount and secure their horses, in order to start preparing the gun for firing. It required only ten seconds for a cavalry battery to execute the order to halt and fire, a speed unequaled in Europe. In a meeting engagement, an Austrian cavalry battery could halt and fire two or three times while enduring but a single fire from a French horse battery. However, because not all the gunners rode horses, Austrian cavalry batteries did not have the rapid cross-country maneuverability of the French. Furthermore, because of their lightweight construction, Austrian cavalry guns fired reduced powder charges with a consequent reduction in range and penetration. A canister round from an Austrian piece had only four-sevenths the number of projectiles a comparable French round held.

There were some 2.8 guns or howitzers, foot and cavalry combined, for every thousand men in the army. As noted, Austrian artillery equipment tended to be lighter than that of the opposing French and thus had shorter range but, except for the cavalry batteries, greater mobility. Two problems hampered its effectiveness. The artillery lacked a tradition of massed fire, a tactic that the former artillerist Napoleon Bonaparte had proved successful on numerous battlefields. Worse, individual batteries tended to be commanded by elderly officers who lacked the drive and dash to use their weapons in a modern style. They were usually cautious in their tactical positioning and often failed to coordinate the guns in the manner needed for a true combined arms effort.

The French Army

The 1808 Reforms

Along the northern French coast from 1803 to 1805 the awesome war machine known as the Grande Armée came into being. At coastal military encampments the French army and its commanders had an unequaled opportunity to drill in all aspects of tactics. Officers and men alike honed their skills on everything from individual marksmanship to corps-sized exercises featuring live musket and cannon fire at targets. The Grande Armée proved a nearly invincible force in campaigns from 1805 through 1808. But even successful campaigns brought enormous loss, both from combat and from the wastage of disease and exposure. By 1809, such attrition, coupled with the dispersion of the army from Spain to Italy to Poland, meant the Grande Armée was no more. The backbone of any army, its noncommissioned officers, had seriously weakened: "As a rule it is easy to find officers, but it is sometimes very hard to find noncommissioned officers" wrote Napoleon in 1809.[23] While some units retained solid cadres from the old Grande Armée, many were filled with untested conscripts.[24] And, like the Austrian army grappling with Karl's reforms, the French army entered the 1809 campaign with a new and untested organizational structure.

By imperial decree of 18 February 1808 the new infantry battalion was to comprise six instead of nine companies. Each company had 140 men. Four companies were line troops called fusiliers; one was a light or voltigeur company trained for skirmishing, and the last was the elite grenadier company. Unlike the Austrians, the best men were not converged into grenadier battalions. Instead, the grenadiers remained with the battalion where they could lead by example, providing an experienced, reliable cadre upon which the battalion could depend.[25] The infantry companies rendered available by the reduction from nine to six companies per battalion were used to create an extra fourth battalion per regiment. The process of raising this fourth battalion had not been completed by the time the Austrians invaded.[26]

The new battalion structure meant every tactical maneuver had to be relearned. In compensation, the six-company battalion allowed a unit to perform vital tactical maneuvers with greater speed than the less supple nine-company unit. Another advantage was an increase in the percentage of light troops from one-ninth to one-sixth. But the newly created fourth combat battalion also required more officers, a need French military schools could not meet. Napoleon emptied the military academies to provide officers. Saint-Cyr cadets, due to graduate in May, left school to become lieutenants in the field. Many company officers had to be found among the rank and file or from rear-area, administrative, and garrison areas. Overall, these expedients caused a decline in small-unit leadership.

The organizational reforms of 1808 were well conceived. The coming campaign would be their first test in the field.

The Leaders

Forty years old in 1809, the Emperor Napoleon Bonaparte remained the transcendent European military figure. He had never lost a battle; his military genius was unchallenged. Under his leadership the imperial eagle had paraded in triumph through Vienna, Berlin, Warsaw, and Madrid. Consistent success can breed overconfidence, and there is no doubt that Napoleon became afflicted. He overlooked the depth of Austrian emnity and the growing passion of European nationalism. Furthermore, by equating French national ambitions with his imperial goals he failed to recognize how much his country craved peace. His autocratic control squashed dissent, so there was no one to warn him when he went astray. Absent cautionary council, he was developing a tendency toward self-delusion, a tendency that displayed itself several times in the coming campaign. He retained virile good health, remained capable of prodigious work, and had an amazing immunity to fatigue. His strategic brain shone brightly and no contemporary at this time had his battlefield vision, his celebrated coup d'œil.

Equally important, he understood what motivated men. His officers vied with one another to display the requisite gallantry and skill that led to promotion. He encouraged such rivalry in the belief that it produced an officer's best effort. More than any contemporary general, he also understood the motivations of the rank and file. He had an uncanny ability to circulate among them, proffer rewards and promotions, and by so doing inspire thousands to valor. His presence on the battlefield invariably produced deafening roars of *Vive l'Empereur!* even among the grievously wounded.

Napoleon has been justifiably criticized for failing to impart to his immediate subordinates, the marshals, his theory and knowledge of war. Yet the seven marshals who participated in the Ratisbonne campaign displayed talents unmatched by any group of subordinates in any other contemporary army. They had risen to their positions via a rigorous meritocracy. Napoleon was nothing if not a good judge of men. He demanded that his high-ranking officers possess what he called "squareness," a balance of character and intellect. By character he meant physical courage, perseverance, and daring.[27] And in this regard Napoleon's subordinates far outshined their Austrian counterparts. However, the confused fighting along a wide front would test everyone, causing the Emperor and his marshals to make important mistakes. Since we will meet the Emperor's subordinates on the battlefield, suffice it to say that the marshals provided Napoleon with gifted leadership.

At lower command levels, generals dreamed that they too might someday earn a marshal's baton. While an Austrian general knew his prospects were limited by birth, the French officer knew his future depended on his skill and bravery. Throughout the army were officers of great ability, eager to advance up the chain of command. One officer would achieve the ultimate reward, the promise of a marshal's baton, during the campaign. As at the corps level, French divisional and brigade commanders surpassed their Hapsburg counterparts.

The French Staff

Imperial headquarters was a complex organization far exceeding its Hapsburg counterpart in sophistication and efficiency. It was rigidly centralized in the person of the Emperor. Napoleon's amazing grasp of detail and thorough, meticulous nature set a demanding standard for the staff. Foremost in meeting this challenge was Marshal Alexandre Berthier, the chief of staff. He occupied a thankless position that inflicted enormous psychological stress, as well as occasional physical batterings when Napoleon lost his volatile temper. Although many authorities denigrate Berthier as nothing more than a glorified clerk, he had the vital task of rapidly translating the Emperor's wishes into written orders. With Berthier present at headquarters, the staff worked like a well-oiled machine, a tribute to his peculiar genius. Forced to suppress his personality for the sake of duty, Berthier sought some release through fashion. He and his staff set the style for the rest of the army. If they switched from black to white fur-lined pelisses, the army's dandies hastened to follow suit. In the exhausting routine of meticulous detail work, it was the only flamboyance permitted the staff.

For special staff assignments there were the official aides-de-camp, headed in the 1809 campaign by Mouton, Rapp, and Savary. These were officers who could be absolutely trusted to perform any duty, regardless of obstacles, with intelligence and bravery, or die trying. They "were expected to be equally capable of leading a charge, negotiating a treaty or cooking a chicken."[28]

An indispensable aide was Bacler d'Albe, who headed the Emperor's topographical office and handled all staff duties associated with Napoleon's planning sessions. He updated daily the situation map, on which he marked every formation with different-colored pins; helped perform time and distance calculations; and maintained the notebooks containing details of every French and enemy unit. On campaign, at night before Napoleon slept, and in the predawn when he awoke, his last and first discussions were with d'Albe.

In sum, the French staff had an organization filled with talented personnel who contributed enormously to French success. Staff mistakes could and did occur, but never with the same frequency as with the Austrians.

The Three Arms

The French Infantry French infantry regiments included ligne (line) and légère (light) units, but by 1809 the distinction had lost its original meaning. They were interchangeable components of the larger brigades, divisions, and corps. The French army continued to operate using the corps system. Unlike the Austrians', the French corps were not symmetrical. This was by choice as Napoleon liked to vary his corps' strengths in order to confuse enemy intelligence estimates. Thus strengths ranged from Oudinot's smallish Second Corps, with 32 battalions, 23 squadrons, and 42 guns totaling 21,298 men, to Davout's large Third Corps, with 70 battalions, 40 squadrons, and 75 guns totaling 51,968 men. Being more experienced, the French corps was more flexible. This allowed the Emperor to create ad hoc corps formations in response to battlefield dynamics. Thus, after the first day's fighting on 19 April, we see Napoleon taking half of Davout's infantry along with some of his cavalry, adding them to some reserve formations, and creating a new corps under the command of Marshal Lannes. Such battlefield improvisation was impossible in the Austrian army.

Napoleon relied upon his infantry's justifiable renown for rapid marching. He made careful logistical preparations to enable them to perform such marches. For example, in a long letter in early April he meticulously established a supply system to provide his men with ammunition. He detailed where supply depots should be located, which fortresses should be stocked with reserve ammunition, how many supply wagons should be assigned to each unit, and numerous other factors in order to "sustain three large battles the size of Austerlitz" without the disadvantage of an overly cumbersome supply train. Through it all, and in contrast to the Austrians, the Emperor kept in mind the salient importance of traveling light and reminded his supply officers to eliminate all excess baggage.[29]

French marching ability is well illustrated by the activity of the 105th Regiment. The third day in March found the unit massing in its camps at the Baltic coastal fortress of Danzig. Thirty-nine days later, having marched 420 miles as the crow flies, the regiment arrived in Bayreuth to join Davout's corps. It rested on five different days. For the balance, day after day, it marched twelve to fifteen miles.

Not all French units were capable of the sustained endurance of the veterans. Marshal Oudinot explained that he had to regulate his corps march so that the battalions covered not more than sixteen to seventeen miles per day because his young conscripts were not yet hardened to war. Still, an average day's march for the "soft" French conscript matched an Austrian soldier's maximum on his best day.

If the French infantryman's most valuable weapon was his feet, his musket, of course, was an indispensable adjunct. No Continental army was renowned for its marksmanship, although French and Austrian alike did practice. French officers' correspondence is laced with references to the importance of live firing practice. Davout complained that a lack of powder prevented his men from firing practice. Berthier ordered Oudinot to make sure his young soldiers received target-shooting practice.

In the French tactical system, the infantry battle began with the voltigeur company. The first two ranks (some 90 men per battalion) deployed in what was called skirmish order. Skirmishers worked in two-man pairs, with one always keeping a loaded musket to protect the other as he reloaded. According to the book, about fifteen paces separated each pair. In reality they spread out according to the nature of the terrain and used every scrap of cover for shelter as they blazed away at the enemy. In the attack they glided forward from tree to rock, ditch to hedge, using thoroughly modern fire and movement tactics. Because they presented such a dispersed, elusive target, volleys from opposing formed troops did them little harm. If the opponent charged, the voltigeurs fell back, firing, toward the intervals between their own formed troops. When the enemy retired, out they came again to resume their sniping. The company's third rank occupied a reserve position seventy-five paces to the rear. This reserve sent men forward to replace losses and served as a focal point when the bugles sounded the call to reform.

Screened by the voltigeur's fire, the other five companies stood shoulder to shoulder in three-deep formation. Like the Austrians, French commanders preferred the tactical solidarity offered by the three ranks even though they recognized that the third rank could use its muskets only inefficiently. In 1809, the latest effort to solve this problem recommended having the third rank simply exchange its loaded muskets for the discharged weapons of the men in front. While the front ranks fired, the third rank would merely load. This proved unworkable in combat.

In a firefight the front rank knelt (the front Austrian rank remained standing), the second fired over its heads, and the third fired whenever opportunity arose. At battle's start, the officers regulated their fire so a constant rolling discharge went from right to left (such fire was thought particularly to madden charging horses, sending them off in terrified disorder). As losses piled up, muskets fouled and confusion reigned; firing slowed and became unregulated; each soldier loading, some aiming, and all squeezing triggers as fast as possible.

Eighty thousand conscripts of the class of 1810, called up before their time to meet the Austrian crisis, entered the depots by 15 January 1809. Local authorities found it increasingly difficult to send fit men to the army.[30] In addition, many deserted en route at the first opportunity. A British prisoner of war recalls watching the 1809 conscripts heading for the front: "There was hardly a day that large parties of refractory conscripts were not brought in and out. . . . It is strange . . . that soldiers thus dragged in chains to their respective regiments should leave but few places from the Mediterranean to the Narva unconquered".[31] Hastily sent to the Army of Germany to fill depleted units, they were the poorest physical specimens to enter the army to date. Never before had so many immature, half-trained, or untrained conscripts been in the ranks.[32]

Basically, French infantry relied upon the same formations—line for combat, column for maneuver, square when confronting cavalry—as the Austrians. While conscripts diluted their ranks, on balance they remained devoted to the Emperor and skilled in war. The Bavarian countryside, where the fighting would take place, was rolling and heavily forested. It was terrain well suited to the supple, fluid French infantry tactics and the genius of the individual French soldier.

The French Cavalry: *L'Arme Blanche* Individual training and equipment mattered a great deal more for the cavalry than for the infantry. One infantryman, standing amid hundreds of others, would not know whether his musket fired straight or even, in the general din, whether it fired at all. His single shot seldom made the difference whether he survived or not. Such was not the case for a cavalry trooper.

During the frequent outpost skirmishes and the occasional intense hand-to-hand grappling of massed mounted charges, equipment made a life-and-death difference. Following one of the campaign's first cavalry combats, a French officer observed: "Our new sabers are dull and useless, they bend like lead, the round hilt turns in the hand, causing it to strike with the flat rather than the edge."[33] Since equipment came from many manufacturers, other troopers were more pleased with their blades: "The 2d regiment of chasseurs . . . still carried the sabers of honor that the regiment had obtained in Cremona during our old wars in Italy; they were long, straight, and very slender, the wounds they inflicted were murderous."[34] A sword's quality mattered because, unlike the infantry, cavalry frequently engaged in hand-to-hand fighting.

French heavy cavalry comprised cuirassiers, carabiniers, and dragoons. Cuirassiers were big men wearing heavy metal casque helmets, encased in front and rear metal breastplates and knee-high stiff leather boots. They were the battlefield descendants of the armored knights of the Middle Ages. Because of their size and their equipment's weight, they rode much-larger-than-average horses. The carabiniers had not yet been fitted with the cuirass. Their origins reflected a mounted-fire tradition that they exhibited on the battlefield, firing a carbine volley into the enemy before drawing swords and charging. The Army of Germany had twelve cuirassier and two carabinier regiments, normally kept in reserve for the decisive moment. Then, as the enemy wavered, they thundered forward to complete the victory.

At the other end of the mounted spectrum (dragoon regiments did not participate in the campaign) were the French light cavalry, the dashing *beau sabres* of Europe. Thirteen chasseurs à cheval and four hussar regiments comprised this contingent. Taught to think of themselves as a cut above the plodding heavies, they acted accordingly, on and off the battlefield. Off the battlefield, drinking, gambling, wenching, and dueling were expected. Some of this free-spirited behavior carried over to the battlefield. Intended to operate in the army's van, they both screened friendly troops from prying hostile eyes and scouted the enemy. These were the traditional light cavalry missions and the French performed them unevenly. Bravery they exhibited in spades, but attention to duty they sometimes lacked. On many battlefields the French light cavalry failed to keep track of enemy movements, thus causing their foot-slogging brethren to experience too many unwelcome surprises.

All French cavalry regiments were smaller than their Austrian counterparts. Like the Hapsburg horse, they maneuvered by squadrons with the troopers formed in two-deep ranks. Unlike the Austrians, each regiment had only three or four squadrons. Given that a squadron of 250 men occupied about 165 yards of front, the command and control problems associated with a French regimental charge were much easier than with an Austrian six- or eight-squadron regimental charge. French regiments were quite simply handier tactical instruments than the bulkier Austrian units. More important, French cavalry customarily participated in multiregiment charges. The heavy cavalry, in particular, delivered most of its blows in massive groups. Given roughly equal equipment, training, and courage (and such was usually the case when French trooper met Austrian), bigger numbers would win. French cavalry had one other intangible asset compared to the Austrians: a tradition of victory under Napoleon that made it a confident, aggressive force.

The French Artillery Napoleon had entered the army as a gunner, so it is not surprising that he lavished great attention upon the artillery. In 1809 the artillery was still in the process of implementing reforms begun in 1803. Lighter-weight, more mobile six-pound guns were replacing the old four- and eight-pounders. Because they were made with the highest-quality material and incorporated several technical advances, they almost matched the eight-pounders' firepower. In terms of mobility, they compared favorably with the four-pounders while having superior firing performance. Similarly, improved howitzers replaced the older Gribeauval models. Neither the Second nor the Third Corps had yet received any six-pounders. Both retained the eight-pounders. Conversely, the Fourth Corps had no eight-pounders, having instead a combination of the new French six-pounder and captured Austrian six-pounders.[35]

A French battery comprised six guns and two howitzers. The Emperor's goal, only partially realized in time for the campaign, was to have each infantry division supported by one foot and one horse six-pound battery. In corps and army reserve were the "Emperor's daughters," his beloved twelve-pounders. Like the heavy cavalry, they were intended for a reserve role until the situation ripened. Committed at the decisive point, they would batter a hole in the enemy's line and pave the way for victory.

French horse artillery exhibited dash unlike any other Continental horse gunners. In part this was due to equipment; only the British caisson design equaled the ease with which the French caisson with battery in tow could gallop across a field and sharply turn to position the gun for firing. Furthermore, all French gunners rode horses, which increased a battery's cross-country speed. From the time the battery officer gave the order, it took a mere

seventeen seconds for a moving horse artillery battery to take position and fire.
Technical considerations aside, the effectiveness of French horse artillery came
from the battery officers' bold leadership.

At campaign's start, the ratio of guns and howitzers per 1000 soldiers was
1:8, a figure that did not meet Napoleon's ideal of two per thousand. This
deficiency would not become apparent until the campaign moved from the
wooded Bavarian countryside around Ratisbonne to the open plains outside
Vienna.

The French Allies

More than ever before, the conduct of the French allies assumed extreme
importance in the coming campaign. The first Austrian blows would fall on
the Bavarians. For days the French center would be held by Bavarians, Württembergers, and a division raised from the Rhenish princes. The Austrians saw
this as an opportunity and tried to present the war as a struggle of all German
peoples against the French. These efforts worried the French leaders, who
wondered to what extent they could rely upon their allies.

A week after the war started, Marshal François Lefebvre, the French
commander of the Bavarian Corps, wrote headquarters that he urgently
needed a regiment of French light troops to perform outpost duty. The marshal
reasoned that the outpost troops were in close contact with the Austrians and
thus most vulnerable to enemy blandishments to desert or even change sides.
French troops could screen the allies from such temptations. In the event, the
French allies performed reliably and often extremely well. But Lefebvre's
concerns were a real fear at the time, and in them can be seen the seeds of a
growing schism between French war aims and the national aspirations of her
Germanic allies. French allies contributed 31 percent of the Army of Germany's strength. However, as the Austrian offensive caught Napoleon un-
prepared, his French forces dispersed, his Germanic allies played a major role
at the campaign's start. Much depended on their performance.

Lefebvre's Bavarian Seventh Corps had 24,334 infantry arrayed in three
divisions. A total of 3269 cavalry and 76 guns supported them. France and
Bavaria had a history of alliance and cooperation dating back to the 1700s.
Furthermore, Bavaria and Austria enjoyed a historic emnity, intensified by
Bavaria's acquisition of the Tyrol following the 1805 war. Bavarian agents had
detected Austrian agents traveling about the Tyrol planting the seeds of revolt,
which did little to persuade them to accept Austria's overt role as liberator of
the oppressed German peoples. Although French officers had some doubts
about Bavarian steadfastness, in the event the Bavarians solidly adhered to the
alliance. The rank and file cared little about such political considerations but

could understand the need to fight when an ancient enemy invaded their territory.[36] Bavarians were loyal to their king; if he was pro-French, so were they. They were a thoroughly professional army. If they rarely displayed prodigies of valor, they were steady and every bit the equal of their Austrian opponents. Yet Napoleon judged the Bavarian regular inferior in spirit to a French conscript. During one operation on 21 April, he shuffles the order of march so that a division of French conscripts replaces a division of Bavarians in the army's van. He delicately explains that the substitution is to take advantage of "French impetuosity."[37]

A notch above the Bavarians were the tough Württembergers of the Eighth Corps. Their commander was the French General Dominique Vandamme, an irascible, hard-to-please officer. Yet Vandamme's after-action reports are full of praise for his men, a sure indication of some outstanding battlefield conduct. On the approach to Eckmühl, the Württemberg Light Brigade showed French-like mobility, covering fifty miles in thirty-eight hours during which they fought several combats. Slightly over 10,000 infantry, 2214 cavalry, and 16 guns made up this fine corps. At the other end of the spectrum was Rouyer's Confederation of the Rhine Division. In spite of a desperate situation that required every available musket, Napoleon chose to assign them to line-of-communications duties. We can only suppose that he judged the men from Anhalt, Arenberg, Mecklenburg-Schwerin, and numerous other small Rhenish territories unequal to the challenge of open combat. A total of 3820 Germans filled the ranks of Rouyer's division. Masséna's Fourth Corps had a substantial allied contingent made of sterner stuff. A Hesse-Darmstadt brigade was in Saint-Cyr's division, a Baden brigade comprised more than half of Legrand's division, and both nations contributed troopers to the light cavalry division. These were good soldiers, capable of outstanding performances. While French historians and writers have historically found great fault with their army's allies, they found little to quarrel with regarding allied conduct during the Ratisbonne campaign.

In campaigns past, the French army had entered combat boosted by months of propaganda. However, an important consequence of the Hapsburg surprise attack in 1809 was that Napoleon's extensive propaganda apparatus did not have time to perform its duties. In the police state that was France, the government controlled all means of public information. Normally, government machinery prepared the country for war through newspapers, official pronouncements, and handbills. These writings had the prime goal of instilling public enthusiasm for war. When time permitted, officially inspired whispering campaigns, speeches, rallies, and martial fetes further stoked popular spirit.

A second propaganda goal was to enlist allies. Napoleon knew that British and Austrian agents circulated among the restive peoples of French-occupied Germany; French propaganda sought to limit their influence. With enough advance warning French propaganda also sought to demoralize the enemy. In the case of Austria, these efforts would be directed at the potentially weak members of the Austrian empire, the Hungarians and Poles. However, before the crisis on the Danube there was no time for French propaganda to accomplish its goals, and thus Austrian strategic surprise had largely negated one of Napoleon's important weapons.

However, some of the Emperor's propaganda efforts did have time to bear fruit. In 1808, French scholars nationwide received instructions to encourage male students to volunteer for the military before their official conscription date. Similarly, Napoleon did not overlook the church's influence. The clergy was commanded to extol the glories of war to young, impressionable parishioners. Bombarded in school and in church, many young men responded to the call to arms. The horrors of service in Spain were not yet readily apparent to the masses. Consequently, young Frenchmen marched off to their assembly areas in Bavaria in search of glory. The well of French martial patriotism, while drawn deep, was not yet empty.

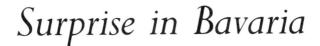

CHAPTER III

Surprise in Bavaria

Military science consists in first calculating all the possibilities accurately and then in making an almost mathematically exact allowance for accident. Accident thus always remains a mystery to mediocre minds and becomes reality for superior men.

The Battle for Intelligence

The years preceding war's outbreak witnessed intense Franco-Austrian competition for strategic information. Both sides put enormous effort into understanding the other's military capacity and plans. In this struggle Austria enjoyed significant advantages. For four years Austrian diplomats and military men alike targeted France as the most likely opponent in a future war. They could afford to concentrate most of their resources toward this end. Napoleon, on the other hand, had to divide French attention and resources. Everywhere he gazed he saw restive allies such as the Bavarians, sullen neutrals like Prussia, and outright opponents in the Iberian Peninsula. Wherever water lapped a European shore, British agents could be actively recruiting and financing opposition to Napoleon's rule. In France itself royalist cells worked in the shadows to plot the king's return. Always in the background was the possibility that the man who had risen to be emperor on the power of his soldiers' bayonets could be violently displaced. Thus it was an uneven competition, with Napoleon forced to watch in all directions while the ascendant Austrian war party kept an unblinking gaze on the main chance.

Geography also favored Austria in the area of strategic intelligence. Prior to war's outbreak it had had several years to establish secret routes of correspondence and to position spies and informers. Austria reaped great benefit from the fact that the French line of communications stretched long distances through unfriendly territory. French reports from the farflung outposts of the Empire were thus vulnerable to interception. When Marshal Davout, billeted with his corps in peacetime cantonments in central Germany, wanted to communicate with France's Polish allies, a messenger had to pass first through unfriendly Prussia and then across Galicia, territory possessed by Austria four years previously.

In addition to intercepting messengers, Austrian agents and sympathizers could easily observe French military movements in occupied territory. In Prussia, patriotic Prussian officers happily passed to Vienna important intelligence based on personal observation. Throughout the Confederation of the Rhine, civilians and military men who retained old allegiances provided intelligence and prepared partisan bands who were to erupt in revolt once the war began. Austria made skillful use of its resources and without a doubt bested the French in the prewar intelligence competition. The extent of Austrian success is highlighted by the fact that just three days before the war began, Davout learned that one of his trusted messengers was actually an Austrian agent.

Another indicator of the degree to which Austria won the battle for intelligence is shown by the lack of preparedness of the French intelligence service, a deficiency best illustrated by the case of the French master spy Karl Schulmeister. Schulmeister's timely information had contributed immeasurably to Napoleon's smashing success against Austria in 1805. In 1808, sensing the winds of war, the spy volunteered to abandon a comfortable retirement and resume his profession. But the Emperor did not believe war likely and failed to organize his espionage service as he had in 1805. Not until 23 February 1809 did Napoleon authorize the creation of an intelligence bureau at Munich, the communications hub of south Germany. There was hardly time to begin operations before the Austrians attacked. Had Schulmeister been on duty, he might have provided a warning.

The result of Austria's triumph in the battle for intelligence was that the Hapsburg decision for war came as a tremendous shock to Napoleon. Austria had achieved strategic surprise.

By midwinter 1809 French military men realized that war was a near-certainty. The battle for intelligence shifted from the grand strategic—Will Austria fight? Will Russia support France?—to specific questions about when the war would start and the composition of the rival armies. Since he was stationed nearest Austria, Marshal Davout had the major military intelligence-gathering role. He organized special bureaus at important communications centers near the Austrian border to intercept correspondence with Vienna. One interception told of Karl's departure from Vienna for the front, a movement Davout correctly interpreted as a sign that war would begin shortly.

However, Napoleon required more precise information about the timing of the war's outbreak. Just before the Austrian invasion, his ally the Bavarian general Carl Wrede sent word that all communications with Bohemia and Austria were being rigorously intercepted by the Austrians. Consequently, Wrede himself began to intercept all letters dispatched to Vienna. One intercepted letter claimed that the Austrian war declaration would come on 8 April.[1] Although Davout, Wrede, and other front-line officers penetrated the Austrian veil in time to learn that an attack was pending, it was too late for Napoleon to make strategic adjustments. The specific timing of the Austrian attack surprised him, and this surprise led to near-fatal complications.

The uncertainty over when Austria would attack caused Napoleon to linger in Paris rather than join the army in Bavaria. He knew enemy agents would note his departure and did not want to do anything that might hurry Austrian war preparations. Instead he entrusted the opening maneuvers to a subordinate.

Complementing Marshal Davout's activities, French diplomats in Austria strained every nerve to determine when Archduke Karl would leave Vienna, figuring that his departure would signal imminent war. Even the movement of Karl's carriage was deemed significant. Thus a French diplomat reported that on 22 March a well-connected source revealed that both Karl's and Kaiser Franz's carriages and stable had left Vienna. A French spy whose report is signed with an enigmatic X—undoubtedly an Austrian national in French pay—wrote from Vienna on 27 March: "The time when hostilities will commence is still unknown. . . . One must consider Karl's departure as a signal for war; but there is a very great mystery surrounding his departure, as well as that of the Emperor."[2]

In an effort to curb intelligence leaks, as early as 1808 Austria and Bavaria set up patrols on opposite sides of the border. They were so vigilant that a British officer, attempting to escape from French prison, wrote that the Austrians "seemed to watch with the eyes of an Argus."[3] In spite of such efforts, diplomats and travelers provided a wealth of military intelligence used by both sides to deduce the enemy's order of battle.[4] In early March, for example, a French diplomat in Vienna sent a list of Austrian regiments that had traversed the city for the past two weeks on their way to the front. Another French diplomat managed to arrange his travel itinerary so that he visited important Austrian posts along the Bavarian border. He thus provided small details like "30 grenadier companies are concentrated around Linz . . . the Linz landwehr exercise every Sunday, and those in Bohemia have just received their flags."[5] Austrian diplomats performed similar service in France and among the French-allied states.

Since both sides recognized the intelligence leaks caused by travelers and diplomats, both considered the enemy's efforts to plug such leaks important indicators that war was near. When, on 24 March, the Austrians arrested a French courier (an elderly French officer residing in Vienna whom the Austrians evicted for security reasons and who was pressed into service by the French ambassador to carry intelligence back to France) Napoleon himself considered it a very significant step. He immediately ordered that all officers assigned to the army in Germany leave immediately for their posts.

Then as now, newspapers provided valuable reports of a country's military operations. Both sides made arrangements to have the latest papers smuggled out of the country for analysis by military men. For example, three days before the war's first major engagement, Davout informed headquarters that he had just received the latest papers from Vienna.

In addition to strategic intelligence provided by various forms of espionage, once war began the opponents acquired battlefield tactical intelligence from a variety of sources including prisoner and deserter interrogation, civilians, and hired spies. During the campaign's first days, the French brigadier Baron de Piré sent a spy out past his picket line to scout an enemy patrol his troopers had encountered during the day. The spy returned with the information that Piré's patrol had engaged fifteen Blankenstein hussars, fifteen Merveldt uhlans, and 200 jägers. Behind them stood four infantry regiments and four landwehr battalions. From colonel to emperor, leaders on both sides recognized the value of being able to divine what was on the other side of the hill.

By war's eve the French had assembled a detailed order of battle for Karl's army. It listed commanding generals from brigade up to corps, the names of the regiments and the total number of battalions and squadrons in each command. French staff officers carried this invaluable information in special notebooks that accompanied Napoleon in the field. Certain details of this estimate were incorrect.[6] Yet in sum, when the French calculated that the Austrian army comprised 184 battalions and 164 squadrons, they were off by only a single battalion.[7] It had been an impressive achievement.

War Plans

Archduke Karl doubted that his army was ready for war. Yet as supreme commander (Generalissimus)* he was in charge of devising a war-winning strategy. He could make the main effort in one of two theaters, Italy or the Danube Valley in Germany. In wars past Austria had tried both. For the 1809

---

* See page ix for table of Austrian ranks.

campaign Karl chose the Danube Valley. In previous campaigns Austria customarily sent major forces to support secondary efforts. Indeed, Napoleon counted on Karl making such a dispersion of force. Instead, showing fine strategic ability, Karl created an unprecedented Hapsburg concentration of force on the main front.

Karl planned one diversionary effort in Poland. It involved 40,000 men commanded by Archduke Ferdinand who massed his troops in Galicia. By and large these were second-line troops assigned the task of defending Austria's Polish possessions. The possibility also existed that if Ferdinand defeated the Polish forces who were allied with France and only numbered some 17,000 men, the Czar would cast his lot on the Austrian side.

Archduke John commanded the army in Italy. Although his force numbered nearly 100,000 men, only half were regulars. The balance comprised landwehr, Hungarian Insurrection forces, and other reserve formations. John had the triple mission of reconquering as much of Italy as possible, containing the French forces occupying Dalmatia, and raising the Tyrol in revolt. This left Karl with a formidable force of nearly 200,000 regulars grouped in eight corps—a much larger force than Napoleon anticipated encountering. With this allocation of strength, Karl added concentration of force to strategic surprise. None of Napoleon's earlier opponents had done so well.

Karl's first idea was to make an early attack with his main force on the French Army of Germany before French reinforcements arrived. Accordingly, during March he concentrated his best units in Bohemia. Karl planned for them to debouch from the Bohemian mountains, overpower any enemy encountered—hopefully catching Davout's corps in its peacetime cantonments—and advance to cut off French forces in north Germany. His bold plan had several advantages (see Map 2). It would quickly lead to a decision; this was important since the Austrian army could not base itself in Bohemia for very long for logistical reasons. The attack from Bohemia had two other advantages: There were few good defensive positions available to the French to check the Austrian attack, and an attack from Bohemia might stimulate a Germanic uprising among the restless peoples of Franconia, Hesse, and Saxony. The Bohemian alternative was "a daring plan and could have had decisive results—if launched about 20 March and carried through with speed and decision."[8]

The Bohemian plan also had certain weaknesses. In addition to its difficult logistics—poor roads, few resources to feed an army, and distance from Austrian bases on the Danube—the plan left the Danube Valley open to a French counterinvasion directed at Vienna. It would leave a wide strategic gap between Karl's forces in Bohemia and those of Archduke John in the Tyrol and in Italy. Accordingly, considerable strength would have to be detached to provide a link with John and to defend the Danube.

These problems led Karl to consider an alternative, an attack south of the Danube (see Map 2). Here the army could use the river as a main line of communications. There were many well-stocked fortresses to serve as bases. Karl could better protect the Tyrol and defend against a French attack out of Switzerland. He would be closer to John and be positioned to block a French drive on Vienna. On the debit side, valuable time would be lost transferring the army from Bohemia to the Danube's south bank. Once there, the army would have to cross several smaller rivers that provided the French excellent defensive positions. Also, numerous Bavarian fortresses dotted the countryside, giving the enemy additional defensive resources.

In sum, Karl had two choices: a bold attack out of Bohemia or a cautious advance south of the Danube. Bickering among the staff impeded careful balancing of the two plans. In February the feuding became so ugly that Karl dismissed his chief of staff. This officer had been the most prominent supporter of the Bohemian plan. Given that the original decision for war was based on the belief that France could not both fight a war in Spain and maintain in Germany an army strong enough to resist a surprise Austrian invasion, it would seem Karl should have followed his original instinct and chosen the Bohemian option. But underlying all planning was the recognition that the monarchy's integrity depended upon the preservation of the army. Bold options could be considered on paper, but in the breach the state's stifling conservatism prevailed. So Karl issued orders to transfer his army south over the Danube.

The Austrian march south demonstrated that the reformed Hapsburg army still could not move quickly. After a mere two-day march, several corps halted to allow the baggage train to catch up so that bread could be baked and the army fed. Thus it was for the remainder of the march: waterlogged days of trudging through the mud separated by frequent stops to refit. During the twenty days preceding the actual border crossing into Bavaria the four front-line Austrian corps averaged seven idle days. Even on march days, the large artillery train greatly encumbered the army, while the Austrian generals, unused to the new corps structure, marched in the old formal style and so further reduced the rate of advance.

Unlike the French, the Austrians did not live off the land. Karl feared provoking popular resentment and worried that widespread foraging would erode discipline. Consequently, a huge supply column trailed each of the combat corps. These columns included heavy field ovens to bake daily rations. Their necessary presence governed the speed of the Hapsburg march. It was not, as the situation demanded, a whirlwind descent into Bavaria.

Meanwhile, across the lines, Marshal Davout, engaged in his own flank march south to Ratisbonne, first detected the Austrian maneuver on 27 March. He informed Napoleon, who now recognized that the French mobilization was a step behind the Austrians. The later the war came, the more time Napoleon had to catch up. As noted, he feared that his own departure to the front would precipitate an early Austrian attack. Consequently, he ordered his chief of staff, Marshal Louis-Alexandre Berthier, to take command until the outbreak of war.

The fifty-six-year-old marshal was an officer of vast experience. He had served on Rochambeau's staff during the American Revolution. He had campaigned with Napoleon in Italy, where he displayed fine tactical prowess and front-line leadership. Since 1796 he had been an indispensable figure at Napoleon's headquarters, serving as chief of staff with unsurpassed energy and attention to detail. Years of suffering the Emperor's moods and whims had taken a heavy toll on the once-dashing officer. In recent years he had been reduced to acting as a staff clerk, a role he performed superbly. When Napoleon assigned him the task of guiding the Army of Germany, he supposed that the job merely required administrative talents. He doubted the Austrians would move fast enough to cause Berthier to make combat decisions. It was another critical error of judgment that contributed to Napoleon's crisis on the Danube.

On 30 March the Emperor dictated a long, rambling set of instructions to guide Berthier in his absence. In them lay the seeds of a first-class disaster. They began with a review of the general situation. Napoleon asserted that Austria would not make war without withdrawing her ambassador and without making a formal declaration of war. Thus France would have some advance notice before hostilities began—a mistaken assumption. Napoleon continued by saying he doubted the war would begin before 15 April. Based on this assumption, the balance of his instructions detailed what preparations should be completed by the fifteenth.

Distilled with hindsight, the instructions can be summarized by two contingencies: If the Austrians move before the fifteenth, the French army should concentrate to the rear around Donauworth; if the attack comes after the fifteenth, the concentration should center on Ratisbonne (see Map 2). This key conditional order lies buried in the middle of a lengthy set of instructions full of digressions. It only stood out later, after several unexpected things happened.

The Fog of War

Although they would be physically apart, Napoleon relied upon a most advanced communications system to keep his chief of staff on a short leash. Back in the days of the Revolution, the wizard-inventor Claude Chappe had designed a semaphore system to link Paris with the frontiers. It consisted of a series of signaling stations located within sight of one another. Every station had a movable central arm at each end of which hung a secondary arm. The combination of these arms in different positions enabled messages to pass from station to station. Lanterns hanging from the arms at night permitted communication in the dark. With good visibility a message traveled over twenty miles in a mere seven minutes, easily outdistancing a mounted courier. Chappe's amazing system, contemporarily referred to as a telegraph, provided officials in Paris incredibly up-to-date information and allowed them to direct events from afar accurately.[9]

Throughout the late winter of 1809 the telegraph running through Strasbourg carried a heavy load as the field forces in southern Germany received orders from Paris. Then, during the first crucial days of April, as Karl's forces drew near the Bavarian border, a stormy period disrupted operations. Mist and fog imperiled the French army to a greater extent than the creeping Austrian advance. Delays in transmission coupled with dispatches entirely lost helped produce a fog of war that first disoriented, then thoroughly rattled the hapless Berthier.

At the root of the trouble lay Napoleon's increasingly characteristic over-confidence. He hadn't wanted to believe war with Austria was possible. Once proved wrong, he doubted Austria could attack before 15 April. He did not realize that a revitalized Hapsburg army was capable of more energetic maneuver. On 3 April, the ever-vigilant Davout again provided important intelligence: "Diplomats, travelers, deserters, all agree that the Austrians are marching with a part of their force from Bohemia to the right bank of the Danube."[10] The dispatch also warned of Prussian plots to seize French fortresses in Germany once the war began and reported that the ex-elector of Hesse-Cassel was in Prague raising a band of men who were in communication with partisans in Westphalia. Encouraged by British gold and Austrian agents, Europe was growing increasingly restless under the heel of the French conqueror.

Neither sure of the Austrian invasion's timing nor of its location, Napoleon prepared two plans. As in his original instructions to Berthier, he predicated the first upon the supposition that the Austrian attack would come before the fifteenth. It directed a safe, rearward concentration behind the Lech River (see Map 2). The order went by telegraph on 10 April. Unknown to Napoleon, the Austrians invaded the same day. He also did not know that a weather-created breakdown kept this vital message from reaching Berthier until the sixteenth.

The Emperor amplified his wishes with a longer order as soon as he finished dictating the telegraphic order. In one sentence it repeated the instruction to withdraw behind the Lech if an attack came before the fifteenth. But the balance of the order detailed a second plan that assumed the attack would come after the fifteenth. It recommended a more aggressive forward deployment around Ratisbonne and contained a key clause regarding Marshal Davout's Third Corps: The marshal "will place his headquarters in Ratisbonne; his army will be gathered one day's march around that city, and that under all circumstances."[11]

Dispatched by mounted courier, the second order reached Berthier two and a half days ahead of the telegraphic dispatch it was meant to interpret. Had the telegraphic message arrived first, what now happened would never have occurred, but years of intense clerical service for the Emperor had beaten all creative powers from the once-dynamic chief of staff. During the war's first days, Berthier would maintain his balance under pressure. When he received the written orders sent from Paris that seemingly contradicted everything to date, the chief of staff acted without pausing to reflect on the consequences of his orders.[12] Berthier focused on the *and that under all circumstances* and dutifully ordered Davout, who was about to unite with the main French army, to countermarch to Ratisbonne.

Recognizing that events had surpassed his ability to cope, the despairing Berthier wrote to Napoleon: "In this position of affairs, I greatly desire the arrival of your Majesty."[13]

Napoleon Bonaparte as he appeared in 1809.

Czar Alexander I. Skillfully remained neutral in 1809.

Joseph Fouché, Minister of the Police. A masterful schemer, he "needed intrigue like food."

Karl Talleyrand-Perigord, Minister of Foreign Affairs. The indispensible traitor.

Marshal Andre Masséna, duc de
Rivoli. Gave a poor performance as
commander of IV Corps.

Marshal Louis Davout, duc d'Auerstadt.
Commanded the superb III Corps,
Europe's most able subordinate.

Marshal Jean Lannes, duc de
Montebello. Provided top-notch
advance guard leadership.

Archduke Karl. Reformer and able
strategist, his plan created Napoleon's
"Crisis on the Danube."

Clemens Metternich-Winneburg.
The unsurpassed diplomatic genius
of his era.

FML Johann Hiller, Karl's
detested rival, commander of
VI Corps.

FML Friedrich Hohenzollern-
Hechingen, commander of III Corps.
Karl considered him his best corps
leader.

FML Franz Rosenberg, commander of
IV Corps, which defended alone at the
climactic Battle of Eckmühl.

Saint-Sulpice's cuirassiers support Saint-Hilaire below the Teugen-Hausen ridge, 19 April.

Teugen-Hausen. Austrian crestline from Saint-Hilaire's position. The hollow is just beyond wheat field.

Teugen-Hausen. U-shaped woods and Austrian-held crestline from the hollow. Up this slope charged the Terrible 57th.

CHAPTER IV

The Master Arrives

In war, men are nothing, one man is everything.

The Invasion of Bavaria

The Archduke Karl proceeded with his own plans, ignorant that Berthier's blundering would give him the perfect opportunity for a decisive thrust. On war's eve he issued a manifesto written by a German nationalist that was designed to inspire his own men to valor and Napoleon's allies to desert:

> Companions in arms, the eyes of the world, the eyes of all who still retain a sense of national honor are focused on you. . . . Europe looks for freedom under your banners . . . your German brethren wait for redemption at your hands.[1]

On 9 April Austrian messengers carried word to the French that the Hapsburg army intended to advance and treat all who resisted as enemies, decidedly not the formal and time-consuming procedure Napoleon had anticipated. The Austrians were behaving in typical French, but atypical Austrian, style. The next day Austrian troops poured across the Bavarian border and war began.

Two Austrian corps remained north of the Danube. Commanded by GdK (full cavalry general)* Heinrich Bellegarde and totaling nearly 50,000 men, they were to attack any troops encountered and then march south on a broad front in the general direction of Ratisbonne, where it would link up with Karl.

---

* See table, page ix.

On the main front, Karl led over 150,000 men in six corps west across the Inn (see map 2). Detached on his left was a 10,000-man division assigned to capture Munich. Farther south, the Tyrol exploded into violent rebellion. Austrian agents had carefully planned the revolt, which took advantage of Tyrolean hatred of the Bavarians. Quickly the rebels captured most of the key posts and massacred their Bavarian garrisons. By their actions, the Tyrolese severed French communications with Italy while linking Karl's army in Bavaria with Archduke John's army in Italy. In Italy and Poland the Austrians launched secondary offensives. The result was a war whose front extended from Warsaw to Milan. The cockpit of combat was in the Danube Valley, however, and here the best troops and best leaders concentrated.

The only French formation initially confronting this formidable Hapsburg host was Davout's Third Corps, which contained more veterans of the Grande Armée than any other French force. While other Grande Armée formations went to Spain, the Third Corps had luxuriated in billets throughout Germany. There the men found the food and drink ample and the women agreeable.[2] The Austrian threat summoned them from their blissful idyl and to war they marched once more. They were to the Army of Germany what the Tenth Legion had been to Caesar—a veteran, totally dependable fighting force.

Before the war's outbreak, Davout—ably seconded by his set of superb divisional commanders—had shown great activity in tracking Austrian movements. A combination of spies and vigilant border patrols identified the Austrian buildup south of the Danube. Six days before the invasion divisional commander Louis Saint-Hilaire reported to Davout that at least three Austrian corps had crossed to the Danube's south bank, that one corps commander had had his headquarters near the Bavarian frontier for the past three days, that 6000 head of cattle were being gathered, and that many pontoon boats had been sighted. This information, contained in just one of numerous reports, clearly showed that a major Austrian effort was imminent. In response, Davout planned to evade Bellegarde north of the Danube and march south past Ratisbonne to join the main French army.

Meanwhile, directly in Karl's path lay the border fortress of Passau and three Bavarian divisions. The nearest, commanded by Deroi, guarded the Isar River crossings at Landshut (see Map 2). The Isar provided an excellent defensive position, squarely blocking Karl's intended advance. Surprised by the early Austrian invasion, the French were unable to support Deroi and thus the Bavarian general could not take advantage of the position. He would have to fight a solitary delaying action while behind him the balance of the French army gathered. At Ingolstadt a Württemberg and a Confederation of the Rhine division massed, supported by a weak French infantry division and a powerful unit of heavy cavalry. In southern Bavaria, Marshal Masséna was rapidly collecting two corps comprising 50,000 men. Dispersed over a very long front, uncertain whether the Austrians would attack from Bohemia or along the Inn, the French army stood off-balance and vulnerable. Both armies were marching toward a central location between Ratisbonne and Ingolstadt. Here the inevitable collision would take place.

After crossing the Bavarian border on the tenth, Karl marched his army westward. He detached a second-rate force comprising mostly landwehr to blockade Passau. The action started well when unwary ceremonial guards opened the city gates to Austrian scouts. The Austrians happily occupied the city but found the fortress a tougher proposition. Passau was well stocked with food and munitions thanks to Napoleon's prescient prediction, delivered to Metternich back in February, that it would play a front-line role in any future war.[3] A Bavarian battalion confidently manned its walls. Karl consequently chose to bypass it; Passau's fate would be determined by battles farther westward. Westward marched the Austrians, none too swiftly. Hampered by heavy rains, they averaged a mere eight miles per day.

During the leisurely Austrian advance, commanders on both sides sent out patrols ranging from ten-man cavalry detachments to small mixed forces of horse and foot. The patrols vied to screen the movements of the main body while trying to ascertain the enemy's strength and location. Collisions between rival patrols produced numerous combats. Reports of these skirmishes filtered back to the generals, who passed them up the chain of command. At headquarters, officers analyzed the reports, taking note of uniforms and regimental names. Combined with prisoner interrogations and deserters' tales, an enemy order of battle emerged.

Characteristic of the small combats flaring up along the 150-mile front was an encounter on 13 April near Amberg, a road junction north of the Danube much needed by both Davout and Bellegarde. At 3:00 A.M., the French colonel Meda led his First Chasseurs à Cheval on a reconnaissance. He advanced carefully, expecting to meet the Austrians at any moment. Around 6:00A.M., as his men climbed up a small defile, scouts spotted a squadron of the Merveldt uhlans massed across the road. Meda sent his cavalry forward while fifty light-infantry voltigeurs who accompanied his unit moved into a nearby ravine to flank the Austrian position.

Suddenly a second uhlan squadron charged in column down the road. The uhlans' surprise attack threatened to drive off the French cavalry and capture the infantry. Meda instantly ordered his elite squadron to countercharge in column. The two columns collided. The chasseurs drove their horses between the uhlans' lance points. At close quarters they could use their sabers while the uhlans could not bring their unwieldy lances to bear. An intense melee followed, with troopers on both sides receiving wounds. One young Frenchman took two lance wounds in the belly and a saber cut in the face. Additional uhlans plunged into the elite squadron's flank, throwing the French into disorder until a straggling fire from the voltigeurs in the ravine checked the Austrian flank attack.

The fighting escalated when a gray-clad Austrian jäger company emerged from a nearby village to attack the French light troops. The combination of the voltigeurs' musketry and carbine fire from the mounted chasseurs stopped the jägers. Meda's second squadron galloped up to the road, where the elite squadron engaged the uhlans. The Austrians wavered at the sight of the French reinforcements and withdrew into the village. Meda aggressively sent his fifty voltigeurs forward in column while his horsemen moved toward the village's side entrances. The advance seemed to overawe the uhlans, who abandoned the village as the impetuous voltigeurs entered. It was a trap.

From windows and doors a hail of bullets struck the small French column. An entire jäger battalion, hidden in clever ambush, poured its fire against the hapless voltigeurs, driving them out of the main square. The uhlans returned to press the battered French. Meda retired from the field, having lost one chasseur killed, four officers and twenty-four troopers wounded, and a number of infantrymen killed or captured. He nevertheless carried off several prisoners, including one valuable informant who had served as secretary to the colonel commanding the Austrian advance guard. Thus, although Meda paid a stiff price for his little fight, he accomplished his goal of locating the Austrians and bringing back news of their plans.

Such skirmish actions produced myriad intelligence reports for the generals to digest. The reports moved up the chain of command to arrive at supreme headquarters anywhere from several hours to several days after the events took place. Thus, amid great uncertainty, small threads of hard information had to be woven together to divine larger motives. The man who had performed this work better than any other for the past thirteen years was about to arrive.

To the Front

At 7:30 P.M. on 12 April an officer dismounted in front of the Elysée Palace. He hurried inside to find Napoleon and deliver Marshal Berthier's latest dispatch from Bavaria. The Emperor read it and then spoke to his entourage: "They have passed the Inn; it is war."[4] Until midnight he dictated orders to the minister of war regarding measures necessary to defend the coast against the English; advice to his step-son, who commanded the army in Italy; and lengthy instructions to his brothers—the rulers of Holland, Spain, and

Westphalia—concerning how a Bonaparte should behave in this moment of crisis.

He slept for two hours and awoke to order his large traveling carriage prepared. To the surprise of some, the Empress Josephine appeared at 4:15 A.M. In the past, the soft, creature-comfort-loving Josephine had always avoided the disagreeable rigors of accompanying her husband to war. Yet Fouché and others had alerted her to the fact that Napoleon's affection was increasingly tempered by a dynastic imperative to produce an heir. It is a sign of Josephine's great desperation that she undertook the journey. Yet, willful to the end, she delayed Napoleon's departure as she took an excessive amount of time over her toilet. It is a sign of Napoleon's continued affection for his wife that he tolerated her behavior. In the dawn hours of 13 April the Emperor Napoleon departed Paris to conduct his fifteenth major campaign, his fourth against Austria.

After a twenty-three-hour nonstop journey the carriage reached Bar-le-Duc, where it stopped for predawn breakfast at the Oudinot household. The master of the house was absent in Bavaria, where he commanded a corps attached to Masséna's command. After a hurried meal, Napoleon embraced Oudinot's daughter and promised to take greetings to her father. Then the journey resumed.

In moments of crisis Napoleon traveled fast and hard. This instance was no exception. A day earlier one of Lannes' young aides, Marcellin de Marbot, had set off from Paris to join the army in Bavaria. Although Marbot was well known for his speedy travel, the Emperor's carriage beat him to the front by two and a half days. Napoleon went without rest, catnapping aboard his carriage and pausing only to pick up fresh relays of horses.

At 4:00 A.M., 15 April, the carriage arrived at Strasbourg on the Rhine.[5] Napoleon hopped down and demanded news about the Austrians. Josephine, staggering with fatigue, demanded a bed. Napoleon dictated orders until 1:00 P.M. Informed that the Austrians had halted all diplomatic traffic, he ordered Metternich's arrest along with all Hapsburg agents in the Confederation of the Rhine. Turning to problems more immediate, he continued arrangements for Strasbourg to serve as a war depot and rallying point for troops hurrying across France to meet the Austrian invasion. The elite men of the Imperial Guard would gather here. Normally the Emperor campaigned with his Guard, using it as an ultimate reserve to protect against disaster. Picked troopers of the Guard cavalry served as his escort and guarded his tent at night. The unexpected suddenness of the Austrian invasion caught Napoleon before he had assembled his beloved Imperial Guard. He left orders for the Guard to rally as quickly as possible. He could not wait; he had to press on alone.

Not only did he leave his Guard behind, he also bade au revoir to Josephine. At forty-six years of age she manifestly was unable to keep up with the Emperor's schedule of sleepless travel. Before he would see her again he would spend sweet nights with the superb Marie Walewska. Walewska's child, conceived that summer, would prove to Napoleon that he remained potent and that Josephine therefore must be barren. Consequently, for the star-crossed lovers Napoleon and Josephine ahead lay divorce and ultimately a new, much younger wife capable of giving Napoleon what he felt he needed most, an heir. Also in the future veterans would grumble that the Emperor's luck, and theirs, was never the same after he abandoned the cherished Josephine. Still, in 1809, however briefly, he went to war with her at his side.

The carriage traveled swiftly across Bavaria. West of Munich it encountered the Bavarian king, who had been forced to flee his capital when the Austrians approached. The Emperor descended from his carriage to greet his ally. The distraught king embraced him with great emotion. When Napoleon asked for news from the front, the king replied: "Sire, the Tyrol which you have given me is on fire. The Austrians are maneuvering between the Isar and the Danube."

"Rest assured," responded Napoleon, "you will return to Munich in a few days. I will have at my side your son, Prince Louis; all will be well."[6]

The imperial carriage galloped through the Donauwörth gate at 5:00 A.M. on the seventeenth. Napoleon entered Berthier's headquarters and walked into a chaotic situation. According to an eyewitness, his first words were "Where is the enemy?"[7] Berthier had left for the front and no one remained who could inform Napoleon of either his army's disposition or Karl's whereabouts. The Emperor sat down at Berthier's desk to peruse his chief of staff's correspondence. Such had been the French disorder for the past few days, full of order, counterorder, march, countermarch, that he was barely able to piece together his own army's probable locations. Having arrived with the expectation of finding his army safely concentrated, he found instead that it was widely dispersed and in great peril.

Berthier's letters told him little about the Austrian scheme of maneuver. South in the Tyrol all was confusion. The Bavarian king's claim that the Tyrol was on fire was apparently all too true. Rebels had seized important mountain passes, interdicting all French and Bavarian communications. A letter from Marshal Masséna revealed that French officers traveling south to join their units in Italy had been unable to penetrate the mountains. The news was similarly grim around Munich. The Austrian force that had captured the Bavarian capital and forced the king to flee for safety could now be identified as something more substantial than a mere raiding group. Reports from various Bavarian units deployed along the Isar indicated that major Hapsburg units had seized river crossings at Moosburg, Landshut, and apparently Straubing. Davout's reports spoke of contact with the Austrians on both banks of the Danube.

In this depressing situation Napoleon detected opportunity. He still believed his original plan to mass his army behind the Lech River was the appropriate counter to the unexpectedly early Austrian invasion (see Map 2). Masséna's assembling troops remained poised along the Lech in accordance with this plan. However, the lack of firm intelligence regarding Austrian dispositions made planning difficult. Consequently he sent trusted officers to all his major commands to collect information. In addition he wrote his corps commanders. He told Davout: "I impatiently await news of the enemy. Which Austrian corps has debouched from Landshut? Where is it heading? Where are the other enemy columns marching, which you and General Wrede have met?"[8]

Although Napoleon preferred a rearward concentration behind the Lech, his innate aggressive spirit caused him to advise Davout to seize any favorable opportunity to attack and punish the Austrians debouching from Landshut. He called this force the Landshut column, a misleading term that underestimated its actual strength. Napoleon did not know it, but the Landshut column comprised the Archduke Karl's main force. Regardless, the Emperor already conceived of the Landshut column as the target for a pending counteroffensive.

Napoleon mounted his horse at 10:00 A.M., 17 April for a tour of Donauworth (see Map 2). Wearing his simple, green chasseurs à cheval uniform without medals or any indication of rank, he rode about the town's perimeter to examine its crumbling fortifications. Inspection completed, he issued orders for their immediate repair. Although he was considering operations against the enemy's rear, he took this characteristic precaution to ensure that his own line of communications would be secure. Several eyewitnesses describe how relaxed and confident the Emperor appeared.[9]

The inspection had apparently given him an opportunity to reflect further upon the strategic situation. Napoleon had been in Donauworth for only a few hours and had been forced to plan with very limited intelligence. Most commanders would have concentrated their forces while collecting information. Yet Napoleon now entertained a deep flank thrust by Masséna's corps against the Austrian left rear. While Masséna could form the basis for a safe, rearward concentration, he might instead become an offensive thunderbolt. Not yet certain which he preferred, the Emperor returned to headquarters to issue an alert order to Masséna to have his men cook four days' rations and prepare for rapid movement.

Shortly thereafter his anxiety-ridden chief of staff and acting commander of the Army of Germany, Marshal Berthier, appeared. Surprisingly, considering the terrible muddle Berthier had concocted, Napoleon greeted him with good-natured understatement: "Bonjour, Prince, I have had to change many of the dispositions you have taken."[10] Berthier happily handed over the command of the army to his leader and the two spent the remainder of the day in familiar fashion, Napoleon dictating orders and Berthier acting as a contented chief clerk.

Sifting through updated reports, Napoleon deduced that Davout must be around Ratisbonne. If so, it appeared that he was isolated and in grave danger of being overwhelmed by a converging attack from the Landshut column and the Austrian formations operating on the Danube's north bank. Accordingly, the Emperor dispatched an aide to locate the marshal, warn him of his peril, and order him to rejoin the main army at Neustadt. Since he would probably have to abandon Ratisbonne, Davout was also to destroy the stone bridge spanning the Danube. No one at Donauworth realized that the destruction of the bridge was impossible. On 11 April one of Davout's divisional commanders had warned Davout that the bridge's massive construction prevented demolition. Amid the frantic maneuvering this important detail never penetrated up the chain of command. Furthermore, Napoleon's message did not reach Davout until the afternoon of the nineteenth, at which time all of the Third Corps except for one regiment had departed the town. Yet having issued the order, Napoleon based all future plans on the belief that the demolition had been performed.

By the afternoon of the seventeenth Napoleon had abandoned his original plan to defend behind the Lech River. He felt that the immediate situation presented a fine opportunity to destroy Karl's army. Masséna would indeed take the offensive. The Emperor ordered the French forces to concentrate in three masses: Masséna's two corps at Pfaffenhofen, the German allies and some French detachments around Ingolstadt, and Davout around Neustadt (see Map 3). The Bavarians would screen the concentration by defending a sixteen-mile front in the middle. This concentration should be completed on the eighteenth and would allow the French to take the offensive the next day, a plan that proved hopelessly optimistic. Davout did not receive his orders in time, his corps was not where Napoleon guessed, and the bulk of the Austrian army lay on his flank about to attack. Masséna, on the opposite wing, failed to concentrate his divisions on receiving his alert order and only sluggishly complied once the march orders arrived. One day after Napoleon's arrival, the French position had continued to deteriorate.

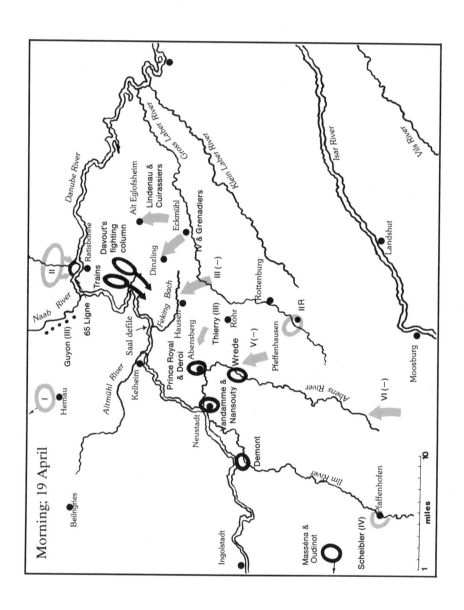

Morning; 19 April

Approach March

The advance of the Hapsburg force Napoleon labeled the Landshut column had triggered the campaign's first serious combat on 16 April. At the campaign's beginning Karl hoped that the Bavarians would rally to the Austrian cause. Indeed, one of the prominent Bavarian generals, Carl Wrede, had distinguished himself against the French while under the Archduke's command nine years earlier.[11] When probing uhlans brought word that Bavarian infantry was resisting the Austrian advance at Landshut, Karl realized his hopes were not to be.

Accordingly, his army advanced on the important Isar River crossing at Landshut at 8:00 A.M., 16 April 1809. Somehow, the reformed, leaner Hapsburg army could not set off any earlier. Karl assigned GM Josef Radetzky the task of capturing the bridging site. One of a new breed of Austrian officer, the hard-charging Radetzky welcomed his opportunity. He began forming his infantry for the advance when Bavarian artillery opened fire from across the river. Adding to the Austrian discomfort, a battalion of Bavarian infantry, distinctive in crowned leather helmets and cornflower-blue uniforms, fired from an island in midriver. Realizing the situation required a full-scale river assault, Radetzky set about organizing it with a sure hand.

When Archduke Karl arrived at the front at eleven o'clock he found Radetzky's artillery firing from the high ground overlooking the Isar. The artillery was clearly dominating the opposing Bavarian guns. Soon, the eleven surviving Bavarian guns displaced to the rear. Austrian pioneers advanced to the river to begin construction of a bridge, only to be driven back by Bavarian musketry. Radetzky responded by lining the river bank with the tough light infantry of the Gradiskaner Grenzer Regiment, and the grenzers drove the enemy marksmen under cover. The pioneers resumed work, completing the bridge by 1:30 P.M.

The Hapsburg advance guard eagerly crossed the Isar. The spirit of the advance affected even the staff officers. Captain Simbschen, aide-de-camp to a corps commander, led two companies of grenzers against a Bavarian outpost guarding the crossing point. Outnumbered and having received word that another Austrian force had outflanked Landshut by using a more northerly crossing, the defenders retired all along the front. While Karl ordered the Austrian main body to cross, Radetzky dispatched a squadron and a half of cavalry to pursue the retreating foe. The first important skirmish was over. For a price of fourteen killed, sixty wounded, and forty horses disabled the Austrians had gained their river crossing. Upstream, at Moosburg, FML Hiller completed his crossing at 11:00 P.M. Seventeen miles downstream, the Aus-

trian Fourth Corps slowly made an unopposed march over the river at Dingofl-
ing. Farther toward Ratisbonne a detached brigade from the Second Corps
commanded by GM Veczay crossed the Danube at Straubing. Somewhere
ahead lay the isolated, outnumbered French army. For the remainder of the
day the Hapsburg army tramped over the gently swaying bridges.

Bavarian pickets detected all of these crossings but were unable to identify
units and strengths; Napoleon would use their incomplete reports the next day
to plan his counteroffensive. On the evening of the sixteenth, the initiative lay
with the Austrians. Archduke Karl could content himself with the fact that a
difficult operation, a river assault, had come off without a hitch. Yet his
position offered something much more. Because of Berthier's confusion the
French army lay scattered across a seventy-five-mile front with Davout danger-
ously exposed around Ratisbonne. Only a tenuous cordon of Bavarian troops
linked Davout with the main French force. Karl occupied a central position
where he could turn and attack either the French left or right. Alternatively,
he could push against the weak center and interpose his army between the two
French wings, then pounce on one before turning to defeat the other. Many of
Napoleon's finest maneuvers had been designed to place the French army in
such a central position. This time French blunders had given it to the Austrians. However, Karl failed to capitalize on this golden opportunity. Possibly
he did not even realize the potential inherent in his position. He explained his
plan for the seventeenth in a letter to his brother, Kaiser Franz: "I am uniting
the army corps tomorrow in a position beyond Landshut."[12]

On the seventeenth Karl sent a message to Bellegarde's detached command
operating north of Ratisbonne describing his plan—or rather his march
schedule, since the message explained the direction of march without address-
ing how the Archduke planned to defeat the French army. At this point Karl
had yet to come to grips with this central problem. He merely ordered the
main body, comprising five army corps, to head west to cross the Danube
between Ratisbonne and Ingolstadt. It would continue and reunite with
Bellegarde's two corps at a road junction west of the Danube.

During the day Karl's army maneuvered according to this scheme. Five
corps cautiously crept along the roads emanating from the central hub at
Landshut. Days of rain had reduced secondary roads to muddy farm tracks.
Movement was confined to the main highways. Advance guards gently pressed
the Bavarians, who in turn were under orders to retire westward. By evening
Hapsburg pickets advanced west along the Landshut–Siegenburg and
Landshut–Rohr roads to secure positions along the Abens River (see Map 3).
In the direction of Ratisbonne, another Austrian force reached Eckmühl while
Veczay's brigade that had crossed the Danube at Straubing assembled on the
Landshut–Ratisbonne road. Further welcome news came from Munich where

FML Jellacic proudly announced he had entered the Bavarian capital on the night of April 15–16. The only blot on Karl's horizon was the information that Hiller, perhaps already showing a lack of cooperation with his rival and superior, Archduke Karl, had spent the day resting his corps at Moosburg. Nonetheless, as the historian F. L. Petre comments: "The position of Napoleon's army was now, thanks to Berthier's misunderstandings, hazardous in the extreme."[13]

During the night of 17–18, April Karl learned that French prisoners reported Napoleon's arrival in Donauworth. Whether the speed of Napoleon's journey unsettled the Hapsburg commander is unrecorded. In any event he saw nothing in the news to cause him to change his planned march west over the Danube.

Sixty miles away, at French headquarters, a constant stream of intelligence arrived on the night of the seventeenth/eighteenth as Napoleon's exploring officers returned. The Emperor learned that the Austrian force emerging from Landshut, the Landshut column, was larger than he expected. He wrote his marshals: "It appears the Archduke Karl with three army corps is between Landshut and Ratisbonne."[14] He also knew that a major Austrian force was at Moosburg while a detachment maneuvered near Munich. Finally there was Bellegarde's force, which, if it continued, would cut the French line of communications. With more accurate information, Napoleon began to grasp the strategic situation. He correctly inferred that Karl would strike at Davout while fending off the Bavarians with a flank guard. His strategic insight anticipated what Karl would do, for in fact the Archduke would not conceive this plan until late morning on the eighteenth.

Napoleon recast his own plans. He based his strategy on the time-proven French ability to march colossal distances rapidly and the equally proven inability of the Austrians to do the same. He ignored Bellegarde's threat. Instead, he counted on the speed and violence of his own counteroffensive to threaten the Austrian rear and force Karl to call off the Austrian attack against the French rear. It was a calculated risk by a master strategist determined to seize the initiative rather than react to his opponent's maneuvers. To this end Davout would march to rejoin the main army, the Bavarians would defend the center, and Masséna would drive deep into the Austrian rear in the direction of Landshut. In effect, Napoleon was prepared to hold off Karl with the weakest third of his army, his Germanic allies, while his two French wings performed flank marches across the front of a large, undefeated enemy. It was a plan of stupendous audacity that promised great results: If Masséna set off from Pfaffenhofen before daybreak of the nineteenth, Karl would be lost. He would be trapped by Masséna controlling his line of communications, Davout and

the Bavarians forming a united shield blocking his front, and the Danube—
with the bridge at Ratisbonne destroyed—providing an impassable barrier on
the Austrian right. Writing to his corps commanders, Napoleon reaffirmed
that the eighteenth would be a day of preparation, a day of approach marches
as his units got into position to spring the trap. The next day would be the day
of decision.

The Austrians resumed marching on 18 April, according to the Archduke's general notion to pass the Danube and rejoin Bellegarde. Austrian
scouts had begun to detect Masséna's buildup south and west in the Augsbourg
area. Karl ordered Hiller to engage the attention of this French force without
becoming involved in a battle. Hiller in turn ordered Jellacic's force at Munich
to rejoin him to assist in this task.

The meanderings of Jellacic's division were a microcosm of the Hapsburg
army's operational method. In early April, with war just days away, it was
completely reorganized for detached service.[15] The reorganization disrupted
the division's command relationships. At a time when the Archduke should
have been concentrating every available soldier for decisive battle, he instead
gave Jellacic's 10,000 men the vague mission of advancing toward Munich to
observe the enemy and link the Tyrol with the main army. Unopposed, Jellacic
occupied the Bavarian capital and sent the Bavarian king fleeing. From
Munich Jellacic could have sent flying columns to fan the flames of the
Tyrolese rebellion and to incite German nationalists to revolt. Instead, he sat
until receiving Hiller's order to return. Dutifully Jellacic countermarched
while Hiller's corps waited motionless on the eighteenth for him to arrive.
Then Karl sent new orders telling Jellacic to go back to Munich! Not only had
Jellacic's division failed to contribute anything to the Austrian effort, its
movements had upset Hiller's arrangements for protecting Karl's left flank. In
1808 Napoleon had written: "It should not be believed that a march of three or
four days in the wrong direction can be corrected by a countermarch. As a
rule, this is to make two mistakes instead of one."[16] In 1809 Archduke Karl
proved he did not understand this maxim.

Yet at 11:00 A.M., 18 April, it seemed to Karl's optimistic staff that
Jellacic's absence would merely deprive his men of a share of the pending glory.
Earlier the Archduke had directed Veczay to advance toward Ratisbonne to
determine conclusively if Davout remained near the town. When Veczay's
scouts reported affirmatively, Karl realized he had too fine an opportunity to
ignore. As Napoleon had anticipated, the Archduke redirected his corps to
crush Davout's isolated command. Karl ordered nearly four corps to perform an
approach march to intercept Davout, whom he correctly supposed would be
marching south to join the Bavarians. Bavarian deserters, picked up near
Abensberg, informed the Austrian Generalissimus that the three Bavarian

divisions were massing behind the Abens River directly to his front (see Map 3). Consequently, he ordered the Fifth Corps to advance to the Abens to fend them off. Karl believed that his left was not immediately threatened and that Hiller's corps could adequately protect the army's left.

Like Napoleon, Archduke Karl expected the nineteenth to be the day of decision. If Karl completed his approach marches quickly, he had an outstanding opportunity. However, as the authors of the West Point study guide observe, any delay risked the possibility that "the French dispersion might tighten into a trap."[17]

During the eighteenth the concentration of French forces Napoleon had ordered did not occur. Orders to Masséna dispatched at noon and 1:00 P.M. on April 17 did not reach the marshal until about 7 o'clock. Had Masséna displayed initiative by immediately concentrating his command he might have been able to accomplish the next orders he received. Instead, Masséna displayed much less energy than in past campaigns. When he received specific instructions at 2:00 A.M., 18 April, he fell hopelessly behind schedule. These instructions required the van of his corps to reach Pfaffenhofen by day's end. Although Masséna and Oudinot marched all day, not until dawn of the nineteenth would French troops enter Pfaffenhofen. Masséna was partially to blame for his failure of initiative. More importantly, Napoleon had placed unrealistic demands upon his soldiers' marching ability.

On the opposite flank Davout likewise failed to arrive at his objective during the day. In fact, he could not even begin the march. When Napoleon ordered the Iron Marshal to march to join the French center, he had incorrectly believed that Davout's entire corps was well concentrated around the town. His error regarding Davout stemmed from his analysis of the confusing orders and counterorders Berthier had issued in the days following the outbreak of war. When Davout received Napoleon's instructions on the morning of the eighteenth, Friant's infantry division was more than twenty miles northwest of Ratisbonne and Saint-Sulpice's division of cavalry was more than twelve miles away. Davout would have to wait for them to arrive at Ratisbonne before setting off south.

From Davout's perspective it was not at all clear that his outlying troops would reach the safety of the Ratisbonne perimeter before being snapped up by Bellegarde's two corps. For the past four days the action north of the Danube had involved a perilous tactical minuet featuring French efforts to evade Austrian forces who, in turn, tried to intercept them before the French found safety at Ratisbonne. That any of Davout's units remained north of the Danube was due to Berthier's orders misinterpreting Napoleon's plan. In consequence, the French had to toil toward Ratisbonne over terrible secondary roads while the

Austrians descended upon their flank. Several times Davout's veterans secured critical road junctions just ahead of the Hapsburgs. At that, only the French cavalry's ability to screen the corps' flank and prevent Bellegarde from accurately following their line of march allowed the corps to reach Ratisbonne.

Although Berthier's orders had plunged the French Third Corps into disorder, they had the unintended consequence of confusing GdK Bellegarde. When he had invaded Bohemia on the tenth, Davout's units were within one day's march of Ratisbonne while his were no closer than four days' march. He could hardly have anticipated that Davout would not cross the Danube to safety and thus remain vulnerable for eight days. So he marched southwest with his own and half of Kollowrath's corps rather than south directly toward Ratisbonne. He kept one eye to his right, where the Saxons, another French ally, presented a distant threat. Only slowly did he appreciate the opportunity to cut off part of Davout's corps before it escaped via Ratisbonne.

On the fifteenth Bellegarde shifted his line of march to concentrate more force at the key town. The next day one of his divisions contacted French forces outposting the north-bank suburbs. During the sixteenth and seventeenth Austrian forces tightened their embrace of the key Stadt-am-Hof suburb, which was the northern terminus of the stone bridge spanning the Danube. Davout matched the Austrian maneuvers by entrenching a bridgehead on the heights overlooking Stadt-am-Hof, a position the French had to hold in order for Friant and Saint-Sulpice to rejoin the corps.

However, on 17 April the Austrian commander, FML Klenau, skillfully positioned several artillery batteries to enfilade the French fortifications. When his howitzers set a key village on fire the French had to abandon part of their line. From the heights Klenau observed with satisfaction the French evacuating their defenses and hurrying over the stone bridge to Ratisbonne.

On the eighteenth Davout's men clung to a reduced perimeter that included a commanding height overlooking Stadt-am-Hof. Yet Hapsburg batteries had closed the range to the extent that a French staff officer carrying orders over the bridge had to pass through a stiff bombardment to complete his mission. The remainder of Kollowrath's corps invested the French perimeter during the day, but not before Friant's panting infantry and Saint-Sulpice's horse reached Stadt-am-Hof and crossed the river to safety. While Bellegarde responded to Karl's orders to proceed south to link up with Hapsburg main body, Kollowrath massed his corps for a full-scale assault. He planned to attack the next day.

So it was that Davout's corps assembled in Ratisbonne, having so narrowly won the race against Bellegarde, still a march short of where Napoleon expected them to be. Moreover, at Ratisbonne they stood vulnerable to a new and much larger Hapsburg force—four corps led by Archduke Karl—bent on their destruction. Coupled with Masséna's situation eighty-some miles to the south, it meant that the concentration of force the Emperor expected to have complete by the end of the eighteenth had barely begun.

Knowing none of this, Napoleon had dictated an order to Masséna on the morning of the eighteenth. It reiterated that Masséna should arrive at Pfaffenhofen and then "fall upon Archduke Karl's rear. . . . Everything leads to the belief that between the 18th, 19th, and 20th all the affairs of Germany will be decided."[18] In his near-illegible scrawl, the Emperor appended a footnote: "Activity, activity, speed! I commend them to you."[19]

By late afternoon on the eighteenth Napoleon rode to Ingolstadt, to be closer to the scene of the coming battle. Communications with Ratisbonne were difficult (Hapsburg patrols were interdicting the Abensberg–Ratisbonne road) and the Emperor remained unaware of Davout's plight. It was worse than he could have imagined.

While Napoleon worried about the absence of news from Davout, a particularly active Hapsburg cavalry captain set off in the evening to patrol near Abbach, which lay on the Abensberg–Ratisbonne road. He intercepted a French horse-drawn ambulance bound for Neustadt. Prisoner interrogation revealed that Davout had evacuated Ratisbonne but remained just outside that town. Better yet, another patrol captured a courier from Marshal Lefebvre. He carried that marshal's message to Davout describing Lefebvre's dispositions and plans for the nineteenth. Most important, the message indicated that Lefebvre would try to attack the Austrian left flank in order to assist Davout.

The Archduke's 11:00 A.M. decision to make an approach march to attack the French Third Corps had placed his cavalry in position to sever communications between Davout and the balance of the French army. Aggressive patrolling had netted a great intelligence windfall. Aware of Davout's position and forewarned of Lefebvre's planned attack, Karl issued detailed orders to destroy Davout.

CHAPTER V

The Tenth Legion

The issue of a battle is the result of a single thought. The adversaries come into each other's presence with various combinations; they mingle; they fight for a length of time; the decisive moment appears; a psychological spark makes the decision; and a few reserve troops are enough to carry it out.

Ridgetop Battle

Ignorant that they were Karl's target, Davout's men rose in the damp predawn chill of 19 April and prepared to march. Because of Davout's foresight, the complicated maneuver began without a hitch. The preceding day he had ordered a topographic engineer to thoroughly reconnoiter the available roads. During the evening he assembled his commanders to explain the next day's movements. This wonderfully gifted set of divisional commanders would become known to history as "Davout's immortals" because of the length of time they served in the same corps and the skill with which they accomplished their assignments.

Three of them, Friant (Davout's brother-in-law), Morand, and Gudin had been with the Third Corps since its formation as part of the Grande Armée in 1803. Karl-Etienne Gudin was Davout's favorite. In a past battle Davout had had to replace Gudin temporarily when the latter received a severe wound. Unnerved by the loss, Davout had stormed: "Before I would remove this heroic general from command of his brave division which he has led at least twenty times to victory, I will break my Marshal's baton."[1] Davout had almost equal confidence in Friant and Morand. Saint-Hilaire, although a relative newcomer to the corps, was also an officer of proven ability. Even with such an able quartet Davout had left nothing to chance as he told them to watch while the engineer traced on a detailed map their expected routes of march (see Map 3).

82

There was only one good road. It ran parallel to the Danube from Ratisbonne to Abensberg. The wagons of the baggage train would have to follow it. Their progress regulated the rate at which the entire corps could advance. Of critical importance to the French was the narrow Saal defile where the road passed through a rocky gap between the Danube and the broken terrain of the Feking Brook. If the Austrians seized the defile, Davout would be trapped against the Danube. If he could clear the defile, his corps would emerge into open terrain and re-establish contact with the rest of the French army. Here too Davout had taken precautions, by ordering a French battalion to hasten through the night to secure the defile.

So, in the gray half-light of the following day, the baggage train trundled slowly along the rain-soaked river road toward Saal. To avoid congestion and protect the vulnerable, slow-moving wagons, three combat columns marched east of the river road to place themselves between the train and the Austrians. They toiled over hilly secondary roads that connected the area's many small villages. Nearest the baggage were Morand's and Gudin's divisions. Farther to the east moved Saint-Hilaire and Friant, who were in turn protected by the third combat column comprising a flank guard under Montbrun. Should any of the columns encounter the Austrians, the broken, wooded terrain would make it difficult to coordinate their maneuvers. In essence, Davout was attempting an exceedingly delicate operation: a flank march across the front of a sizable enemy force whose positions were unknown.

The restrictions of the terrain also hampered Archduke Karl's plans. He wanted to come to grips with Davout as soon as possible but he also did not know his foe's exact location. The last reported French position had been outside Ratisbonne. Accordingly, Karl turned his army toward Ratisbonne in hopes of crushing Davout against the dual barrier of Kollowrath, whom he presumed to be advancing upon the city from the north, and the mighty Danube. Terrain difficulties impeded Karl's efforts. Numerous ridges and woods covered the ground within the key triangle formed by Eckmühl–Abensberg–Ratisbonne. The closed terrain provided few vantage points from which a commander could survey his lines. Major formations could maneuver in close proximity without realizing the nearness of the enemy. These conditions forced commanders to rely extensively upon their subordinates' initiative to see a plan through.

Karl's plan hinged on the activities of three combat columns (see Map 3). The first, comprising Hohenzollern's Third Corps, set out toward the Feking Brook. Rosenberg's Fourth Corps supported by twelve grenadier battalions formed the second column, with orders to advance on Dinzling. A third column (one infantry division and the cuirassiers) marched directly on Ratisbonne using the Eckmühl–Ratisbonne highway. In between was the First

Reserve Corps, reinforced by division-sized attachments. This force had the mission of linking the columns, and with it rode the Archduke himself. While this host, numbering some 65,000 men, dealt with Davout, the Archduke Ludwig—supported by elements of the Second Reserve Corps—would hold off Lefebvre.

The decision for war made in fevered Viennese councils many months ago, Karl's decision to countermarch and invade Bavaria rather than stick to his original plan to attack out of Bohemia, and Berthier's order for Davout to linger around Ratisbonne had come down to this on the morning of 19 April: Could three Austrian corps defeat one isolated French corps? In pursuit of the answer Karl's army marched at 6:00 A.M.

What might have been a clenched Hapsburg fist immediately began to open into less powerful, separate probing fingers as the Austrian generals dribbled detachments left and right. Sinned against and sinner was Hohenzollern. Fearful of Lefebvre, who threatened his left flank, Karl required a division to preserve communications with Ludwig's corps. Hohenzollern assigned the job to Thierry, whose 6000 men were thus subtracted from the attack as neatly as if they had been felled by French bullets (see Map 3). Hohenzollern compounded this error by making a further detachment of some thousand men whose task was to maintain communications with Thierry. This left him with 18,000 men divided into sixteen battalions and six squadrons for the actual advance.

On the right flank, GdK Johannes Liechtenstein's 20,000 warriors marched toward Ratisbonne and into a vacuum left behind by the departing French. Although they heard the sounds of combat off to their left, they remained true to their orders, ignored the disagreeable uproar, and steadfastly marched on. They failed to encounter any Frenchmen during the day and so too contributed nothing to the fight. Only Rosenberg, leading the middle column, initially kept his men in hand and advanced with his entire force of twenty-nine battalions and fifteen squadrons totaling more than 28,000 men. In sum, before the battle began, the Austrian blow had dwindled from 65,000 to 38,000.

Questing French chasseurs à cheval who led Davout's advance encountered Rosenberg's advance guard near the village of Schneidert at 9:00A.M. The resultant combat alerted everyone that the battle was about to begin. The aggressive Austrian van commander, General Stutterheim, advanced his light artillery and attacked with a battalion of tough grenzers. Scattered shots from the French voltigeurs sheltered in a wood line slowed but did not stop the grenzers. Three officers and thirty-two men of the Deutsch–Banater Grenzers fell, but the battalion swept the woods and captured a few voltigeurs. Rosenberg's column marched on. Soon the crackling of musketry and dull boom of heavy guns announced a brisk fight off to the left in the direction of Hausen and Teugen. The sounds told Rosenberg that Hohenzollern had come to grips with the French.

Hohenzollern's opponents included Davout, who had accompanied Saint-Hilaire's division. The marshal had heard the sounds of the action at Schneidert and ignored it. He realized his left flank might be threatened by an unknown host but stuck true to his primary mission: to extract his force from the Ratisbonne cul-de-sac and link up with Lefebvre. Accordingly, he ordered Saint-Hilaire merely to close up his column and keep marching. Recent rains rendered the poor secondary roads sticky morasses and greatly impeded the French as they ascended the narrow defiles outside Teugen. Suddenly from directly ahead the muffled sound of musketry filtered back through the damp air to the marching column.

Sitting squarely athwart Davout's route of march on a steep, two-tiered ridge running from Teugen to Hausen was Hohenzollern's Third Corps' advance guard division commanded by FML Philipp Vukassovich (see Map 4). Saint-Hilaire's advance guard had bumped into Vukassovich in the village of Hausen. Vukassovich sent a grenzer battalion, supported by a light battalion of the elite Archduke Karl Legion, to flank the village while the next Austrian division attacked frontally. Together they easily evicted the French, chasing them over the wooded ridge and back toward Saint-Hilaire's main body.

Davout saw the French skirmishers come tumbling down the slope pursued by a cloud of Austrian light troops. Still in road column and thus unbraced for the shock, Saint-Hilaire's division stood vulnerable. Davout needed time to shield his forces' deployment. He ordered Saint-Hilaire's lead unit, the Third Ligne, to attack immediately (see Map 4). In the emergency the Third went forward without regard for formation. It advanced upslope in thick skirmish order, a formation that could only be employed by well-trained, reliable units.

To fight in open or skirmish order required individual initiative. The soldiers of revolutionary France had specialized in such combat. Units of the Grande Armée, Napoleon's army of 1805, had trained and maneuvered together so that even regular units could fight in open order. But the Grande Armée had died, consumed in the furnace of combat in Germany, Poland, and Spain. Only Davout's corps, spared the ordeal of the Spanish campaign, retained enough of the 1805 cadre to perform as in the earlier days. They now gave a demonstration of what it meant to have belonged to the Grande Armée.

Two thousand veterans swept uphill into the face of 6000 Austrians supported by twelve guns. The attack could not penetrate the Austrian line but succeeded in its purpose of buying time for the remainder of Saint-Hilaire's division to prepare. The Third fell back, rallied to the sound of the drums, and formed up behind the next French unit, the Fifty-seventh Ligne, nicknamed

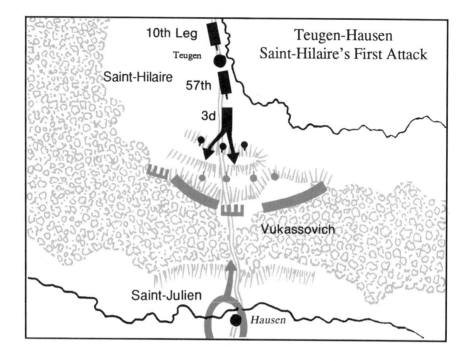

the Terrible. The Fifty-seventh had earned its illustrious name during the early campaigns in Italy. Honed by countless combats, it was one of the army's elite fighting units.

Advancing upslope in three compact attack columns, the regiment drove back the Austrian light troops. The Fifty-seventh gained the first crest of the two-tiered Austrian position (see Map 5). It then descended into an intervening hollow and climbed again to confront the Austrian main line. This protracted maneuver provided an unmistakable target to the massed, canister-firing Hapsburg artillery. Moreover, the white-coated infantry overlapped the Fifty-seventh's flanks and so added their musketry to the defensive fire. Undaunted, encouraged by their officers, the Terrible Fifty-seventh struggled onward. At close musketry range it deployed into line and then resumed its advance, stopping to fire and load every twenty-five paces. Repeated discharges of canister slowed the attack. The Fifty-seventh closed ranks and a furious musketry duel ensued. Thick clouds of smoke obscured the lines and particularly clung in the hollow, thereby sheltering the French wounded just to the rear of the Fifty-seventh's position. The leading French soldiers did not enjoy such protection. Each blast of an Austrian cannon noticeably thinned their ranks, yet inexorably their eagle standards inched forward.

Behind the Fifty-seventh's sacrificial shield the remainder of Saint-Hilaire's

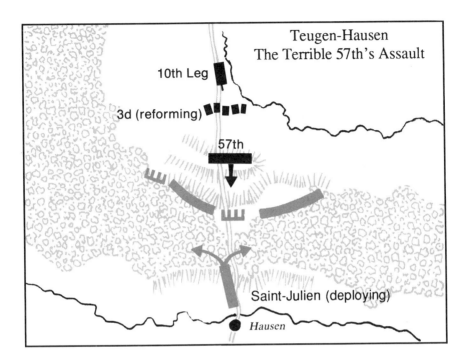

division deployed. From Teugen the French line of sight did not extend beyond the first ridgeline. This allowed Saint-Hilaire's men to use a sheltered approach to combat. Accordingly, the Third Ligne rejoined the fight on the Fifty-seventh's right. Saint-Hilaire directed the Tenth Légère to advance toward a small copse even farther to the right flank (see Map 6). Distracted by combat with the Fifty-seventh and unable to see clearly through the smoke, the Austrian artillery failed to react to this movement until the Tenth appeared through the trees on its left flank. Imperiled, the gunners hastily limbered their guns and withdrew, leaving one piece behind. Sweeping forward, the Tenth overran the battery site and captured the gun, the campaign's first trophy. The Tenth then opened out into skirmish order where it joined the regular skirmishers of the voltigeur companies. Operating as a fast-moving, fire-tinged cloud, they spearheaded Saint-Hilaire's assault.

Along with the Third Ligne, the Tenth Légère continued toward the second crest. Here they met the Austrian main line of resistance, attacked, and were soundly repulsed by overwhelming Austrian musketry and cannon fire. The French withdrew into the woods to lick their wounds while rival skirmishers sustained the fight between the lines.

Saint-Hilaire organized his position with care. Parallel to the Austrian-held crestline, halfway down the slope toward Teugen, Saint-Hilaire deployed

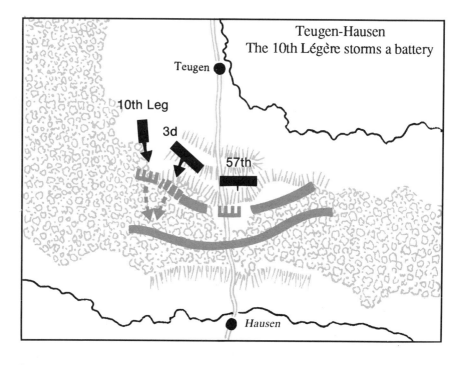

his men along the first crest. Its height almost equaled the Austrian position. For either side to advance, it had to descend into the hollow and then charge up a steep incline. Because of this feature both the Austrians and French recalled that they seemed to have fought uphill against a hidden foe all day as the combat teetered back and forth along the ridge. Saint-Hilaire placed the Third and Fifty-seventh overlooking the hollow, parallel to the Austrian position (see Map 7). Just to the rear, the Tenth Légère deployed en echelon to the right of Teugen. In close support was the 105th Ligne, while the Seventy-second Ligne stood in column in front of the village. Because of a command mix-up, the French artillery was absent somewhere to the rear. Slowly the French skirmishers on both flanks gained ground and penetrated into the woods lining the second, Austrian-held crestline. Because the fighting in the middle stalemated along the hollow, Saint-Hilaire's position gradually assumed a U shape with the open end facing the Austrian position.

With the fighting apparently stabilized along this compact front, a thousand paces separating Teugen from Hausen, Davout sent messengers spurring to order Gudin and Morand to strike Hohenzollern's left flank. He quickly had to modify this scheme when an Austrian attack came roaring into the hollow, up the ridge, and over the French position. Ordering one of Gudin's brigades to countermarch to Saint-Hilaire's direct support, Davout re-entered the combat.

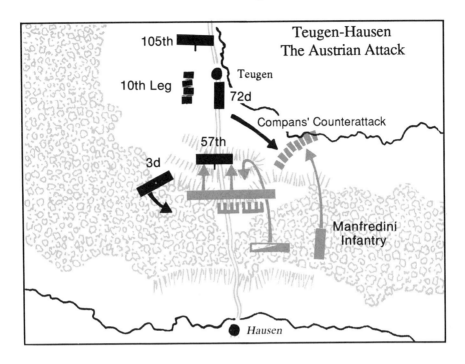

On the Austrian side, Hohenzollern's advance guard and lead brigade were fought out by their combat with the Fifty-seventh and Third Ligne. They could not see past the French-held first ridge and thus the Tenth Légère's flank attack had come as a shock and driven the Austrians back.[2] When the French became disordered by their pursuit, Hohenzollern saw an opportunity. He ordered his next regiment, the just arrived Manfredini Infantry, to form three attack columns and drive through the woods toward the Fifty-seventh's flank (see Map 7). Screened by skirmishers and led in person by the brigade commander, Prince Alois Liechtenstein (one of three brothers serving in the army), the attack penetrated the woods. The Frenchlike formation, compact attack columns spearheaded by light troops, showed the army's progress since Karl's reforms. No longer were the Hapsburgs limited to rigid, linear formations.

As they closed rapidly on the unwitting Fifty-seventh, General Compans (Davout's chief of staff) saw the danger and hustled the Seventy-second Ligne forward (see Map 7). With nice timing Compans waited until the Austrian columns emerged from the woods and began to deploy. He then launched the Seventy-second against the head of the column as it undertook its vulnerable change of formation. The Austrians fell back in confusion.

Undaunted by the repulse of the Manfredini Infantry, Generals Lusignan,

Saint-Julien, and Alois Liechtenstein placed themselves at the front of their infantry and led the white-coated Hapsburgs forward again. Although the ground was poorly suited to mounted action, an Austrian light cavalry regiment joined the attack and bore in against the French infantry's flank (see Map 7). One battalion of the Fifty-seventh calmly formed square and shot the cavalry attack apart. Advancing over the crestline and into the valley, the Hapsburg infantry entered the open end of the U-shaped French position. A battalion of the Third Line that Davout had retained just for this purpose emerged from a small woods at the tip of one prong of the U and crashed into the Austrian flank. Caught in a cross fire and then struck in flank, the Austrians yielded.

Meanwhile, off to Hohenzollern's right, the other Austrian column led by Rosenberg continued its advance on Dinzling. It encountered Davout's flank guard commanded by the cavalry General Montbrun. Montbrun's force included two infantry battalions and nine cavalry squadrons totaling 3800 men. Typical of Montbrun's cavalry was the Twelfth Chasseurs à Cheval, a highly disciplined veteran unit. With such matchless troopers he ably performed his flank-guard role: skirmishing before Rosenberg's advancing column, forcing them to slow and deploy, then dancing out of range before becoming engaged. Like a toreador waving his cape before a charging bull, Montbrun thoroughly occupied Rosenberg's attention for the entire day. As the Austrian Fourth Corps slowly advanced, Rosenberg frittered away much strength to garrison villages and protect his line of communications. Half his infantry and a third of his cavalry had been assigned to this service by the time the corps neared Dinzling. Although Rosenberg could justifiably claim to have reached his objective by the end of the day, the combination of his strict focus on this terrain objective and Montbrun's skillful delaying action kept him from contributing one whit to Hohenzollern's battle.

Fighting alone, Hohenzollern's corps was losing its impetus. Fresh troops could have restored the battle. Around the village of Grub, within easy reach of the battlefield, sat twelve grenadier battalions. In their midst was Archduke Karl. He had retained this elite reserve under his personal supervision so they would be available at the right moment. Now that they were needed, Karl failed to respond. Although located along the spine of a ridge, Grub itself sat in a small bowl. Due to this fact and several intervening treelines, visibility in the direction of Hohenzollern's battle was poor. All Karl could have possibly seen was smoke rising above the trees. In the event it was not enough to stir him into action. He sat sphinxlike at his command post while the battle raged on the heights.

Prince Alois Liechtenstein believed he could win the battle without Karl's grenadiers. He had found what he considered the key to the French defense.

Rather than attack into the mouth of the fire-swept U, he organized an assault against one of the prongs that extended out toward the Austrian lines. He seized a flag of the Würzburg Infantry and led them forward in a column charge. The Austrians advanced without pausing to fire. Bombarded by Austrian artillery and assailed in front and flank by superior numbers, Saint-Hilaire's men ceded the ground they had captured at high cost. However, one of their last volleys inflicted multiple wounds on the brave Liechtenstein, knocking him out of the battle.

Saint-Hilaire's men retreated down from the crestline position that had been the backbone of their defense and continued until they backed up against a shallow marsh. Here they tried to rally, and at this critical moment up rode Davout. The bespectacled marshal spoke energetically, reminding men of their past gallantry and the importance of the situation. He ended his short exhortation with "Today, our lot is to conquer or to die on this ground. Other than this, there is neither salvation nor glory for us."[3] Davout ordered them to return to the attack.

On the Austrian side of the lines it seemed that victory had been gained. The persistent Austrian infantry had suffered. Many of the officers, including several well-known generals, had fallen to French fire. Yet finally, after five hours of combat, the Hapsburgs had driven the French back almost to their original line. The tired yet elated Austrian soldiers cleaned fouled muskets and swabbed out begrimed cannon while talking excitedly about their success. For well over a decade they had fought the French and almost invariably lost. This time, inspired by the new spirit of Germanic nationalism, they had won. As their officers ordered them to reform their ranks they boasted about what they would do to the French on the morrow. Overhead, dark stormclouds gathered and obscured the sun. From in front, the French swept forward again.

The French regained the first crestline. From this position at 3:00 P.M. French cannon fire reverberated along the heights for the first time. The artillery's costly absence had been the result of a staff error that left them back in camp near Ratisbonne without orders. Now, led by Colonel Seruzier, renowned in the corps as "the father of cannon shot," and manned by grizzled veterans, the artillery quickly gained fire superiority along the French left. Maneuvering behind the veil provided by the first ridgeline, Seruzier took a howitzer upslope through the woods (see Map 8). He soon found what he was looking for, a trail leading to a position on the Hapsburg flank. He returned to Saint-Hilaire, explained his plan, and set off with his horse artillery. To cover the artillery's maneuver, Saint-Hilaire launched the Fifty-seventh and Seventy-second into a diversionary attack. In the fading light the French infantry advanced again through the casualty-littered hollow and up the slope. Simultaneously, fresh troops of Friant's division advanced against the Austrian

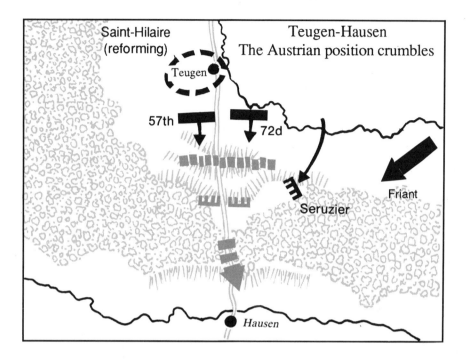

flank. Animated by the brigadier's "You will be a wall of fire" and spearheaded by the grenadier companies, they joined Saint-Hilaire's assault.[4]

Seruzier's batteries took position unnoticed on the Austrian flank. Their canister enfilade ripped into the Hapsburg gun line, killing horses and crew alike. Doubly surprised by Seruzier's guns and the fact that the French refused to concede, the Austrians put up little resistance. They retreated before the French onslaught. Prince Moritz Liechtenstein placed himself at the head of the Kaunitz regiment and counterattacked. Although he fell wounded, his counterstroke halted the French pursuit. At 5:00 P.M. a terrific thunderstorm put an end to the fight.

During the day's fighting the Archduke Karl had failed to destroy Davout's isolated corps. Davout had also failed to accomplish his goal of reuniting with the main army. It was a hard-fought stalemate during which much of the time five French regiments without artillery fought seven Austrian regiments supported by numerous artillery batteries. Looked at differently, the best-trained regular French infantry—the last force that could claim to be men of the vaunted Grande Armée of 1805—had been unable to beat average Austrian infantry. Apparently, tomorrow would decide the issue.

Yet it was not to be so. Rather than continuing the trial on the battle-field, the contest was decided back at headquarters. Toward battle's end,

Hohenzollern reported to Karl that he could not make headway against fierce French resistance and could only hope to hold the woods. When the final French attack nearly swept him from the field, he appended a note explaining he had lost the woods and would try to hold a position on the slopes. Initially Karl ordered Hohenzollern to hold his ground; on further reflection he ordered him to retreat. By failing to order a resumption of the attack, he gave Davout unchallenged use of the river road and thus unbarred the route between that marshal and Napoleon.

Hohenzollern's corps had suffered. The brave Manfredini Regiment lost all its superior officers. In addition to two Liechtenstein brothers, Generals Lusignan and Vukassovich had been wounded. Overall, the Austrian Third Corps' officers had demonstrated a type of front-line leadership that heretofore had been rare in the Hapsburg army. The rank and file stoutly backed them. Total losses for the corps were eighteen officers and 509 men killed; seventy-eight and 2392 wounded, respectively; and four and 462 taken prisoner. One man out of every six engaged had become a casualty. While moderate, these losses were not crippling and cannot account for Karl's decision to retreat.

Davout's casualty list accurately reflected which units had done the fighting. Cavalry and detached units suffered 257 casualties; Gudin, 80; Friant, 317; and Saint-Hilaire, 1700. About one in seven men in Saint-Hilaire's division had been hit. Unlike most Austro-French battles, the French higher-echelon commanders suffered less than the Austrians: No French general was shot this day.

Often a campaign's first battle has a morale importance out of proportion to its military significance. Talk of the battle's outcome spreads quickly, elating the victor and depressing the beaten. Davout's men settled into camp with the familiar feeling of triumph. Across the field, Hohenzollern's men believed that although they had fought as well as or better than ever and their leaders had displayed uncharacteristic front-line leadership, they had been driven back and suffered yet another defeat.

Seizing the Initiative

While the battle along the Teugen–Hausen ridge gathered momentum, Archduke Ludwig sallied off toward Abensberg to contain Lefebvre's Bavarian corps. Because of the intercepted dispatch, Ludwig knew Lefebvre intended to attack Karl's flank. The young archduke's task was to prevent this. GM Thierry's detachment from the Third Corps was the first to strike the enemy (see Map 3). Thierry's mission was to link the Third Corps with Ludwig's Fifth Corps. Thierry set off at 6:00 A.M. in a straggling march that dribbled small detachments Austrian-style along his route of march. He arrived on a commanding hill outside Abensberg. From this vantage point he observed the Bavarians forming heavy road columns as they prepared to march against Karl's left flank. Deciding a reconnaissance was in order, Thierry sent scouting detachments in all directions and ordered forward two battalions of the Kaiser Infantry, four squadrons of dragoons, and a cavalry battery.

This descent off the commanding ground proved a mistake. Following a brief artillery duel, the Austrian dragoon colonel charged the opposing Bavarian light horse. He badly bungled the effort, managing a piecemeal fight that saw only half his force engage at any one time. Consequently, the dragoons were soundly drubbed, losing many of their officers. Thierry sent more troops down the hill and the combat tapered off, becoming a desultory artillery exchange.

On Thierry's left, Archduke Ludwig had marched on Siegenburg in order to defend the Abens River line against Wrede (Map 3). Missing one division, which in the crazy-quilt Austrian offensive arrangement was marching under the First Reserve Corps commander, GdK Johannes Liechtenstein, toward Ratisbonne some twenty miles to the northeast, Ludwig continued until he heard the sound of Thierry's fight. Fearing for Thierry, he ordered his right-most brigade to investigate the trouble. It arrived on Thierry's flank just in time to encounter some of the latter's infantry that had become separated from their parent brigade. They reported that Thierry was in retreat. The brigade continued to Biburg, where it managed to stop a Bavarian effort to cross the Abens. Nonetheless, the brigade's efforts to succor Thierry had at least developed the true situation. The Bavarians had driven a wedge between Ludwig and Hohenzollern.

The architect of this maneuver, Marshal Lefebvre, had spent a challenging day striving to accomplish numerous objectives. First, Napoleon directed him to gather intelligence on the Austrian dispositions. The Emperor ordered the marshal to assign an officer the task of interrogating Austrian prisoners and deserters. This Lefebvre did, and it quickly paid dividends. Four deserters, including one loquacious French-born soldier, detailed the composition of Ludwig's corps. They were only unsure about the name of the uhlan regiment that wore red shakos![5] The deserters also alerted Lefebvre that Ludwig intended to advance on the Abens River line.

In addition to gathering intelligence, the marshal had to hold the Abens crossings so Davout could rejoin him, and if the Austrians appeared vulnerable to attack. Hearing nothing from Davout (the Austrians having temporarily interdicted all communication between the two marshals), Lefebvre arranged his Bavarians along the Abens line (see Map 3). Forty-five minutes later—at 9:45 A.M.—he wrote Napoleon again, informing him that his outpost line had picked up more deserters who told him that the Austrian army had set off at 6:00 A.M. Knowing that part of the Austrian host was directed at him, Lefebvre spent an uneasy morning waiting to hear from Davout. It didn't help when a short message came from headquarters stating that they too "waited with impatience" news of Davout's march.[6]

When at last Lefebvre heard the sounds of Davout's fight at Teugen–Hausen, he set off with soldierly zeal to see what he could do to help his fellow marshal. It was this movement that Thierry had first observed from the heights overlooking Abensberg. So it was that Marshal Lefebvre, liberally interpreting his orders to attack if he spotted an enemy weakness, severed communications between Ludwig and Hohenzollern. Best of all, from the French standpoint, was the last message Lefebvre dispatched to Napoleon at ten that night. He could see Davout's campfires along the Teugen–Hausen heights. Although he still had no direct contact with Davout, he would send a message in triplicate, one to be carried by an officer and the other two by peasants familiar with the countryside, in an effort to communicate with Davout and coordinate their efforts. He ended his dispatch to Napoleon with a simple "I await your orders."[7]

Across the lines Ludwig waited as well. During the evening, as he had for most of the day, Ludwig waited for news of the arrival of Hiller's Sixth Corps. Dark suspicion turned to near-certainty in young Ludwig's mind when Hiller failed to appear. Ludwig believed Hiller's dislike of Archduke Karl superseded other considerations and accounted for his absence. He may have been right.

FML Johann Hiller was fifty-three years old in 1809. He had entered the Austrian artillery service at sixteen but did not see combat until he campaigned against the Turks eighteen years later. Then, starting at the beginning of the French Revolution, he went from an officer of limited experience to a wizened veteran as he participated in all his country's repeated wars against France. Although he won little battlefield distinction, he rose high in the esteem of certain factions within the Austrian government. Along the way he had become a bitter rival of Archduke Karl. Because of the divided counsels that characterized both the Hapsburg government and its military, Karl had to employ Hiller in a position of high command. Thus, on 19 April Hiller was given his greatest opportunity.

His orders for the day were to march to support Ludwig's left. As senior commander he would then take command of the entire Austrian left wing, an impressive force comprising more than three corps. Yet this incentive apparently did not stir Hiller to prodigies of zeal. He had wasted the previous day resting his corps at Moosburg. On the nineteenth he sent a small mixed detachment west to scout Pfaffenhofen (see Map 3). Here they ran into Oudinot's French Second Corps and were attacked, overwhelmed, and forced to scamper back toward Moosburg. Meanwhile, the balance of his corps marched toward Ludwig.

They managed an unopposed eighteen-mile march to Mainbourg and camped for the night. This placed Hiller seven miles short of a link-up with Ludwig. For the Austrian army, even after a day of rest, an eighteen-mile march was a heavy burden. In a similar situation a French corps could have marched the extra distance to join Ludwig. What the French could do the Austrians could not, so Ludwig was left without support. Worse, and inexplicably, Hiller failed to inform Ludwig that his corps had reached Mainbourg and would come no farther on the nineteenth.

Hiller's failure to link up with Ludwig or to inform him of his whereabouts became particularly important when Ludwig read his orders that evening. Dispatched from Karl at 3:00 P.M., the message informed Ludwig that Hohenzollern was heavily engaged with Davout. French prisoners indicated that Davout intended to attack all along Karl's front. This Karl knew because he could see French campfires from the Grub plateau where he sat with his grenadiers. Seemingly, Karl's strategic imagination was entirely confined within the limits of his eyesight. He wrote that except for what he could see, he "could not judge if my columns have arrived at the different places" they were ordered to march to.[8] Given "this uncertitude," the probability that Davout would attack again on the twentieth, and Karl's desire to renew the fight once the situation clarified, Karl required Ludwig to march all night to rejoin him. However, Ludwig's orders were conditional: If Hiller failed to arrive, Ludwig was to remain in position. If Ludwig received a heavy attack, he was to fall back toward Landshut to protect the army's line of communications.

On the night of the nineteenth, knowing his older brother expected his arrival by dawn, Ludwig was off balance. He felt unable to comply with Karl's wishes until he learned where Hiller was. Seven miles from the perplexed Ludwig, Hiller slept blithely, knowing nothing of the complex series of events his inattention to duty was causing.

The nineteenth of April had seen scattered fighting along a thirty-mile front. This would have taxed the capacity of any general of the period. To retain control required a commander to design a plan whose central purpose would see the army through the inevitable confusions inherent in war. In addition, the subordinates had to adjust to changing circumstances while pursuing the plan. On the nineteenth, both Karl's strategic planning capacities and his subordinates' abilities came up well short. By day's end his army lay scattered all over the map outside mutually supporting distance. Worse, although Karl did not know it, he had lost the initiative.

Planning a Counteroffensive

"Activity! activity! speed!" Marshal Masséna had read Napoleon's personal appeal in the early afternoon of 18 April. Heretofore, the prematurely aging marshal had managed a rather indolent campaign. In part, according to one of his staff officers, this behavior was caused by Berthier's confusing orders sent over the preceding days. Masséna possessed a fine strategic brain when he chose to use it. He had sensed Berthier's confusion. Rather than trying to assist a fellow marshal, Masséna had taken advantage of the situation to deliver a lax command performance. When he read Napoleon's personal appeal, appended on the bottom of a daily order, he responded to the goad in the manner Napoleon desired.

Napoleon explained that he wanted Masséna to debouch through Pfaffenhofen and descend on the Austrian rear (see Map 3). While Napoleon applied frontal pressure, Karl would be caught between two fires. Masséna recognized the simple brilliance of this plan, and a glance at his maps showed that it had a very real chance for success. The marshal's problem, however, was that he had let matters drift to the embarrassing point that he didn't know the location of major elements within his corps. He felt compelled to halt outside Pfaffenhofen while he waited for his corps to close up. With growing anxiety he dispatched his top aide, Sainte-Croix, to find the missing Oudinot and his two divisions and inform him of Napoleon's desires.

Seemingly galvanized into action, Masséna sent along the message that Oudinot had to "drive on Pfaffenhofen as early as possible. I think that after having rested your men for a few hours you must put them back on the march, having a strong advance guard, you will reconnoiter well, and have your corps underway at sunrise . . . if necessary you will march all night to share in the glory that waits you."[9] Yet having written these fine words, Masséna waited the remainder of the day for his own corps to close up instead of advancing with the men at hand. Because of his careless dispersion, his outlying units marched all day and well into the night to join his main force. A regiment of Hesse-Darmstadt light horse covered more than seventy miles; during a two-day period one of his infantry divisions marched some sixty-five.

Supported by such herculean feats, at dawn the next day, 19 April, Masséna advanced on Pfaffenhoffen and there, at last, he found Oudinot. Faithful to Masséna's urgings, Oudinot had marched most of the night. Hurrying beneath the moonlight, his young soldiers sang a newly popular song written by Napoleon's stepdaughter. The romantic song spoke about soldiers leaving their sweethearts as they departed for war:

You leave me to search for glory
My tender heart will follow your path.
The night stars, with their peaceable radiancy
Cast their light on the tents of France![10]

It must have stirred mixed emotions among the conscripts heading toward their first fight.

At 4:00 A.M. Oudinot's unit arrived to find the village defended by a force estimated at 4000 men. In fact it was a mere outpost (Scheibler, the force Hiller had sent to scout Masséna; see Map 3) comprising some 1200 infantry.[11] Oudinot attacked with an infantry division supported by the chasseurs à cheval of Colbert's light cavalry brigade. The cavalry were veterans, renowned armywide as the *brigade infernale*. Charging with characteristic dash, they easily overwhelmed the Austrians. Fighting in their first battle, Oudinot's conscript infantry helped capture over 200 prisoners and experienced the satisfaction of seeing their enemy fly from the shock of combat. For green troops at the beginning of a campaign, nothing could be better. They would fight with much greater confidence in the future.[12] On the other side, the pernicious Austrian habit of using entire battalions and squadrons as outpost troops (a force too large to evade combat easily and too small to offer an adequate defense) when a mounted picket was more appropriate had reaped the inevitable result.

When Masséna encountered Oudinot's men they were resting on their laurels. He was furious, castigating Oudinot for the cardinal sin of failing to pursue a defeated enemy. Oudinot explained that his men were fatigued from their heavy marching. Even as they argued Oudinot's Baden troops began straggling in, having marched all night to join the main body. Prodded by Masséna, Oudinot launched a tepid cavalry pursuit. Masséna himself felt content to wait in the village as his units slowly concentrated.

Napoleon had spent the first half of the nineteenth at Ingolstadt digesting reports and sending orders. He realized Davout had fallen a day behind schedule but hoped he would complete his march to Neustadt during the nineteenth. When around noon he read Masséna's report about the skirmish at Pfaffenhofen, his confidence soared. The fact that Masséna also was not as far advanced as the Emperor had intended did not cause him to seriously revise his basic strategic plan. Indeed, by return courier Napoleon dispatched an order that expanded upon that marshal's role. He told Masséna: "According to the news I receive today, I shall direct you on Landshut; and, then, Prince Karl will find he has lost his line of communications."[13] However, in case the Bavarians needed reinforcing, Masséna was to hold Oudinot available for a rapid march to the Abens line. The Emperor concluded by referring to the Austrians as "that scum which you beat this morning."[14]

Just as he completed dictating this order the sounds of cannon fire at Abensberg caused the Emperor to leave in haste for the front. The "scum" were apparently attacking. Because he departed so quickly he did not wait to sign the fine copy of the order. This omission, coupled with poor French staffwork, meant that several hours later Masséna received two slightly contradictory sets of orders regarding the exact placement of his forces. In Masséna's view the confusion was a characteristic and certain sign that the orders originated with Berthier. The absence of Napoleon's signature seemed to confirm this impression. Consequently Masséna decided he did not strictly have to obey. He returned to his previous lassitude, asking little from his soldiers for the rest of the day. From eight in the morning until dusk he advanced only another four miles in the direction of Moosburg, hardly "Activity! activity! speed!"

Meanwhile, Napoleon arrived closer to the combat at the village of Neustadt. Having outstripped his stables during his journey from Paris, he rode a horse borrowed from Masséna named Patience. Patience was exactly what he needed for the rest of the day. He learned that Davout and Lefebvre were engaged but received no details of their fights. In fact, all word concerning Davout was secondhand since no intelligence came from that marshal himself. Uncertain as to Davout's fate, Napoleon ordered Masséna to send one of Oudinot's divisions to Neustadt to support the center. Then he waited some more.

Restless, he rode to a nearby camp occupied by a Bavarian division. He encountered the division commander, the king of Bavaria's son and heir to the throne. During his brief conversation with the king a few days back he had commented on the importance of having the son assume a field command. He now spoke similar words to the son himself. Patting him on the shoulder and complimenting him for his presence, the Emperor said: "Here you see how one must be King! Otherwise, if you were to stay at home, each of your men would do the same; and then, good-bye to the state, good-bye to glory!"[15]

Evening and darkness only brought increased anxiety. An imperial aide found Napoleon resting uneasily: "He was lying on a wooden bench, his feet next to a wood-burning stove, and his head on a soldier's knapsack, having a map spread out before him."[16] Impatiently he asked for news of Davout. Because the Austrian attack had cut the Ratisbonne–Abensberg road, Davout's couriers had to ride a circuitous route to bring his messages. Lacking information, the Emperor circulated among his entourage. Shortly after midnight the Emperor again wrote Masséna and this time told him to send

Oudinot's entire command to strengthen the French middle and left. Finally Lefebvre's 10:00 P.M. dispatch arrived announcing that Davout's corps could be seen on the Teugen–Hausen heights. Vastly relieved, Napoleon set to work in the predawn hours to refine his counteroffensive.

He correctly deduced that the Austrian line of communications went through Landshut. Since his earliest campaigns in Italy, he had learned that the surest way to defeat the ponderous Austrians was by threatening their rear and their line of communications. Accordingly, he prepared a two-fisted drive on Landshut. Marshal Masséna's orders would stand; his Fourth Corps would descend on Landshut with over 40,000 men. Lefebvre, with 27,000 men, would break out of his Abens River bridgehead and make a frontal attack toward the same objective. Napoleon did not know Davout's precise status because Davout's dispatch from Teugen on the night of the nineteenth did not reach imperial headquarters until midmorning of the twentieth. Absent total knowledge but unlike the equivocal Karl, Napoleon stuck to his plan.

Of critical importance, although no one yet realized it, was the massive stone bridge spanning the Danube at Ratisbonne. The bridge rested on enormous pillars designed to stand up to the pounding they took each spring when the Danube's floodwaters propelled large ice floes into the abutments and under the bridge. When Davout had evacuated Ratisbonne he left the Sixty-fifth Ligne behind to hold the town and destroy the bridge if the Austrians appeared on the far shore (see Map 3). When Kollowrath's Second Corps did arrive, French engineers found that the stout bridge resisted their demolition charges as well as it resisted ice. Unable to destroy it, the Sixty-fifth prepared a defense.

The regiment had been hand-picked by Davout for this task. The marshal wanted to give its colonel—the Baron de Coutard—an opportunity to earn promotion. Coutard had been in tight situations before. In 1800 he had distinguished himself during the memorable siege of Genoa. At that time the French defenders had displayed iron-willed resolve in the face of disease and starvation. Such an experience could be assumed to prepare a commander for the special isolation of a siege. However, something beyond military logic influenced Davout when he chose a commander at Ratisbonne. Coutard was Davout's cousin.

During the nineteenth it appeared Davout had chosen well. The action began when Kollowrath's patrols probed the French fortifications on the high ground overlooking Stadt-am-Hof. To their surprise they found some of the trenches empty. When they advanced upon the few manned redoubts, the French hastily fled downslope to Stadt-am-Hof. From the commanding heights Kollowrath examined the scene and saw that the masses of French soldiers who had been camped around Ratisbonne for the past three days were gone. He advanced his artillery and opened fire against the suburb.

Coutard's 2000 men were insufficient to defend the extensive fortifications on the heights. He wisely withdrew to Stadt-am-Hof and prepared to make his stand. The constricted terrain greatly aided his effort by channeling the attackers against one gate leading into the suburb. The gate was the focal point of the fight. Plunging artillery fire from the heights bombarded the gate's defenders. The Sixty-fifth could make no effective reply; it simply had to endure. Covered by the artillery, a battalion from the Froon Infantry Regiment formed serried column and assaulted. Simultaneously, several companies of Tyrolean jägers worked their way around the gate to fire at the defenders in flank.

The attack carried the gate and forced the defenders back into the houses lining the main street leading to the stone bridge. From doors and windows a hail of point-blank musketry lashed the whitecoats. Undaunted, the men of the Froon Infantry accelerated their pace and drove downhill toward the bridge. Not even pausing to return the fire, they tried to carry the suburb by shock alone. They reached a second gate guarding the bridge itself. The medieval iron portcullis was raised; the open archway beckoned. Suddenly, from a stone tower flanking the gate an unseen foe discharged a lethal volley. It knocked down the standardbearers and the officers at the front of the column. In disarray, the battalion halted. From the tower in front and the houses on both sides of the street musketry tore into the motionless target. It was more than the battalion could stand. It broke, some men surrendering while others fled through the gauntlet of fire up the street and out the first gate.

For the remainder of the day the dull boom of the Hapsburg guns reverberated in the Danube Valley as the artillery methodically pounded the suburb, but no follow-up assault came. The Sixty-fifth had put up a tremendous fight against a brave, though poorly supported, assault. By day's end, Coutard proudly reported to Davout that during a ten-hour fight his regiment had repulsed the Austrians while capturing two flags and 400 prisoners. However, over half the Sixty-fifth were casualties and ammunition had run so low that the survivors were reduced to taking bullets from the wounded, the dead, and the prisoners. Coutard ended his message with the promise to hold if Davout sent him more ammunition.

By the end of the nineteenth, lack of ammunition had become a pressing problem for Davout's entire corps. The corps' trains had not managed to accompany Friant's rear guard when that general had force-marched to Ratisbonne on the eighteenth. Instead the trains had traveled south to safety and were separated from the Third Corps by the Danube. Nonetheless Davout tried to meet Coutard's need, but he now paid the price for having abandoned his line of communications back to Ratisbonne. The ammunition wagons dispatched to Coutard failed to find a way through Austrian lines to the beleaguered city. Davout's cousin was on his own, defending with few remaining bullets a bridge he could not destroy against an enemy who outnumbered him ten to one.

CHAPTER VI

The Battle of Abensberg

*A general's principal talent consists in knowing the mental-
ity of the soldier and in winning his confidence.*

Cordon Defense

The terrific storm that ended Davout's battle along the Hausen ridge ushered in
a cold and rainy 20 April. Around the French campfires foragers returned from
predawn plundering expeditions. Typically, the army had outstripped its supply columns, so the soldiers had to supplement their bread rations with
foodstuffs taken from nearby Bavarian villages and farms. Familiar with
Napoleon's way of war, veterans had little trouble finding root crops, chickens,
and the like to contribute to the communal soup pots whose aromatic fra-
grance gave the French camps a special flavor. The new soldiers eyed the
veterans' campfires hungrily and went without. Lacking the know-how to care
for themselves, sheltered only by a blanket from the April rains, the young
men began a winnowing process that hardened the survivors into lean, durable
warriors capable of withstanding enormous privation.

At the Austrian encampments the soldiers fared better. Landshut had
become an enormous magazine filled with supplies of all sorts. Endless wagon
columns trundled back and forth to the front lines to feed the men and horses
and replenish ammunition. However, having well-stocked bivouacs carried a
risk: the vast supply trains clogged the road net behind the Austrian lines. If
the soldiers should have to march quickly it might prove difficult.

Archduke Karl rose on the twentieth to consider developments along a
vast front stretching from Hiller's left at Pfaffenhofen across the Danube where

Kollowrath and Bellegarde operated. Unlike Napoleon, he had few able subordinates who could display sound initiative under confusing circumstances. Only he could rectify yesterday's mistakes. Having seen his offensive fail to prevent Davout from linking up with the French center, Karl focused his attention on rejoining the Austrian forces operating on the far bank of the Danube. To this end, Karl himself would conduct a strong force toward Ratisbonne. Meanwhile, the corps in contact with the French along the Abens would retire (see Map 9).

The Archduke had initiated this retreat when, on the preceding evening, he had ordered most of Hohenzollern's Third Corps to fall back toward Leierndorf, a village west of Eckmühl on the Gross Laber River. This took the Third Corps out of direct support of the three Austrian corps to the south, including Ludwig's Fifth Corps. However, Ludwig remained under orders to support Hohenzollern. Karl should have advised Ludwig of Hohenzollern's move immediately. Instead, he waited until 7:30 A.M. on the twentieth to inform his younger brother that Davout's link-up threatened Ludwig's right flank and that he had just taken away the force that could have protected this flank. According to Karl's new instructions, Ludwig should retreat through Rottenburg and take up a defense behind the Laber (see Map 9). Hiller would defend at Pfeffenhausen. The major problem with this order was the timing: Dispatched at seven-thirty, it could not be expected to reach Ludwig until mid- to late morning. It would take even longer to arrive at Hiller's headquarters. Karl had simply taken too much time to make a decision. He now relied on the French giving him a grace period so his orders could take effect.

After a five-hour sleep, Napoleon rose at 5:00 A.M. and began the day in characteristic fashion by calling for Bacler D'Albe, Berthier, and the maps. His two staff officers reviewed overnight developments and assured the Emperor that the Austrians remained in position behind the Abens. Napoleon believed the campaign's climactic battle would occur today. Yesterday's surprise Hapsburg attack against Davout, coupled with Masséna's inexplicable slowness, had forced him to postpone the destruction of the Austrian army by twenty-four hours. Moving his pins about the situation map, he judged the situation remained ripe for his favorite maneuver: *la manoeuvre sur les derrières*, the advance of envelopment.

Napoleon erroneously thought that the balance of Karl's army stood directly before him blocking the roads to Landshut and that Ludwig's corps was just one element of this host. Accordingly, he would personally oversee the frontal pinning attack using his Germanic allies and a special ad hoc shock force to be commanded by the aggressive Marshal Lannes. Davout and Lefebvre would envelop the Austrian right. Masséna's two corps had the critical task. Masséna would march toward Landshut to occupy the strategic

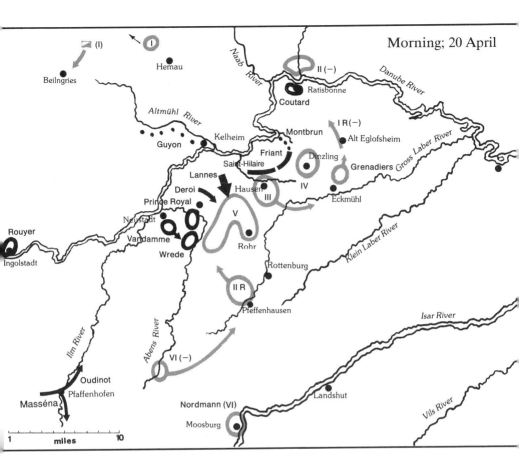

curtain formed by the Isar River. The marshal would occupy all crossing points and thus isolate Karl from his rear depots and separate him from any reinforcements. Trapped against the elbow of the Isar and Danube, Karl would have to fight without supplies or surrender.

Orders went out from imperial headquarters to put this plan into effect: Masséna to march via Freising to Moosburg and Landshut; Vandamme to take command of the Württembergers and attack through Siegenburg; Lefebvre's Bavarians to provide a link between Vandamme and Davout; Lannes to take three of Davout's infantry divisions and a cavalry division and attack toward Rohr—which left Davout (see Map 9).

The problem here was that the Emperor simply did not know the status of Davout's corps. Davout had fought on the nineteenth in isolation; only during the night had he been able to establish tenuous contact with Lefebvre. Communications remained so difficult that Napoleon did not receive Davout's evening reports on the nineteenth until the morning of the twentieth was well advanced. Napoleon had to plan in a vacuum, although he knew he could rely on Davout's good judgment. In any event, Napoleon believed Davout's front was of secondary importance. The campaign was to be won by the pinning attack over the Abens River and by Masséna's capture of the Isar River crossings. Riddled with mistaken assumptions, this strategy could be disastrous against an active opponent.

At 6:00 A.M. Napoleon descended into the courtyard, where he found his escort mounted and ready. Normally cavalry of his Imperial Guard provided an escort squadron. But, as we have seen, the speed with which Napoleon's crisis on the Danube had developed forced the Emperor to leave his bodyguard behind in France as he hurried to the front. Absent the Imperial Guard, today Napoleon deliberately chose to remain with his Germanic allies. They were a potential weak link in his plans, so he worked to ensure that his personal presence inspired them. By honoring the German cavalry as escort troops he converted a necessary expedient to a morale-boosting opportunity. It was not a risk-free decision: the Bavarian and Württemberg chevaulégers would have to protect him from surprise and ambush. Such events were possible because a dense Danube fog, thickened by intermittent rains, clung to the Bavarian countryside, reducing visibility to a few hundred yards. All along the ill-defined front line both sides were sending out early-morning patrols to scout the shrouded woods and hamlets. But the escort performed its duty well, allowing Napoleon to reach a hillside overlooking the Abens River valley without incident.

There he established his headquarters. Ever attentive to the morale power of his army (it was Napoleon who proclaimed "the morale is to the physical as three is to one"), he had dictated an order of the day for circulation among the Bavarians. He now called for the Bavarian officers to gather around while he delivered this order. It was a characteristic gesture of which only he, among all European generals and statesmen, seemed capable:

> Bavarian soldiers! I do not come to you as French Emperor, but as protector of your country and the Confederation of the Rhine. Bavarians! Today you fight alone against the Austrians. No French serve in your front ranks . . . I am entirely confident in your bravery. . . . For two hundred years Bavarian flags, protected by France, have resisted Austria. We are going to Vienna, where we will know how to punish Austria for the harm she has so often done to your country. Austria wants to partition your country and disband your units and distribute you among their regiments. Bavarians! This war is the last you will fight against your enemies; attack them with the bayonet and annihilate them![1]

Square in the path of the Bavarian–French assault was Archduke Ludwig's Fifth Corps. His brother's orders of the nineteenth governed the twenty-five-year-old Ludwig's conduct in the early morning of the twentieth. He knew his corps was supposed to retreat and close on Karl's left flank. However, he was not to begin this movement until Hiller's Sixth Corps appeared. Trying to accomplish both objectives placed Ludwig in the awkward position of defending in place behind eight miles of the Abens River with one eye looking rearward in anticipation of a retreat. Ludwig was reluctant to commit too many men to a front-line defense lest it prove difficult to extricate them once Hiller arrived. Consequently, he spread his units out in a cordon defense blocking the two main roads leading to Landshut. It was a characteristic Austrian defense and one that Napoleon scorned, for by trying to hold all the Austrians were not strong anywhere.

GM Radetzky held Ludwig's left at Siegenburg (see Map 10). Radetzky's four battalions and twelve squadrons of the advance guard division blocked a Bavarian advance along the main road running back through Pfeffenhausen and on to Landshut. At Biburg, the next village downstream on the Abens, Bianchi commanded his own brigade and portions of Thierry's. Near Offenstetten were the remainder of Thierry's brigade, three-and-one-third battalions, and half a dragoon regiment. Thierry belonged to the Third Corps but was temporarily attached to Ludwig. Thierry blocked an advance from Abensberg toward Bachel. At Bachel itself was Pfanzelter's Third Corps detachment of one grenzer battalion and two hussar squadrons. Bachel was a key position sited athwart the second of two major roads running south toward Landshut. Backstopping the Bachel position were Schustekh's four hussar squadrons (see Map 10). He would be joined by a mixed arms detachment working its way cross-country from Mainbourg.

The Second Reserve Corps occupied the heights around Ludmannsdorf (Map 10). Even this elite reserve was fragmented. It retained its five grenadier battalions, but only four of sixteen dragoon squadrons remained. In sum, not only were Ludwig's men dispersed, they had also lost their organizational structure with even individual battalions splintered between different commands. Enfeebled by the previous day's combat, Ludwig had seventeen battalions and sixteen squadrons to guard the Abens line until Hiller arrived from Mainbourg. Given time this dispersion could have been corrected, but time was the one thing the opposing general cherished above all. The muffled popping of skirmish fire rose in intensity as the French and Bavarians advanced out of the predawn mist.

At first the situation revealed to Ludwig as he gazed through the mist toward Siegenberg did not seem grave. His soldiers manned a low ridge overlooking the Abens crossing. In the valley below Wrede's Bavarian sappers made a half-hearted effort to lay a new bridge across the river. Although the Abens was exceedingly narrow at this point, the Bavarians displayed a decided lack of zeal. The little energy they possessed dissipated quickly when Ludwig directed a battery of twelve-pounders to bombard the bridging site. Its fire prevented the sappers from making any meaningful progress. Satisfied matters here were well in hand, when the young Archduke learned that the French were attacking on his right against Thierry he set two battalions marching cross-country toward Kirchdorf to Thierry's support. He then ordered the Second Reserve Corps to advance to Siegenberg to replace them (see Map 10). With this decision Ludwig committed most of his reserves before the battle began. He now had to depend on Hiller for further help, and herein lay a major problem. Hiller's antipathy for Karl was known armywide, yet much depended upon Hiller's ability to overcome his feelings and behave in a soldierly fashion.

Hiller had received Karl's message of the previous day informing him to march to support Ludwig and then take command of the entire three-corps wing operating along the Abens. For once an Austrian movement began in a timely manner when Hiller had his Sixth Corps under way at dawn. A major road ran eight miles directly from Hiller's encampment at Mainbourg to Ludwig at Siegenberg. Hiller feared to march along this road. He worried that he would expose his left flank to any French formations in the direction of the Danube and then be forced to fight with the Abens River cutting across his rear. An aggressive, cooperative commander might have taken the risk. (In fact, there was no French force in position to prevent the movement.) Hiller preferred a cross-country march along secondary roads to Pfeffenhausen (see Map 9). Once there he planned to take in events before deciding where to proceed.

While Hiller marched and Ludwig perfected his deployments, the Austrian officer on the spot, GM Ludwig Thierry, sent a dawn patrol from Offenstetten toward Abensberg (see Map 10). The patrol did not go far before it struck Bavarian pickets who seemed to occupy every path leading through the broken terrain. Although unable to penetrate the enemy screen, the rising sunlight revealed all the Austrians had to know. The patrol observed the road from Ratisbonne to Abensberg choked with fast-moving enemy columns. They belonged to Marshal Lannes, although the Hapsburgs did not know this. One of Thierry's staff officers brought up a dragoon patrol who managed to slip between the enemy pickets and thoroughly scout the French columns. He reported to Thierry that the French were deploying in great strength. A French outpost commander like Montbrun would have brazened it out and at least tried to delay the enemy advance. Thierry chose to retreat.

Lannes

Forty-year-old Marshal Jean Lannes had traveled a great distance to lead the French advance toward Bachel. He exemplified the possibilities inherent in

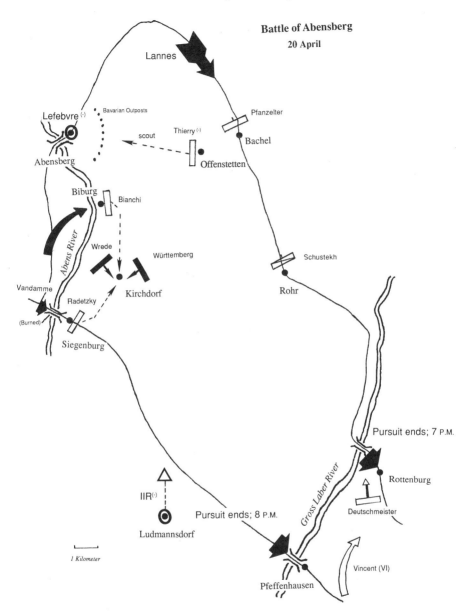

Battle of Abensberg
20 April

Lannes

Lefebvre (-)

Bavarian Outposts

Pfanzelter

Thierry (-)

scout

Bachel

Abensberg

Offenstetten

Biburg

Bianchi

Abens River

Wrede

Württemberg

Schustekh

Vandamme

Kirchdorf

Rohr

Radetzky

(Burned)

Siegenburg

Pursuit ends; 7 P.M.

IIR (-)

Gross Laber River

Rottenburg

Pursuit ends; 8 P.M.

Deutschmeister

Ludmannsdorf

1 Kilometer

Vincent (VI)

Pfeffenhausen

revolutionary France's meritocracy. He had abandoned his civilian life as an apprentice dyer in 1792 to become a soldier. Showing amazing bravery (none surpassed his displays of courage on the battlefield) and sound tactical judgment, he became a general just three years later. He had continued to develop as a soldier and was appointed one of the original marshals. More than just a gifted leader, Lannes was one of Napoleon's few friends, the only officer permitted to address him with the familiar *tu* instead of the more proper and formal *vous*. According to an admiring subordinate, Lannes was "very kind, but passionate . . . his ambition boundless, his activity extraordinary, and his courage undaunted."[2] Most recently he had supervised the horrific siege of the Spanish town of Saragossa, which his men had captured only after a building-by-building fight more akin to the World War II struggle for Stalingrad than usual nineteenth-century warfare. When danger mounted on the other side of Europe, Napoleon summoned him to Bavaria. He had just arrived on the night of the nineteenth. So quickly had he traveled that he left behind his staff and his mounts.

On the morning of the twentieth, riding a borrowed horse, he listened while the Emperor gave verbal instructions to assume command of a new corps formation comprising Morand's and Gudin's infantry divisions, Nansouty's and Saint-Sulpice's cuirassier divisions, and a brigade of light cavalry. Gesturing toward the objective, Napoleon told Lannes to attack down the road toward Rohr while Lefebvre's Bavarians applied frontal pressure.

At 8:00 A.M., as Lannes' hurrying columns worked their way forward, Thierry fell back toward Bachel where he expected to find Pfanzelter (see Map 10). To his dismay he found Bachel already occupied by Lannes' cavalry. Unknown to Thierry, Pfanzelter had received orders from his corps commander, FML Hohenzollern, to rejoin Third Corps. Here was a penalty for the Austrians having broken their corps into uncoordinated detachments; inevitable confusion would occur. Worse, Thierry's four dragoon squadrons, sent forward to scout, failed to rejoin the Austrian infantry as they marched through the wooded terrain to Bachel. They were not available to protect the infantry just at the moment they were most needed.

Seemingly abandoned, what the soldiers in Thierry's Kaiser and Lindenau Infantry Regiments most needed now was cool leadership to react to the shock and draw the strung-out columns in tight to form square. They did not receive it and instead scattered into the woods to escape the French cavalry. They marched back to Rohr, where they hoped to find a second chance under the shelter of Schustekh's cavalry.

Meanwhile, questing French chasseurs à cheval spearheaded Lannes' advance, followed by two infantry divisions with artillery. The heavy cuirassiers, "the mass of iron," brought up the rear. The march was not as rapid as it might have been. Lannes worried that the fog-shrouded hills along his left concealed enemy formations. In fact, the Austrian Third Corps was well placed to menace Lannes' left flank but failed to do so because Karl's orders called for the corps to retreat. However, the threat existed, so Lannes slowed his advance while infantry regiments deployed out of road column, climbed the slopes northeast of the road to Rohr, and probed the many small villages and woods that might have hidden a Hapsburg force. Finding nothing, Lannes' column continued toward Rohr, marching past potato fields, occasional farms, and frequent woodlots. His light cavalry had just reached its outskirts when they encountered their first serious opposition. The leading chasseurs à cheval fired their carbines to warn their comrades, turned, and galloped back to their supports. Breathlessly they reported to their officers: Austrian cavalry were advancing at the trot.

The Hapsburg horse belonged to Schustekh. While Thierry struggled to extricate his infantry from Bachel, Schustekh had held his position on the Rohr heights. He had every right to expect that Pfanzelter, positioned in Bachel—and therefore between his command and Lannes' French—would provide him timely warning of any French advance. Instead, Pfanzelter's departure from Bachel to rejoin Hohenzollern meant that Lannes' cavalry appeared before Rohr without warning. Surprised, Schustekh made the soldierly decision to charge the French van with his four hussar squadrons.

The Austrian charge experienced initial success, tumbling the French chasseurs à cheval backward upon their supports. But the French had superior numbers, and their commander, General Jacquinot, soon led them forward to overlap the Austrian flanks. The Hapsburg hussars performed a neat tactical retreat back upon their grenzer supports and took up a new position south of Rohr. Here Thierry's dispirited and disorganized infantry joined them.

They arrived in Rohr in great disorder and found, to their surprise and dismay, that the French cavalry had again beaten them to their objective. On the far side of Rohr they saw Schustekh standing firm for the moment, but how to join him when nearly surrounded by large numbers of French cavalry proved an unexpected and daunting problem.

Jacquinot exploited Thierry's confusion superbly. While some of his squadrons continued to face Schustekh, the remainder bluffed charges against Thierry's infantry to keep it pinned in the open. Meanwhile, the Thirteenth Légère, Gudin's leading infantry unit, hustled into position to attack Thierry. A French artillery battery hastily deployed. The three arms—cavalry, infantry, and artillery—were in place for a combined arms assault. The artillery fired several salvos of canister to open a breach in the Austrian formation. The Thirteenth Légère charged the wavering whitecoats and the Austrians broke in panic. Jacquinot's light cavalry scooped up nearly 300 prisoners before the Austrians reached the safety of the woods.

The surrounding hills channeled Thierry's survivors through difficult defiles. To cover their retreat, Schustekh resolved to charge again with his hussars. Simultaneously Thierry's four dragoon squadrons, who had finally reappeared, attacked the French flank. The double attack succeeded in overthrowing the leading French cavalry regiment. The Hapsburg horse swept forward in pursuit only to find French cuirassiers, summoned to the front to help clear the way, charging in against the hussars' flank. Under cover of this charge, the French cavalry rallied and returned to the fray. Now it was the Austrians' turn to be caught in front and flank. Outnumbered and outmaneuvered, they broke and fled. They galloped through their own infantry, plunging Thierry's none-too-steady men into renewed disorder. GM Thierry frantically tried to rally his troops. To set an example, he dismounted on the road and commanded his men to stand fast with him.

The fear of the French cavalry was upon the Austrian warriors. They threw down their muskets, shouldered their general aside, and fled toward Rottenburg. Thierry's gesture proved worse than futile; in the general disintegration of his command the French cuirassiers captured most of his infantry and snatched up the forlorn Hapsburg general himself. Thierry's failure had been complete. Lannes' pursuing cavalry surged forward all the way to Rottenburg. There they found Hohenzollern's trains and the wounded from his earlier battle against Davout. All in all, Lannes' command seized over 3000 prisoners and four cannon.

While this terrific French pursuit was taking place, FML Johann Hiller arrived in Siegenburg to meet Ludwig and take command of the entire three-corps wing operating south of the Laber. Sensitive to his own inexperience, aware of his brother's dislike of Hiller, and prickly about his royal bloodlines being subordinated to a plebeian, Ludwig proved anything but a dutiful lieutenant. Reviewing events, Hiller learned that Schustekh and Thierry were opposed by superior numbers of French but did not yet know the extent of the debacle. He sent an order back to his advance guard commander, FML Karl Vincent, to take two brigades and four squadrons of Rosenberg Chevaulégers to Rohr to support the right flank.[3]

Vincent's men found passage toward Rottenburg, where they planned on picking up the main road to Rohr, very difficult (see Map 10). The two brigade batteries with their sixteen guns impeded progress as the Austrians tromped along poor, sodden farm tracks. After a four-mile trek Vincent neared the outskirts of Rottenburg, where he witnessed a spectacle amazing even on this day of Hapsburg surprises. Jamming the vital road leading to the front were wagons, caissons, horses, and the associated rear-area impedimenta that accompanied the Austrian army. Seeing a gap in the torrent of moving vehicles, Vincent entered the road and marched west against the flow. Another wagon train appeared, heading toward Vincent's toiling soldiers. A wagon wheel broke, a caisson overturned, vehicles from side roads penetrated the Austrian column. Hopelessly intermixed, Vincent's command ground to a halt.

Some lightly wounded Hapsburg hussars and dragoons came riding east.

They had fought with Schustekh and brought frightening news of unopposed French cuirassiers sabering Austrian wagon drivers and teamsters. Punctuating their tale of woe was the sound of scattered musketry. Apparently the French were just ahead. Vincent advanced toward the firing, clearing a way through the Hapsburg trains by main force. Nearing the hamlet of Rottenburg he spied the French cavalry hacking at a throng of routing Austrians. FML Vincent quickly learned he had contacted Thierry's and Schustekh's units, the formations he had been supposed to support.

Vincent determined he would fight to save the trains and Thierry's and Schustekh's routing remnants: "The danger was imminent, and General Vincent, seeing the enemy rapidly advancing on the Rottenburg heights, decided to occupy the village at the run with his leading brigade."[4] To gain time for his units to deploy, he ordered his cavalry to charge. Four chevauléger squadrons with about five hundred troopers attacked the French cavalry van. Thousands of French cuirassiers stretched back behind this van toward Rohr, but at the point of decision the Austrians had the edge. They were formed troops acting in concert charging individuals who heretofore had been happily sabering running, unarmed infantry. Glancing up to see the thundering wave of advancing enemy cavalry, the French reined in, reversed direction, and galloped back on their supports.

This brief check gave Vincent time to deploy his men on the heights behind Rottenburg. His artillery unlimbered and began bombarding the French as they in turn maneuvered from road column onto the adjacent fields. Vincent's second brigade arrived and with it appeared Hiller. Hiller had displayed commendable energy to first ride to Siegenburg to apprise himself of events along one of the roads to Landshut and then on to the second artery at Rottenburg, where he arrived just in time to intervene at a critical moment. Hiller quickly studied the situation through his glass and conferred with his staff. His chief of staff insisted that before them was but a feeble enemy detachment. Swayed by his optimism, Hiller sent this staff officer to order Vincent's left-hand brigade to attack through the woods and turn the French right flank.

At 7:00 P.M. the Austrian brigade advanced, led by the vaunted Deutschmeister Infantry (see Map 10). This regiment was special; many of its rankers and all the officers belonged to the Teutonic Order. Its inhaber, or regimental proprietor, was current head of the order. The Deutschmeister Infantry attacked with great élan, penetrating into the woods, where it encountered Bavarian infantry. At first it was no match; some 300 Bavarians surrendered during the initial onslaught while the balance fled from the woods. There they met the formidable presence of their French commander, Marshal Lefebvre. Napoleon had chosen Lefebvre for this command partially because he spoke

German. Lefebvre now employed his linguistic skill to shame the shaken Bavarians into rallying: "The Emperor is near and is watching you; will you fail to justify his confidence?"[5]

These words, coupled with the sight of rapidly advancing reinforcements that included a French regiment, checked the Bavarians' flight. The French and Bavarians charged into the dark woods and a tremendous twilight firefight ensued. Heeding their officers' hoarse cries to close ranks, the Deutschmeister Regiment traded volleys for as long as they could endure. Their ranks visibly shrank while their opponents' numbers seemed to grow even larger. Bested at last, the Deutschmeister Regiment retired back to its starting point, minus 600 men who had fallen. Although defeated, the regiment had halted the enemy pursuit.

Collapse of the Abens Position

Largely independent of the fight southward along the road to Rottenberg was the action at Siegenburg and Biburg. The Bavarian General Wrede and Vandamme's Württembergers had the assignment of forcing a crossing over the Abens and attacking Ludwig's Austrians. Wrede permitted himself to be delayed all morning at Siegenburg while his men half-heartedly tried to rebuild the bridge. Wrede then attempted to outflank the Siegenburg position by crossing downstream at Biburg (see Map 10). Here he encountered GM Bianchi's command. The terrain did not favor the Austrians. The feature best suited to a protracted defense, a stout monastery, stood on the Bavarian side of the Abens. Nonetheless, Bianchi thwarted the Bavarian effort to force a crossing. Around noon Wrede dispatched a courier to report to Napoleon.

The courier found Napoleon with his headquarters staff on a plateau west of Bachel. The Emperor and his staff were eating a hastily prepared cold lunch while trying to warm themselves against the raw chill before a roaring bonfire. The Bavarian courier reported that Wrede could make no progress against a formidable position manned by Bianchi's entire command. Napoleon turned to Berthier: "What force is it?"

Berthier opened the notebook documenting the Austrian order of battle. Laboriously compiled from the reports of French spies, diplomats, and travelers and constantly updated with intelligence gleaned from prisoners and deserters, the invaluable notebook allowed Berthier to reply: "Brigade Bianchi, Fifth Corps, Regiments Duka and Giulay, six battalions, fine soldiers."[6]

The Emperor briefly reflected and then spoke: "Monsieur Wrede is strong enough to defeat them. Let him display the zeal necessary to reconquer his country."[7]

Stimulated by the Emperor's words, Wrede managed to cross the Abens at Biburg (the defenders had withdrawn to a stronger position slightly to the rear at Kirchdorf) and to deploy for a set-piece assault. The Austrians had been reinforced in late morning by two battalions from Ludwig and had enjoyed ample time to prepare their defense. More than nine battalions, a brigade battery, and a reinforced squadron of dragoons occupied the Kirchdorf heights (see Map 10). The Bavarians attacked with spirit but could make no headway. The infantry reformed while the Bavarian artillery began methodically to hammer the Hapsburg position.

Upstream at Siegenburg, Vandamme's Württembergers had replaced Wrede's division and likewise had been unable to force a river crossing. Discouraged from a useless frontal attack, Vandamme retired, marched parallel to the Abens to Abensberg, and then followed in Lannes' wake on the Rohr road. During this march his men passed beneath Napoleon's headquarters. The Emperor rode down to the column and addressed them in the same manner he had spoken to the Bavarians earlier in the day. He reminded them of their victories against Austria when they had fought with Frederick the Great. He concluded: "The time has come to triumph once more, and to take the fight to Austrian soil."[8] When the Württemberg General Neubronn translated these stirring words to the eager soldiers, they reacted with the type of enthusiasm more typical of French troops.

Inflamed by the Emperor's oratory, the Württembergers advanced east of the Kirchdorf position, where they maneuvered to take Bianchi in flank (see Map 10). Shortly after 2:00 P.M. the Württembergers went into action. The Konig jäger battalion and Wolff's light infantry advanced in column toward the Austrian right flank. Their maneuver had not gone unnoticed; some Austrian infantry turned to face them and opened fire. Coolly the Württembergers deployed into line. Their commanders, wishing them to distinguish themselves in this first combat as members of the Confederation of the Rhine, prominently took position at their head and led the charge. Behind them, the Württemberg artillery deployed very professionally even though Hapsburg round shot bowled over several battery horses and killed a handful of gunners. Bombarded and charged, the Austrians recoiled before the Württemberg infantry closed to contact.

With Wrede's Bavarians joining the advance, a cross-country hunt ensued. Wrede received an order from Napoleon to advance and seize Pfeffenhausen (see Map 10). It was difficult because the Austrians conducted a tenacious fighting retreat from ridgeline to ridgeline. At one point Wrede had to commit his Sixth Légère and Second and Seventh Ligne regiments to attack a wooded rear-guard position. A hot firefight took place. Firing battalion volleys, the Bavarian infantry slowly forced the Austrians to withdraw.

At dusk, after a ten-mile advance, Wrede's Bavarians neared the objective; Pfeffenhausen with its important bridge over the Laber that led to Landshut. To animate his flagging troops, Wrede placed himself at the head of the Sixth Légère and led it toward the village. The Sixth advanced at quick step and charged through the streets toward the bridge. All was confusion. Several hundred Austrian soldiers, many of them lightly wounded, mingled aimlessly in the streets. Tardy Austrian teamsters flogged their panic-stricken horses while Austrian staff officers worked to burn the bridge. The Bavarians captured many prisoners, baggage and ammunition wagons, and even an aide to GM Bianchi, but they did not capture the bridge.

After a weak morning performance Wrede had shown commendable energy. The Württembergers had put in a solid performance for the entire day. All had responded to Napoleon's exhortation and none more so than the commander of the Württemberg Light Brigade, who had his horse shot out from under him and an aide-de-camp killed as he exposed himself recklessly to inspire his men. Overall, victory had been easy and losses light. Nothing could be better managed to give the soldiers of the Confederation of the Rhine confidence for future battles.

From Ludwig's viewpoint, the Bavarian–Württemberg pursuit had been a near thing. Although GM Radetzky had skillfully deployed his grenzers and uhlans to cover Ludwig's retreat, it had taken the commitment of the grenadiers of the Second Reserve Corps to finally stabilize the situation. By the narrowest margin the Fifth Corps trains had escaped the potential trap of the Pfeffenhausen defile. Even so, Ludwig had to use some of his cavalry in a police role to sort out the bewildering array of vehicles that choked the road running east to Landshut. By 10:00 P.M. the bulk of his corps rallied behind Pfeffenhausen along with a brigade from the Sixth Corps. Behind him toward Landshut, the grenadiers slept by the roadside. The absence of news from his brother, Archduke Karl, troubled Ludwig as he tried to prepare for the morrow.

The Abens position had been well suited to a determined defense by a small force willing to hole up in one of the many stout villages blocking the roads and to dare to kill or be killed. Later in the campaign Lannes' men would show this kind of tenacity at the Essling granary. New to war, uncertain of his mission, Ludwig proved unequal to the task.

Four miles away in Rottenburg, Hiller likewise awaited communication from Karl. In fact, Austrian couriers carrying orders from headquarters rode to Rohr, where they conveniently fell into French hands. Without central direction, Hiller pondered what to do given the partial disaster that had overtaken the Austrians on the road between Rohr and Rottenburg. In the late afternoon he had received a report from Ludwig that the buildup of enemy strength at Kirchdorf was overwhelming. Ludwig's report, and the unsettling news from the far left around Pfaffenhofen that a large French force commanded by Masséna was menacing his line of communications, convinced Hiller that he had to retreat. He decided to retire all the way back through Landshut and unite his three corps for a defense behind the Isar River.

It was a critical decision that influenced the remainder of the 1809 campaign. With this decision Hiller removed his three corps from any possible direct support of Karl. He was not to rejoin his commander until after Vienna had fallen to the French. Demoralizing losses aside, this separation of the Austrian Army was the major strategical outcome of Napoleon's offensive on 20 April.

Ratisbonne Beleaguered

Napoleon had won a memorable victory along the Abens, but the success of his intended *maneuver sur les derrières* depended more on the performance of his two flanking corps commanded by Davout and Masséna than on the frontal pressure he himself directed. In particular, his plan's success hinged on Masséna.

A series of overnight orders had reached Marshal Masséna in Pfaffenhofen on the morning of the twentieth and clarified the confusion that had returned this indolent man to a state of lethargy. On the seventeenth Napoleon had believed he would unite his forces on the eighteenth and destroy Karl the following day. Because Davout's union with the French center had been sternly contested by Karl's offensive and Masséna had failed to draw close enough, the Emperor postponed the day of decision by twenty-four hours. Today, 20 April, would occur the much-sought-after decisive battle. Accordingly, Masséna was to send Oudinot with two divisions to reinforce the French center at Abensberg. The rest of Masséna's wing, four infantry and one cuirassier division and one light cavalry brigade, were to march on Landshut if possible, and if not on the Isar bridge at Moosburg. In either event, Masséna would act as the anvil upon which Napoleon and Davout crushed the Austrians.

Neither Masséna nor Oudinot's infantry fired a shot during Napoleon's supposedly critical day of the twentieth. Both faced unopposed marches. Oudinot did not join the French center in time to participate in the running encounters along the Abens. Masséna turned in another lax performance, making a leisurely march toward Freising, well south of the assigned objectives at Moosburg and Landshut. One of his divisions did not depart Pfaffenhofen until 11:00 A.M. The marshal himself preferred the comfort of his rear guard instead of riding with the van. By nightfall Masséna's infantry, heavy cavalry, and artillery lay scattered around Freising; only his light cavalry had neared Moosburg.

On the opposite flank, Davout's two remaining infantry divisions had an easy day. The infantry occupied the heights they had captured the evening before. Patrols probed the woods screening the Austrian positions. Davout correlated their reports and wrote to Napoleon that he continued to face close to 40,000 Austrians. Strangely, this force seemed content merely to observe Davout's outnumbered force.

Davout's pickets did detect some Austrian movement along the front. On the right, toward Leierndorf, skirmishing revealed the Austrian Third Corps occupying some advanced posts. Their presence was due to Hohenzollern's decision when he had received orders to close on Karl's main body. First he had withdrawn Pfanzelter from Bachel and thereby unwittingly allowed Lannes an unopposed march to Rohr. Then he had slowly marched across the Laber. Hohenzollern outposted some of the hamlets overlooking the Laber Valley and waited until nightfall for further instructions. Like his fellow corps commanders, he had found no new orders forthcoming, and in the absence of instructions his corps contributed nothing to the Austrian cause on the twentieth.

The other movement French pickets observed involved a curious transfer of Austrian forces in the direction of Ratisbonne. Montbrun, whose command screened Davout's left, tried to investigate this movement. He carried out the light-cavalry scouting duties in his usual aggressive style, and in so doing nearly lost a considerable portion of his command. Forced by the closed terrain to maneuver in narrow column, his light troops moved between the trees seeking to discover enemy intentions. Suddenly, musketry flailed the column from an adjacent woodlot as Austrian infantry sprung an ambush.

The French tried to escape, only to encounter another hidden enemy. Multiple mounted attacks failed against the well-protected infantry. Soon the woods surrounding the light troops flickered with musket fire. The grave situation forced Montbrun to consider a desperate expedient: He would abandon his infantry, form a cavalry spearhead, and cut his way to safety. Fortunately, the Austrians mysteriously retired before administering the coup de grâce. It had been a near-fatal "embarrassment for an officer who was not seeking a fight," but rather merely "wanted his Marshal's approbation" for a successful reconnaissance.[9]

The major event of the day on Davout's front took place in Ratisbonne. During the night of the nineteenth, Coutard had struggled to prepare for renewed combat. A dispatch from Davout arrived to inform him that he could expect an ammunition convoy—welcome news since his men had been reduced to stripping the wounded and slain of their ammunition in order to keep firing.

Throughout the twentieth Coutard's Sixty-fifth Ligne fought bravely while the colonel himself kept hoping against hope that the promised ammunition convoy would come. Outnumbered ten to one, bombarded from the dominating heights across the Danube, the Sixty-fifth fought until it exhausted its ammunition. Convinced his men could do no more, Coutard entered negotiations with the enemy to determine conditions of surrender. He tried to stall to give Davout a last chance to send help. He asked the FML Karl Kollowrath for a twenty-four-hour truce. If no French assistance arrived within that time, he would surrender. Kollowrath commanded some 20,000 men, most of whom had not yet fought. Coutard had fewer than 2000 effectives. It is a testament to the cerebral power of Karl's key lieutenants that Kollowrath agreed to the truce.

Delighted and relieved, Coutard returned to Ratisbonne only to learn that another enormous Austrian force was advancing on him from the south. It was Prince Johannes Liechtenstein's First Reserve Corps, dispatched by Archduke Karl to ensure the capture of the town (see Map 9). Apprised by the French that a truce existed, Liechtenstein curtly replied that it did not encompass his force and that he was preparing an assault. At wits' end, seemingly abandoned, Coutard surrendered at 5:00 P.M.

An hour later the Sixty-fifth Ligne marched from Ratisbonne with all the honors of war and laid down their arms. The officers signed a parole and were free; the men became prisoners of war. The regiment's cherished eagle standards became Hapsburg trophies. At 10:00 P.M. Coutard's kindly captors permitted him to write to his cousin commander. Undoubtedly humiliated by events, Coutard tried to explain what had happened: No help "having penetrated to us, all our munitions having being used up, having to my front the division of General Kollowrath, surrounded by General Liechtenstein and menaced by a triple attack that I could not repulse without ammunition, I saw myself reduced, after several summons from these two generals, to surrender the town today, at 5:00 P.M."[10]

In fact, Davout had not entirely abandoned his cousin. On the night of the nineteenth the Emperor's aide Savary had reached Davout's headquarters to explain Napoleon's plans. For the first time Davout learned of the importance within Napoleon's scheme of campaign of the Ratisbonne bridge. He immediately dispatched his own aide, Commandant Trobriand, to Ratisbonne with orders for Coutard to hold hard against all comers. Trobriand completed the mission in an amazing three hours and returned to inform Davout of Coutard's desperate status. Davout ordered Trobriand to conduct a small ammunition convoy to Ratisbonne so Coutard could maintain his defense.

At this critical juncture, French staffwork failed. Somehow, the infantry escort did not rendezvous with the convoy, so Trobriand had to make the journey unprotected. By 8:00 A.M. on the twentieth, Trobriand's convoy had entered the plain via the river road leading to Ratisbonne. Scouting in advance, Trobriand found an Austrian cavalry force occupying a woodlot that blocked further advance. He galloped back to warn his men, but it was too late.

The Austrian picket of about 200 cavalrymen charged the convoy. They hacked to pieces the defenseless teamsters. On the verge of capture, Trobriand spurred his horse over a wide ditch and galloped toward Ratisbonne. The Austrians pursued right up to the city's walls, where the combination of French musketry from the parapets and the speed of Trobriand's horse enabled the aide to escape.

Trobriand immediately went to Coutard to explain what had occurred. He again emphasized to the beleaguered colonel the importance of either defending or destroying the Danube bridge, but Coutard was helpless to comply. Trobriand's failure was to haunt Napoleon's efforts to destroy Karl's army in the coming days.

On the evening of the twentieth Napoleon believed that the French continued to hold Ratisbonne. This misconception, coupled with the day's success along the Abens, put him in an excellent mood. Twenty-four hours earlier he had begun a carefully staged series of scenes to enhance the fighting prowess of his Confederation of the Rhine soldiers. On the battle's eve he had particularly encouraged the Bavarian heir to the throne, the prince royal. The successes on the twentieth justified Napoleon's efforts. Pleased but still striving to create an impression, this consummate actor gave one last performance for the benefit of his German allies. This time he embraced the prince royal in front of the Bavarian officers, and said: "I'm so sorry I don't speak German, in order to thank these brave soldiers in their mother tongue."[11]

The Emperor's order of the day had promised the Bavarians that they would fight in the front rank without French aid. Losses showed that he had kept his word. Lannes' French corps lost 215, the Württembergers another 146, while 746 Bavarians had fallen in combat. Two to three thousand more French soldiers surrendered at Ratisbonne. Of all the Austrian army only Hiller's wing had engaged in significant combat. Hiller's losses were considerable: 25 officers and 467 soldiers died, and 63 and 2156 had been wounded respectively. Worse, close to 4000 Austrians had been captured along with eight flags and twelve cannons.

At different crucial times during the day, Austrian corps commanders had found themselves operating without orders from headquarters. FML Kollowrath ended the day riding to headquarters to ask what to do next. The other commanders, who were either too far from headquarters or too near the French to leave their command, had to use their own initiative. Subordinate initiative had never been a hallmark of the Hapsburg army, and this day had been no different. Everyone relied upon the brain at the top. During the twentieth that brain apparently suffered an epileptic seizure that rendered Karl incommunicado. An efficient staff might have filled the void, but staff rivalry dating back to the chief of staff's dismissal at the beginning of the campaign left no one in position to take charge.

Consequently, in the words of a frustrated Austrian participant, the "different corps and detachments . . . had conducted themselves bravely and with fortitude, in spite of the remarkable chain of events . . . which left them everywhere inferior when in contact with the enemy."[12] Outnumbered at the points of decision, the Austrians suffered serious losses. Of greater importance was the morale impact of the day's battle. The French and their allies now had the initiative and were buoyed by victory. The Austrians were discouraged by defeat and found themselves hounded rearward by a foe led by the feared Napoleon himself. Tomorrow gave every indication of more of the same.

CHAPTER VII

------••◄◦❧◦►••------

The Landshut Hunt

*The bayonet has always been the weapon of the brave and
the chief tool of victory.*

Davout's Ordeal

The Emperor stirred in his chair in the predawn light of 21 April. Disdaining a
bed, he had catnapped in the chair for two hours, the only sleep he would get
over a forty-four-hour period. Immediately upon waking he consulted with his
staff and began dictating orders for the coming day to Marshal Berthier. He
planned to couple a relentless frontal pursuit with a flank attack from Masséna.
He believed that Masséna would reach Landshut by 3:00 P.M.—sheer fantasy
since the balance of Masséna's command was on the wrong side of the Isar
more than twenty miles from Landshut.

As soon as Marshal Berthier transcribed the Emperor's intentions into
written orders, mounted couriers galloped away from headquarters in Rohr to
carry instructions to all the distant commands. To Wrede: March on Landshut. To Lefebvre: "Pursue the enemy with sword against his kidneys and
before this evening inform the Emperor that you have captured the enemy's
parks, baggage, and wounded."[1] Here was an order the one-time grenadier
could understand with relish. To Davout: "You have but a screen of three
regiments before you. . . . If you hear cannon fire confronting Lefebvre . . .
you will support him. . . . Once your rear is cleaned up, you will march on
Ratisbonne; you will attack Bellegarde and Klenau. You will pursue and drive
them into the Bohemian mountains."[2] What the deluded Napoleon failed to
recognize was that Davout faced not three regiments but more than three
corps.

122

Across the lines, on the night of 20–21 April, Archduke Karl realized that events had not transpired as he had wished. He now had to make plans based on very incomplete information. This required strategic imagination, a type of mental flexibility that proved beyond the Hapsburg Generalissimus. The opportunity to crush Davout remained. Instead of making an appropriate plan and following through, Karl decided to wait, to acquire more information, to reunite his forces. Only then would he resume the offensive. It was as if more than a decade of fighting the French had taught him nothing. He could not have believed that a French army, particularly one led by Napoleon himself, would sit still while he marshaled his resources and collected his thoughts. Yet he proceeded as if that were exactly the case.

The puzzling absence of news from Hiller troubled Karl the most. He did not know the extent of the disaster experienced by his left wing and clung to the hope that he could reunite with Hiller around Rottenberg. His dispositions for the twenty-first showed that he would do little to make this hope a reality. He massed his forces between the Danube and the Gross Laber and awaited developments. If he and Hiller were to rejoin, it would be up to the subordinate both to plan and to execute the maneuver.

Couriers departed Karl's headquarters at Alt Eglofsheim on the morning of the twenty-first carrying instructions to Bellegarde's two-corps wing operating on the Danube's right bank. To date the balance of the powerful First and Second Corps had been ineffectually feeling for Napoleon's line of communications in the direction of the Altmuhl River west of Ratisbonne. So far their hesitant probes had found nothing. The capture of Ratisbonne was all Bellegarde's command had accomplished.

The reason for this lack of contact was that very little stood between Bellegarde and Napoleon's forward base at Ingolstadt. Showing remarkable economy of force, Napoleon had permitted Davout to confront these 48,000 Austrians with a thousand-man force of all arms. The small French force, commanded by Colonel Guyon, provided an intelligence screen along the Altmuhl (see Map 11). Backstopping them was Rouyer's 7400-man Confederation of the Rhine Division at Ingolstadt itself. If matters grew too serious and the Austrians advanced deep into the French flank and rear, Napoleon was prepared to have Rouyer evacuate Ingolstadt, cross the Danube, and destroy the bridges. This abandonment of the French line of communications would not be necessary unless the Austrians showed a great deal more drive than they had heretofore displayed. In the meantime, the thousand French would watch and report.

Napoleon's gamble over his line of communications proved justified, though by the narrowest, when Karl redirected Bellegarde's advance on the morning of the twenty-first. The Archduke commanded the Second Corps,

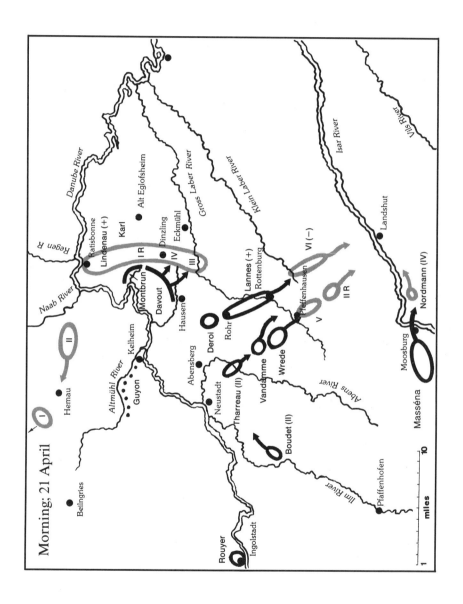

Morning; 21 April

which was nearing Hemau, to countermarch to Ratisbonne and rejoin the main body (see Map 11). This order must have frustrated FZM Kollowrath, who after the capture of Ratisbonne had personally ridden to army headquarters late on the twentieth to receive instructions. Either Karl or his staff had directed the commander of the Second Corps to march on Hemau. Kollowrath had put his men in motion immediately, and they had arrived at their objective after a tiring overnight march. At Hemau Kollowrath received the new orders requiring his return. Meanwhile, the First Corps would replace the Second at Hemau and observe the roads running parallel the Danube. Consequently, 48,000 men neither attacked Napoleon's line of communications nor contributed to the main Austrian effort south of the Danube.

Having disposed of his left under Hiller and his right under Bellegarde, Karl deployed the central force under his direct command. In sequence extending from Abbach on the Danube to the heights around Alt Eglofsheim would be Veczay's brigade, Lindenau's division, and the First Reserve Corps. The Fourth Corps covered the Eckmühl highway from its position around Dinzling (see Map 11). The Third Corps was to take up a position behind Laichling and link up with Hiller's men when they showed up. Typically slow Austrian staffwork prevented orders from reaching the Third Corps until too late. Before the sun had risen, Austrian pickets of the Third and Fourth Corps fired their muskets at the dark shapes gliding toward them. In the mist and gloom the shapes materialized into the outline of French voltigeurs. The combat began.

Before Karl and the Hapsburg staff had drafted plans for the day, Marshal Davout had his men up and on the march. His last orders from the Emperor clearly stated he should attack until otherwise instructed. Later in the morning he would learn the reasoning behind these orders, that, according to the Emperor, he faced a "mere curtain of three regiments." The Iron Marshal knew better, yet—faithful to his orders—he complied with characteristic alacrity. Yet he also knew that it was a dangerous thing to attempt. Not the least of his worries was his shortage of artillery ammunition. His artillery park began the day twenty-five miles distant. Although it forced-marched to the front, it did not arrive in time for the day's combat.[3]

Davout also had to worry about his exposed left flank, which rested upon the shaky foundation of Montbrun's light cavalry. If few Austrians stood between Montbrun and Ratisbonne, as Napoleon supposed, then a light cavalry screen was sufficient. If, on the other hand, Montbrun's belief that a substantial force was poised just beyond his picket line was accurate, Davout's flank stood terribly vulnerable. The terrain over which Montbrun was deployed was hilly and forested. Consequently, during the twenty-first Montbrun's combats and maneuvers would occur independent of Davout's movements. Tactically isolated, Montbrun's success or failure could determine the French Third Corps' fate (see Map 11).

The situation on Davout's right flank was much more secure. At 6:00 P.M. the day before his men had finally made solid contact with Lefebvre's Bavarians. He could expect some degree of cooperation from these troops. Mostly, though, whatever he accomplished would depend upon the performance of his two infantry divisions. Undaunted by the odds—Davout had twenty-nine battalions and twelve squadrons versus forty-five battalions, sixteen squadrons, superior artillery, and a sizable enemy reserve—the Third Corps commander launched his attack.[4]

His first target was the Hapsburg forward position north of Langquaid (see Map 12). Pire's light cavalry led the way, followed by Saint-Hilaire and Friant. The French advance initiated a confusing day of combat in difficult, broken terrain. Coordination on both sides was hard to manage, thus placing an increased burden on small-unit commanders.

At 5:00 A.M. the French encountered a chain of brown-clad grenzers barring the way to the Laber Valley. As dawn broke, Saint-Hilaire's voltigeurs performed a pincers attack through the woods that quickly bundled the startled Austrians back toward Langquaid. Saint-Hilaire continued until he reached the woods near Leierndorf (see Map 12). The opposing commander, Prince Hohenzollern, had his corps awkwardly positioned straddling the Laber, the units on the right bank reaching out toward the vacuum where Archduke Ludwig had last been seen. Since Hohenzollern had not yet received Karl's orders to retreat, the Prince took steps to bolster his left-bank defense against Saint-Hilaire. He went forward with a battalion he placed on the heights outside of Leierndorf and scouted the French columns with a hussar regiment supported by a cavalry battery.

Saint-Hilaire's advance quickly swamped this force, driving them back along the Laber toward Schierling (see Map 12). Later Hohenzollern would learn that Karl's orders called for the Third Corps to retreat in that direction anyway. But what might have been a simple retreat became, now that he was in contact with the French, infinitely more difficult. To complicate matters further, the Prince's outposts across the Laber opposite Langquaid reported they too were under attack. Given the pressure, it is not surprising that Hohenzollern failed to notify his fellow corps commanders of the engagement at Leierndorf.

The soldiers advancing against Langquaid belonged to Lefebvre's corps. Having received Napoleon's straightforward orders calling for an all-out advance, Lefebvre reached Langquaid at about 8:00 A.M. Seeing a poorly formed Hapsburg battalion in the open outside the village, Lefebvre impetuously sent his escort squadron of Bavarian dragoons into the charge. The whitecoats panicked before the sudden onslaught and laid down their muskets in token of

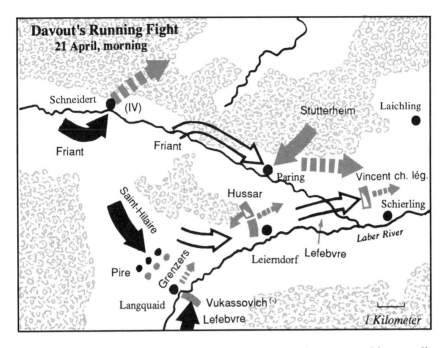

surrender. However, seeing that the dragoons were having trouble actually reaching them to accept their surrender due to marshy ground, the Austrians picked up their weapons. They fired a volley that killed a charging officer and several of his troopers and fled to the east.

Although deprived by this perfidy, an hour later Lefebvre was master of Langquaid. To his front and left he saw Davout's men fighting toward Leiern-dorf. After interrogating some Austrian prisoners he reported to the Emperor that the enemy confronting Davout was present in great strength and that the prisoners claimed that Karl himself commanded.[5] Lefebvre pressed on toward Eckmühl. Before him Hohenzollern retreated along both banks of the Laber.

On Davout's front Friant followed in Saint-Hilaire's wake. With the sun now up, Friant observed that the whitecoats occupied a strong point off to his left in Schneidert (see Map 12). Apparently Saint-Hilaire had not noticed them previously in the half light of his predawn march. Louis Friant had come a long way from his modest beginnings as the son of a wax polisher. A decade of service in the royalist army had provided him a solid military foundation that he exploited to great advantage during the Revolution. He was one of Napoleon's hand-picked officers chosen for the Egyptian expedition. Return-ing to France, he served as inspector general of infantry. The combination of practical and theoretical experience served him well when in 1805 he began a long association with Davout by leading one of the marshal's divisions to glory at Austerlitz. Fifty-one years old in 1809, he was one of "Davout's immortals."

Relying on his experience from countless combat encounters, Friant judged that his division's massed voltigeurs could capture Schneidert. Located in a hollow, the village was poorly positioned for a protracted defense. Friant entrusted the assault to an engineer captain: "The good dispositions taken by this officer, the voltigeurs' courage, [and] we were quickly masters of this curtain of iron."[6] Austrian prisoners revealed that they belonged to Rosenberg's Fourth Corps.

Like Hohenzollern, Rosenberg found himself in contact before he could act on Karl's orders to retreat. One battalion and two squadrons of chevaulégers had occupied the advanced post at Schneidert. The outpost's commander saw and reported Saint-Hilaire's advance against Hohenzollern. Alarmed, Rosenberg dispatched his aide-de-camp, a Captain Kaiser, to Schneidert to observe the French. Kaiser arrived in time to see Friant's voltigeurs vigorously attacking the village. Overwhelmed, the Austrians shed casualties and prisoners as they tumbled back to Rosenberg's line at Dinzling.

Rosenberg resolved to modify Karl's orders requiring the Fourth Corps to defend Dinzling and cover the Eckmühl–Ratisbonne highway. He saw this position a potential trap now that his left-flank support under Hohenzollern had retired and his outpost at Schneidert had fallen. The Prince decided to retreat to Laichling, a position featuring a fine wooded ridge for defense that guarded the highway (see Map 12). While most of his corps hastened back through the wooded defiles, at 8:00 A.M. he sent General Stutterheim with four infantry battalions and a cavalry battery to extricate the Austrians retreating from Schneidert.

As Rosenberg made these decisions, at about 7:30 A.M. Marshal Davout learned from Montbrun that Ratisbonne had apparently fallen. The unwelcome news embarrassed the proud marshal. He had hand-picked Ratisbonne's defender, assigning this post of honor to his cousin, Colonel Coutard. Coutard apparently had let him down and surrendered his command, and this during an era when French troops simply did not surrender to the lowly whitecoats. Ignorant of the details of Coutard's struggle, Davout sent a dispatch to the Emperor informing him of the loss of Ratisbonne. Angered, the Iron Marshal turned his attention back to affairs along his front.

To his left Davout heard the sounds of Friant's combat. After capturing the Austrian outpost at Schneidert, Friant advanced toward Paring (see Map 12). In the woods west of Paring he encountered Stutterheim, sent forward by Rosenberg to bolster the retreating Schneidert garrison. Friant waited until Stutterheim emerged from a wooded lane onto cleared farmland. Then he attacked.

Stutterheim fought hard and skillfully to hold his ground. In the clearing his cavalry battery, commanded by one of the most intrepid Hapsburg gunners, a Lieutenant Zadrazill, dueled with three French batteries.[7] Simultaneously, a single battalion Stutterheim sent to Paring to prevent the French from outflanking his position manfully resisted ever-increasing numbers of French. As Stutterheim viewed the situation, he was being "attacked by infinitely superior forces, and above all by an artillery that was growing constantly, and fired canister without cessation on us. We found ourselves engaged in a difficult, unequal, murderous combat."[8]

To his left, in the Laber Valley Stutterheim saw another heavy column advancing along the river road toward Schierling. Fearful of being cut off by this column and outflanked at Paring, Stutterheim ordered a retreat. The order came too late for the gallant battalion in Paring. At 10:00 A.M. three French regiments charged the village and captured 500 prisoners. Still, Stutterheim had held for more than two hours and thus bought enough time for his corps to occupy its new position in front of Laichling.

The French force Stutterheim spied in the Laber Valley belonged to Lefebvre. Lefebvre had caught Vukassovich's advance guard division awkwardly straddling the river as it tried to cover the Third Corps' retreat (see Map 12). In the French van was Demont's division of conscripts. Napoleon had specified that this unit lead Lefebvre's advance, believing that it would display élan superior to the Bavarians'. A firestorm of shot and shell greeted the young French soldiers in Leierndorf. It came from a twelve-pound battery commanded by one of the many French emigré officers, a Colonel Rousseau, who served in the Austrian army.

Under cover of this bombardment, the Laber bridge burned. The conscripts tried to put out the fire but were driven out of the village as a conflagration, started by bursting Hapsburg shells, rapidly spread from wood to thatch and consumed the village. Unmolested, the balance of Hohenzollern's corps withdrew to Schierling, where they crossed the Laber once again to the left bank at 10:00 A.M. At this point Karl's orders finally arrived. Prince Hohenzollern had done well to extricate his corps from a difficult situation. He had brought them to the position more or less specified by the just-received orders. Understanding Karl's desire to maintain a link with Hiller's command, the Prince now resolved to hold his position.

He received fortuitous assistance from Stutterheim. When Stutterheim began his retreat he perceived that the Bavarian cavalry spearheading Lefebvre's advance in the Laber Valley posed a serious threat. Accordingly, he ordered the battered Vincent Chevaulégers, who had already lost nearly eighty horses to artillery fire alone, to check the enemy horse (see Map 12). The chevaulégers maintained such a solid front that the Bavarian cavalry declined to charge. Thus protected, Stutterheim's men withdrew in good order.

Stutterheim and Vukassovich had managed to cover the retreat of the Third and Fourth Corps, but battles are not won by well-fought rear-guard actions. There had been no coordination between the two corps although their fights took place on some of the same ground. The gallant advance guard divisions had been outnumbered at every encounter. Had the two corps fought in concert, they would have enjoyed numerical superiority.

When Archduke Karl received news of the French attack against the Fourth Corps, he experienced a flash of strategic insight: The balance of the First Reserve Corps, the elite of the army, would march south and take Davout in the flank. The Third and Fourth Corps would hold the Eckmühl–Ratisbonne highway. In Karl's view the Eckmühl–Ratisbonne highway was now the key position. The highway was the major artery linking Karl's forces. The Eckmühl bridge provided the only remaining connection with Hiller and the mysteriously missing Fifth, Sixth, and Second reserve corps.

Across the lines Hiller's counterpart Marshal Davout also faced some crucial decisions. In the late morning Davout received an amazing message from the Emperor. Dispatched at 5:00 A.M., it began: "The past two days have been another Jena."[9] By comparing recent events with the climactic battle against Prussia in 1806, Napoleon did a disservice to both Davout's reputation and his intelligence. Davout had earned the title Duc d'Auerstaedt for his brilliant performance in 1806. Ever after Napoleon remained jealous of him. Now, three years later, he tried to show that he too was capable of tactical virtuosity by sending a misleading, inflated claim. The message to Davout revealed that the Emperor was less interested in reality than in believing that which accorded with his preconceived notions and cast ever greater glory upon his name.

It was an alarming trend for the long-term welfare of France. In the short term, it meant that the supreme commander was telling a devoted subordinate that the situation was well in hand because he, Napoleon, was thrashing Karl's main force and thus Davout must be confronting but "a screen of three infantry regiments."[10] Further, Davout should clean up his rear area, support Lefebvre, and then drive the Austrian First and Second Corps across the Danube into Bohemia. To assist Davout in this insignificant task, Napoleon informed his marshal that he now had Boudet's "fine" division under his command; a division of conscripts to replace the two veteran Third Corps divisions currently chasing the Austrians toward Landshut. Napoleon's entire letter was palpable nonsense. Davout had only to look straight ahead to view the fierce Hapsburg resistance and reaffirm that his leader grossly misunderstood the strategic situation.

Like Davout, Montbrun's day began before the sun rose. During the night a line of campfires had illuminated the sky in front of his pickets. The fires merged into a second grouping on the heights toward Ratisbonne. Together their glow revealed the massing of a formidable Austrian force extending from the Danube to Dinzling (see Map 11).

In a dawn report Montbrun informed Davout that he faced a growing Austrian menace. Deploying his two infantry battalions and three light cavalry regiments, Montbrun decided to concentrate on securing the Abbach defile along the Danube. The defile offered the Austrians a straight-line shot against Davout's flank and rear, thus it had to be held. The remainder of his front presented the cavalier a difficult tactical challenge. His right flank dangled in the air. Worse, the wooded terrain made scouting very difficult. In open terrain cavalry could safely advance far in advance of infantry support. Yesterday had shown that in this part of Bavaria his cavalry had to maneuver on narrow roads between the forests and was vulnerable to ambush from concealed infantry. Montbrun worried that further combat amid such unfavorable conditions would use up his command before they reached "the fine plains of Vienna."[11] Nonetheless, he set out to do the best he could.

Montbrun gave a brilliant display of what a well-led light force could accomplish. With a series of incisive reports gleaned from personal observation and the interrogation of prisoners seized by his active cavalry, Montbrun kept Davout fully apprised of events along his front. In addition, from early morning until 1:30 P.M. he worked to determine what had happened to the French defenders of Ratisbonne. Montbrun stood steadfast at Abbach on his left flank as the afternoon wore on and Austrian strength built up before his vigilant gaze. He tracked enemy movement all along his broad front. When Rosenberg evacuated Dinzling on his right flank, Montbrun sent his troopers forward to snap at the Hapsburg heels. Then he quickly occupied this commanding position with all his available force. He questioned the villagers to learn which enemy forces had passed through the village the day before and who had just withdrawn this day.

Montbrun did all this without command direction. So utterly isolated was he that around 3:30 P.M. he had to inform Davout: "I very much would like to know the direction you have taken in order that I can manage accordingly."[12] Montbrun's stellar performance allowed Davout to concentrate his men for the fight at Laichling. His conduct stands in sharp contrast to the slavish adherance to orders shown by his opponent, Prince Johannes Liechtenstein. While Liechtenstein obeyed the letter of his orders, "to observe the enemy," he failed to recognize Montbrun's weakness and so failed to contribute anything to his country's battle.

Montbrun's conduct permitted Davout aggressively to pursue the Austrians to a wooded ridgeline north of Schierling. For a moment it appeared that the French had behaved rashly—when some Austrian cavalry launched an opportunistic charge against an isolated French battery. Calmly the French gunners repulsed the attack. Capitalizing on this success, the massed voltigeurs of Friant's division then followed hard on the heels of the retreating Hapsburg horse. They marched through rolling farmland planted in potatoes and wheat. On their left loomed a dark-green screen of forest. Friant's voltigeurs darted into the woods to look for hidden Austrians. Finding none, the French continued, expecting to encounter the enemy at each crestline. Finally, after a two-and-a-half-mile cross-country advance, they again confronted Stutterheim's grenzers. Once more the French light infantry demonstrated its superiority.[13] The voltigeurs cleared a ridgeline, thus permitting their commander to see the Austrian main line of defense.

The strength of this new position caused Davout pause (see Map 13). Studying it through his glass he saw the enemy "ranged in many lines having their right wing in the woods and their left on a hill, to the left of Unter-Laichling. They had established on this hill all the artillery it could hold; their right and flank was protected by thick woods, steep, rocky and stuffed with infantry."[14] A chain of Austrian light troops covered the entire front.

The protracted running skirmish back to this main line had given the Austrians time to deploy a formidable defense based on the twin village of Laichling. In Unter-Laichling were two battalions of the Bellegarde Regiment. In a small woodlot between Unter- and Ober-Laichling stood Neustaedter's brigade with two regiments. A grenzer battalion skirmished in the woods in front of the twin village. Farther north, Chasteler's brigade guarded the Fourth Corps' right flank.

Had the Hapsburg defense been better coordinated, Hohenzollern's Third Corps would have filled in on the left between Unter-Laichling and the Laber; Rosenberg sent an aide to Hohenzollern to suggest exactly that. But Hohenzollern declined, citing his orders to hold the heights at Eckmühl. By his unwillingness to display initiative, Hohenzollern abandoned Schierling, a position that, defended, could have tightly stoppered Lefebvre's advance up the Laber Valley.

Instead, Rosenberg had to rely on portions of Stutterheim's advance guard division to occupy the ground, and it was spread thin. One grenzer battalion massed behind Schierling. On the dominating high ground east of Unter-Laichling, the height upon which Davout would soon observe "all the artillery," Stutterheim placed Zadrazill's cavalry battery (see Map 13). In the swampy plain extending to the Laber was the Vincent Chevaulégers in column by squadron. In all, Rosenberg deployed about 16,000 men with his strength concentrated on his right. In uncertain support were elements of the Third Corps back toward Eckmühl. At this point, around 11:00 A.M., Rosenberg faced a Franco-Bavarian combined total well in excess of 30,000.[15]

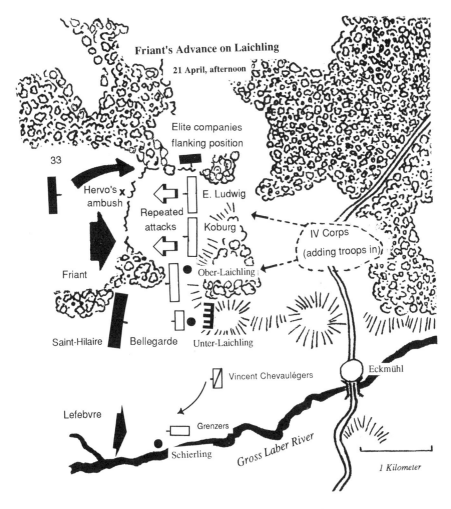

Friant's Advance on Laichling
21 April, afternoon

Had Karl left his early-morning orders in effect, the grenadiers of the First Reserve Corps might have been also available to support Rosenberg. Instead, the Archduke conceived his grand flank thrust and ordered the grenadiers to march south. When they mysteriously failed to reach their objective even though they faced no opposition, it meant that, along with the Austrian forces facing Montbrun on the French left, twenty-eight battalions and forty-four squadrons that should have been available took no part in the combat around Laichling.

The combat began with a vigorous artillery exchange that again featured Lieutenant Zadrazill. From a commanding hilltop the well-served six-pound pieces of his isolated battery tore into the ranks of the Bavarian cavalry. The bounding iron balls carried through to the dense ranks of the French cuirassiers beyond. In response, French and Bavarian artillery began to hammer the cavalry battery in a killing cross fire. The aggressive Zadrazill maintained his position as men and horses fell around him. Seeing the battery's distress, Rosenberg sent a twelve-pound battery to the hill to help Zadrazill hold the position (and thus completed the picture Davout took in through the sweep of his glass).

While the artillery duel raged on, Davout's veterans deployed in front of Laichling and Lefebvre's French conscripts and Bavarians massed in the Laber Valley. Satisfied that he had seen all there was to see from the heights, the Iron Marshal rode downslope to scout between the lines. He recognized that the chase was over. The situation now required something more methodical. He also realized that an attack against such a position, manned by apparently superior numbers (he did not depend upon any contribution from Lefebvre, whose men were just arriving), was no sure thing. Therefore, somewhat strangely given his successes to date, his first thought was defensive. He deployed Saint-Hilaire in a fine position with a deep ravine running along the front. Here he felt they could hold against vastly superior forces.

While the tactical situation might have warranted such care, it proved hard on the French soldiers forced to stand motionless under the Hapsburg guns positioned behind Unter- and Ober-Laichling. A young officer in the Fifteenth Légère described to his brother what it was like:

> The affair of the 21st was very hot; we remained for four hours under fire from three regiments and seven canon; we have already lost 621 men and 10 officers.
>
> My horse was killed between my legs, my scabbard was cut in two by a bit of canister, I received a small contusion on my left thigh, and I was lightly wounded on my right hand; my clothes were pierced in five different places.[16]

Austrian artillery fire did not discriminate between rank. As the cannonade intensified, Davout rode up to consult with Friant. An iron ball toppled Friant's horse; a plunging shell knocked off his hat, landed on the ground nearby, and lay with its fuse sputtering. The shell failed to explode. Unfazed, a nearby grenadier picked up and returned the general's hat. Convinced that "the affair had taken on a more serious character," Davout and Friant planned an assault.[17]

Again Friant maneuvered to outflank them on the right. While this maneuver developed, Davout returned to Saint-Hilaire's division. He wanted them to occupy Austrian attention and so ordered a twelve-pound battery onto a rise to counterbattery the Hapsburg guns. As the battery lumbered forward the marshal spied a column of enemy infantry advancing through a declivity toward the battery.[18] He spurred his horse to the French position and just managed to direct its flank howitzer against the Austrians before they overran the battery. The howitzer belched a round of canister into the front of the column at thirty paces' range. The column halted. The howitzer crew feverishly reloaded, fired, and this time nearly exterminated the column's leading company. The Hapsburgs broke and ran.

The Thirty-third Ligne spearheaded Friant's flanking maneuver (see Map 13). It swung wide through the woods northwest of Laichling and penetrated deep onto the Austrian right flank. The effort stalled when the Erzherzog Ludwig and Koburg regiments hurled attack after attack against the French. During an interval between assaults, the French brigadier general Hervo cleverly deployed his men in a woods-concealed ambush. The next Hapsburg attack had to cross a cleared glade in the woods. Exposed in the open, the whitecoats made unmistakable targets for the fusiliers of the Thirty-third Ligne were hidden along the far treeline. The Thirty-third's fire repulsed the Austrian charge.

Attracted by the sounds of battle, Archduke Karl arrived on the heights behind Laichling. The French effort to turn Rosenberg's right greatly alarmed him. If successful, such a maneuver could sever his force in two. He ordered his personal legion, which he had been keeping in reserve back toward Alt Egflosheim for such emergencies, to hasten forward and block the French thrust—the only assistance Rosenberg received from his chief during the battle. Karl also ordered one of Hohenzollern's brigades, just as it was marching toward the fighting at Ober-Laichling, to bypass the uproar and continue north along the Eckmühl–Ratisbonne highway. Karl intended this brigade to cover the gap between the Fourth Corps and the First Reserve Corps, which was presumably by now preparing to attack Davout's flank. Actually, no French troops were available to exploit this gap. Karl's intervention removed a powerful infantry brigade from Rosenberg's support just as it was about to engage. Having confounded the situation, Karl apparently withdrew.

Unaware of Karl's blunderings, Davout pursued his battle. Confident in Montbrun's ability to screen the void on his left, the marshal looked to his right. As he had anticipated, Lefebvre's corps accomplished very little. Its initial effort focused on Schierling. A Bavarian light battalion formed serried column and charged the village. Stutterheim's grenzers repulsed them. Aided by one of Demont's battalions, a second charge captured Schierling. There the Bavarians waited in shelter while the artillery duel took place. Across the Laber, the balance of Demont's division skirmished inconsequentially with Vukassovich. At one point some Bavarian skirmishers sortied from Schierling. Unlike Davout's advancing units, which could utilize the rolling terrain to make a covered approach to the Austrian position, an advance from Schierling had to traverse level ground. Stutterheim took advantage of the favorable situation to charge the Bavarians with several squadrons of light horse. The chevaulégers drove the Bavarians back to shelter and captured fifty prisoners. This check effectively ended Bavarian enthusiasm for any further advance toward Eckmühl.

So, in the center Davout's tired infantry tried to force the Laichling position alone. Direct assault failed against the combination of heavy Austrian artillery fire from the heights and stout resistance from the Bellegarde Regiment in the village (see Map 13). An effort to advance across the plain toward the left of the village ran up against the Deutsch–Banater Grenzers, who occupied a position behind a small ravine. Although this regiment had suffered severely on the nineteenth, it valiantly maintained its position until dark.

Back in the woods, where his main thrust had been blunted and the Thirty-third forced onto the defensive by the vigorous Austrian attacks, Friant once more sought to turn the Austrian right flank. In the gathering gloom (it was approaching 8:00 P.M.) he organized an ad hoc command comprising the elite companies of the 108th Ligne (see Map 13). He placed them under the command of a reliable battalion commander and sent them deeper into the woods out beyond the Thirty-third Ligne's left flank. From this position they directed an enfilade fire against the attacking Austrians. Their presence discouraged further Austrian attacks. So the battle drew to a close.

Davout dispatched six reports to Napoleon during the twenty-first. Four were annotated copies of dispatches from Montbrun.[19] By combining Montbrun's intelligence with personal observation, Davout felt certain he faced most of the Austrian army. At about 10:00 A.M. he had informed Napoleon "All of the enemy's army is in front of me."[20] After sending this report Davout received Napoleon's letter containing the amazing assertion that the Third Corps confronted a mere screen of three regiments. His confidence in Napoleon shaken, Davout's next report stated the situation plainly, so there could be no possibility of misunderstanding: "It remains certain that the Army of Bohemia is still at this point; that is to say, on your left."[21] The Marshal sent a fifth report at 7:00 P.M. as the fighting along his front began to ebb. To emphasize the gravity of the situation he confronted, he sent Brigadier Piré, a light cavalry general of fine repute, to explain personally the fact that Karl was here, in a great semicircle in front of Davout and Lefebvre.

The Iron Marshal could do no more. His two divisions had fought to near-exhaustion. Ammunition was critically low; the reserve trains would not arrive for at least another twenty-four hours. He knew he could rely upon the skill and bravery of the men in the ranks and the tactical ability and vigilance of his officers. Sad tidings soon confirmed that however tired, his officers remained attentive to duty.

A trusted aide and commander of an infantry brigade, General Hervo, had set out to inspect his advance outposts to prepare for the next day's combat. Suddenly a rattling burst of musketry sounded. Perhaps they were deserters startled by the appearance of a mounted officer, perhaps they were soldiers cut off from retreat by the French outflanking attacks, or perhaps they were just alert Austrian sentries. Regardless, their aim was true and Hervo, one of the distinguished brigadiers of the French army, fell dead. The next evening Friant found time to write a brief eulogy: "General Hervo is no more, but he lives on in the sorrows of his sovereign."[22]

At 9:00 P.M. all firing ended. Two parallel lines of campfires, well within cannon shot of one another, illuminated the sky as the rival forces prepared dinners, cleaned muskets, bandaged their wounded, and awaited a fourth day of combat. For the first time in the campaign the Austrians had managed to hold their position against a French attack. Even though the Fourth Corps had received little help from the considerable numbers of available Hapsburg forces, and even though it faced superior numbers of veteran, well-led foemen, it had tenaciously clung to the Laichling position. The Fourth Corps' performance proved what an Austrian corps could do if it had time to prepare a set-piece defense. The cost had not been cheap: The corps lost eleven officers and 415 soldiers killed and fifty-six officers and 2457 men wounded during the day. The French captured additional hundreds during the Austrian retreat back to the Laichling line. At his headquarters Davout tried to get some fitful rest, recognizing that his men's fate depended on the Emperor coming to his senses.

The Lion of Landshut

To GM Radetzky, the commander of Hiller's rear guard on the Pfeffenhausen–Landshut road, 20 April seemed never to end. Although at Pfeffenhausen the Laber River resembled more a ditch than a flowing body of water, it still restricted vehicular movement. Accordingly, by burning the Pfeffenhausen bridge at dusk and occupying the heights overlooking the crossing Radetzky hoped to delay the Bavarians (see Map 14). His weary men had gotten little rest when, at 11:00 P.M., the Bavarians clambered through the shallows and attacked once more. Reconsidering his situation, Radetzky doubted his ability to hold and ordered a short retreat back to the next position, a hill known locally as the Hornbach, just outside of Pfeffenhausen. From its slopes he resolved to try to block a further enemy advance.

Nearing the Hornbach he encountered units belonging to Archduke Ludwig's corps catnapping on the road. Radetzky commandeered the rearmost infantry battalion and joined it to his forces deployed on the Hornbach. Here they held for several hours as Bavarian pressure slowly increased. At 3:00 A.M.,

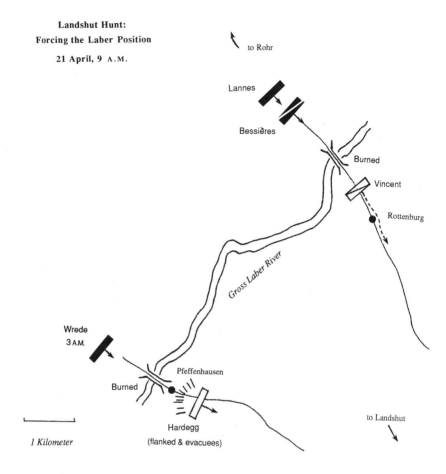

Landshut Hunt:
Forcing the Laber Position
21 April, 9 A.M.

1 Kilometer

21 April, he ordered a subordinate, Lieutenant Colonel Hardegg, to hold the heights as long as possible while Radetzky retired toward Landshut (see Map 14). Hardegg outposted the position with all his forces; two squadrons of Erzherzog Karl Uhlans and five companies of grenzers. Nervously they awaited the coming of dawn.

Two hours later, on the second of the two parallel roads running to Landshut, Napoleon mounted his horse and departed his overnight headquarters in Rohr. Low-hanging clouds threatened to burst open and pour rain on the already soaked roads. Splashing through the mud Napoleon encountered Vandamme's Württembergers marching toward Landshut on the Rohr road. As on the preceding afternoon, he took time to hold an impromptu review designed to put his German allies on their mettle.

Next he passed some Bavarians and Lannes' French divisions. Napoleon complimented Lannes upon his fine conduct during the twentieth. Always eager to surpass himself, Lannes replied: "If your allies, Sire, support me, I will take four to five thousand more prisoners."[23]

Napoleon explained that his plan for the twenty-first was designed to accomplish just such lofty goals and ordered Lannes to proceed without losing a minute. Napoleon's activity, his attention to army morale, the speed of the French staffwork all worked harmoniously to drive the French offensive forward. All stood in marked contrast to Austrian behavior.

A scouting party of French chasseurs à cheval that Napoleon had dispatched to the north returned. They reported an encounter with Austrian soldiers. Napoleon wondered if they belonged to Archduke Ludwig's corps and if they were posted as a link between the Austrian left and center. Dutifully the chasseurs probed again and this time confirmed the Emperor's estimate by capturing men belonging to Ludwig's command. More important, the prisoners revealed that around midnight Thierry's brigade had departed via the Rohr road for Landshut. Napoleon knew that Thierry's brigade was part of the Austrian Third Corps. So, in addition to the Austrian Fifth, Sixth, and Second Reserve Corps, whom he had fought the day before, he concluded that he also faced the Third Corps. Probably major additional Austrian formations were behind these front-line units.

The new intelligence strengthened the view he had expressed in his letter to Davout, that most of the Austrians must be retreating toward Landshut. For the first time, though not by design, the Austrian habit of splintering commands to send detachments hither and yon paid an important dividend by confusing Napoleon about Austrian dispositions. Napoleon firmly believed that a rapid advance would catch and crush Karl's main body. He entrusted one of his two spearheads to Marshal Jean-Baptiste Bessières.

Bessières was one of the notable eccentrics in the French Army. A conservative Catholic who fastidiously powdered his hair in the old style, he hardly seemed the man to lead a slashing cavalry pursuit. That he was brave went without saying; all Napoleonic marshals exhibited great personal bravery. In spite of appearances, he was also a capable cavalry commander. Like Lannes, he had reached Bavaria just the night before after a long trip from Spain. Happy to escape that graveyard of military reputations and serve under the Emperor's eyes again, desirous of returning to the path of glory (he had done little since his great day at Austerlitz in 1805), and eager to display his talents in front of his hated rival Marshal Lannes, Bessières was in the saddle at first light. He commanded the French van on the Rohr–Landshut road (see Map 14). It comprised Nansouty's heavy cavalry supported by the Thirteenth Légère Regiment.

Shortly after 5:00 A.M. Bessières' advance guard contacted the Austrian

Rosenberg Chevaulégers commanded by FML Karl Vincent. The chevaulégers fought well and managed to hold off Bessières for a while. Yet whenever Bessières began to bring his enormous numerical superiority to bear, Vincent had to gallop nimbly away lest his light horse be crushed. The road to Landshut curved through numerous woodlots that offered fine positions to fight a rear-guard action, but the Austrian corps and divisional commanders lacked the will and the wit to take advantage. The French horse steadily advanced to the outskirts of Landshut.

While Bessières drove the cavalry hard, Lannes' infantry rapidly followed in its wake. It was irksome for the dashing Lannes to concede the glory of the front-line pursuit to his rival. Napoleon often used his marshals' jealousies as a goad, and so it proved here. When his lead unit, Morand's division, reached the Laber River on the road to Landshut, it found that the Austrians had destroyed the highway bridge. Bessières' cavalry had swum across. Determined to keep pace, Morand's pioneers swarmed over the smoldering piers. Within twenty minutes they built two passable bridges. Morand's infantry, with Gudin following, pressed on.

Meanwhile, back on the Pfeffenhausen–Landshut road, the Hapsburg cavalier Colonel Hardegg held his position until daybreak as his grenzers, ably supported by his spirited uhlans, checked the Bavarians who tried to cross the Laber. At about 6:00 A.M. Hardegg learned that Bessières had swamped Vincent and thus outflanked his own position (see Map 14). Hardegg prudently withdrew, yet he could not break contact and escape. The Bavarians, joined by French light cavalry, pressed Hardegg's small force vigorously, beginning a series of running combats that lasted the entire march east to Landshut.

The Hapsburgs struck back when they could. At one point the uhlans turned at bay, charged the pursuing French, and drove them back, capturing twenty-five prisoners. But the French merely reinforced their van and the uhlans, having gained valuable minutes for their comrades to continue their retreat unmolested, fell back once more.

As is true with any advancing army, the morale of the French, Württemberg, and Bavarian soldiers marching on Landshut soared. About 40,000 infantry and 9000 horsemen rapidly moved along the twin roads leading to the Isar. They strode past demoralized groups of recently surrendered Austrian soldiers, piles of cast-off knapsacks and muskets, and broken-down baggage wagons still harnessed to drooping teams of tired horses. The prisoners and abandoned equipment clearly delineated the Hapsburg line of retreat leading to Landshut. In past campaigns the French veterans had marched on many similar roads in pursuit of vanquished foes, but for their German allies it was something new: the exhilarating tonic of easy victory and conquest.

The Isar valley at Landshut was nearly three miles wide. Approaching the town, the river split into two branches (see Map 15). The main stream surged along the right bank, separated from the 200-foot-high bluffs by a narrow floodplain. Here stood Landshut, a typical Bavarian town with ornate high-gabled buildings dominated by a modest castle on the bluffs. Several wooden bridges spanned the Isar's eastern branch and connected with a small island in the river's center on which numerous houses stood. From it bridges crossed the Isar's

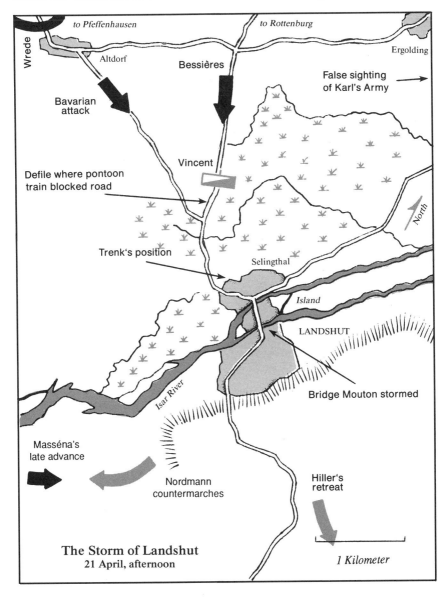

to Pfeffenhausen

to Rottenburg

Wrede

Altdorf

Ergolding

Bessières

False sighting
of Karl's Army

Bavarian
attack

Vincent

Defile where pontoon
train blocked road

North

Trenk's position

Selingthal

Island

LANDSHUT

Isar River

Bridge Mouton stormed

Masséna's
late advance

Nordmann
countermarches

Hiller's
retreat

The Storm of Landshut
21 April, afternoon

1 Kilometer

western branch and connected with the Selingthal suburb. Here the roads to Rohr and Pfeffenhausen joined, and here a tremendous traffic jam was forming.

Since its capture from the Bavarians on 16 April, Landshut had served as the Austrian army's main depot. The transport corps made daily journeys to restock from the depots. The colossal rear-area impedimenta collected at this hub. For two days discouraging news of defeat and retreat had filtered back to Landshut, carried by the croakers of the transport corps, made vivid by the sight of the walking wounded. Now came a fresh alarm: Napoleon himself was snapping at the army's heels.

In this crisis Austrian staffwork, such as is was, collapsed completely. Lacking central direction, everyone tried to retire at once. When teamsters drove their wagons to the main road leading to the Isar bridges they encountered other vehicles from the three combat corps who had been driving all night along the Pfeffenhausen and Rohr roads. A pontoon train jammed a defile, firmly plugging one of the major roads (see Map 15).

Soon wagon teams stood three, four, and five abreast as they choked the rain-soaked road leading to Landshut. Hordes of noncombatants—camp followers, bakers, supply personnel, ambulance drivers, pontoniers—shifted uneasily, always looking back over their shoulders for signs of the dreaded French. Their contagion of fear spread to the thousands of horses who stood pressed together.[24] Drivers flogged the terrified beasts in an effort to get the vehicles moving. The mass quaked and surged, moved forward briefly, and stopped again when it reached the narrow village streets descending to the river.

Ten miles southwest of Landshut the French major Rausonnet led the bearskin-bedecked elite company of the Twenty-third Chasseurs à Cheval to the outskirts of Moosburg. Assigned to scout for the remainder of the regiment, which in turn was the advance guard of Marshal Masséna's corps, he had proceeded with caution until this point. He saw a mixed force of cavalry and infantry milling about in the village. Behind them was an objective worth risking all, a narrow wooden bridge spanning the unfordable Isar River. In preparation for combat, the chasseurs à cheval rolled up their cloaks and slung them bandolier fashion across their bodies, which would provide some protection from enemy saber blows. Drawing saber, Rausonnet ordered the trumpeter to sound the charge. Downslope at the gallop thundered 100 green-clad chasseurs à cheval. Surprised, the Austrians in the village hurried over the bridge. They clambered awkwardly around bundles of kindling on the bridge. Just as the Austrians set torch to the bundles, Rausonnet's troopers reached the bridge's approach.

The French major paused to gaze through the wispy smoke. He saw Austrian infantry lining the far bank. They opened fire as the French troopers eased their mounts to a nervous, snorting standstill. Rausonnet ordered a section to dismount, storm the bridge, and cast the burning stacks of kindling into the river. Without hesitation the troopers of the elite company carried out the order. Better yet, covered by friendly carbine fire, they mastered the bridge's far end within fifteen minutes. Thus it was that when the balance of the Twenty-third Chasseurs arrived they were able to cross the bridge immediately and pursue the flying Hapsburgs northeast toward Landshut. Behind them, marching as only the French could march, came Masséna's infantry.

At 8:00 A.M. back in Landshut, FML Johann Hiller gazed on the ever-growing traffic jam choking the road leading to the Isar crossing. It was a disheartening scene. Perhaps he believed that here was the inevitable consequence of Karl's bungling leadership. Regardless of his feelings toward his rival, Hiller was enough of a soldier to recognize that he needed to take action to buy time for his troops to unscramble and cross the river to safety. He sent a squadron of hussars to his advance guard division commander, FML Karl Vincent, with directions to hold off the French.

When Vincent received this order his running series of rear-guard combats had ended because there was no more room to run. He gathered all the cavalry he could find—two regiments of chevaulégers, two hussar regiments, and one of uhlans—and began to form them in front of the defile blocked by the pontoon train (see Map 15). To his rear his infantry manned the heights on the Isar's near bank.

It was a desperate moment. The small reinforcement sent by Hiller to join Vincent's troopers barely had time to deploy when they spied the French massing on the heights. The Austrians girded for battle. It appeared that the campaign's largest cavalry contest to date was about to occur but, curiously, the French did not attack. Instead, off to Vincent's left, on the Seligenthal–Altdorf–Pfeffenhausen road, came the sounds of combat.

Simultaneous with the arrival of the French cavalry confronting Vincent was the appearance of the Bavarian cavalry at Altdorf (see Map 15). The Bavarian chevaulégers could see a formidable mass of Hapsburg horsemen, Vincent's troopers, deployed below in the plain. Behind them appeared masses of infantry and wagons. The Bavarian general Wrede, operating in the French style with his advance guard, ordered his horse battery to open fire. The battery had discharged a few salvos when Wrede spied a rapidly moving column advancing on his left. It was Bessières. He saw the Austrians react with desperate urgency. Their entire force, except for a thick line of cavalry acting as rear guard, tried to squeeze through the approaches to Seligenthal. The Austrians to Wrede's front joined the panic, abandoning their equipment as they fled. The Bavarians gleefully advanced to scoop up eleven cannon. Inspired, Wrede launched two squadrons of the Third Chevaulégers down the road into Seligenthal.

Concealed within the village were two Hapsburg battalions. Lieutenant Colonel Trenk, battalion commander in the Giulay Regiment (a Hungarian unit), worried that his men appeared shaken. They had seen their front-line comrades collapse in panic. They had heard a constant stream of heavy traffic moving to the rear as most of Hiller's command fled for the safety of the Landshut bridges. Then they saw an overwhelming enemy force massing on the heights before them. Detached from this mass came a galloping force of horsemen heading straight for them. Trenk knew that only his own and an adjacent battalion stood between the enemy and the complete destruction of Hiller's command. He rose to the occasion, steadied his Hungarians, and observed with satisfaction their accurate musketry repulsing the Bavarian horse (see Map 15). From the heights, having seen what appeared to be a heavy volume of fire beat back his probe, Wrede paused to watch the French clear the way.

Inexplicably, they failed to do so. After the flurry of fighting around Seligenthal, nothing further occurred. An hour passed, then a second. In Landshut, Austrian trains continued to pour over the bridges to safety. One of the chances that another Napoleonic soldier, a Prussian named Clausewitz, was to call the friction of war had caused the pause in the French pursuit.

It began when a member of Marshal Berthier's staff galloped to Napoleon's field headquarters with urgent news. Breathlessly the aide told Napoleon that Archduke Karl had appeared leading a large force toward Landshut from the north. Napoleon turned his glass in the direction the aide pointed. It was difficult to see; low clouds provided a poor background for distant views. Yet he could make out soldiers in the indicated direction. Surprised at this sudden turn of events, Napoleon responded: "Very well. It is a fine maneuver! It does honor to the Archduke."[25] He ordered a reconnaissance of the Austrian position and deployed Lannes' corps to confront this unexpected attack.

Foiled in his plans to assault Landshut, Napoleon impatiently awaited the patrol's return. His thoughts turned to Masséna. He snappishly queried his staff for information. Perhaps Masséna could apply flank pressure to dislodge the Austrians in Landshut. There was no news of the marshal. The Emperor became increasingly irritated.

Time passed, and the scouts returned to report that the column was Bavarian cavalry conducting a reconnaissance. Their green uniforms and crested helmets were easily confused with the Austrian design. Napoleon was furious. How, he raged, could four squadrons of allied cavalry be mistaken for an Austrian corps? Precious hours had been lost by the time the damage of the false deployments was undone.

At last the French cavalry under Bessières resumed its advance on Landshut. The Austrian rear-guard commander, FML Vincent, saw their leading squadrons advancing in column along the road. Vincent took advantage of the cramped French formation by charging their van with the Archduke Karl Uhlans and half of the Liechtenstein Hussars. The Hapsburg charge temporarily halted the French. Soon, however, ever greater numbers of French and allied cavalry appeared. Faced with an escalating combat, Vincent paused to examine his position. Remarkably, he had failed to use the several-hour lull to reconnoiter. Consequently, only now did he realize that his troopers stood on marshy ground ill-suited for cavalry movement (see Map 15). They could neither complete their deployment, maneuver where they stood, nor retreat through the pontoon train-blocked defile. Here was blundering of the first order.

Plunged into disorder by the poor ground, Vincent tried to withdraw. His Rosenberg chevaulégers managed to maintain their formation and retreat to the bridge. It was so narrow that only a platoon could cross at a time. With painful slowness the regiment marched to safety. A few of the uhlans and the majority of two hussar regiments followed. Four squadrons of Hesse–Hombourg Hussars and the balance of the uhlans did not make it. They routed through the streets of Seligenthal. Some managed to swim their horses to safety, but the fast-flowing river stymied most. Cornered in narrow alleyways, their backs to the river, they either fell to the enemy's sabers or surrendered while their comrades watched helplessly from the far shore.

When the cavalry fled past them, the Austrian infantry manning the rear guard faced the French alone. The two battalions defending Seligenthal yielded the streets to the French cavalry who galloped in wild pursuit toward the bridge. Fire from doorways and windows emptied a few saddles but could not check the impetuous French. French infantry appeared: Morand's men, their battle fever rising as they charged beneath the eyes of their emperor. The defenders of Seligenthal yielded. The French drew nearer the bridge.

By now most of the Hapsburg artillery had successfully escaped to the island and to the right bank. What remained was frightful chaos: "Hiller's troops battled with great valor, but without unity. Each officer attended to his men and to his honor, hoping to save one while maintaining the other."[26] In the middle of the river, on the Landshut island, Archduke Ludwig and other officers scrambled to bring order to the chaos. They could do no more for the men cut off on the left bank. Someone gave the order to burn the bridge.

Amid the frenzy, Hiller received word from the hapless Nordmann that the French had crossed the Isar at Moosburg. Until now the corps commander had believed he could at least hold the right bank and prevent the French from crossing the river. Nordmann's unwelcome news convinced him that he was outflanked and must continue the retreat. Hiller ordered Nordmann to take four hussar squadrons and an infantry battalion, march back toward Moosburg, and block any French move on Landshut (see Map 15). Ignoring the increasing uproar around the Landshut bridge, FML Hiller drafted orders for his command to retire over the Inn, twenty-five miles to the east.

Jacquinot's light horse spearheaded Bessières' drive on Landshut. The road leading to the Landshut bridge crossed several small, tree-lined canals. The canal bridges constricted the advance of the French chasseurs à cheval. They paused at each obstacle, formed column, and passed the bridges a platoon at a time. At one bridge heavy Austrian fire from a nearby treeline struck them in flank and stalled their advance.

Shortly after noon Marshal Bessières appeared on the scene. A French light cavalryman observed the marshal apparently "Thinking he could accomplish that which we could not" as he launched the elite carabiniers à cheval over the canal bridges.[27] With this charge Bessières crossed the thin line between impetuosity and foolhardiness. The attack collapsed under withering Austrian fire.

Recognizing that the situation required something more than a simple heads-down gallop, Jacquinot dismounted thirty of his men and led them over the bridge in skirmish style. They deployed in front of the Hapsburg position and by so doing managed to attract the enemy fire while other French troops crossed behind them. Austrian resistance collapsed. The whitecoats fled back toward the Landshut bridge. Some scurried to boats and barges along the Isar's left bank. Soon the river was crowded with a miniature flotilla carrying the Austrians to safety.

Bessières' horsemen pressed on. They galloped across the bridge leading to the island, but could go no farther. Looking eastward, they saw the wooden bridge spanning the main channel begin to burn. Napoleon did not know that Masséna's cavalry had already seized a crossing at Moosburg and that Hiller had consequently decided to retreat. He believed he needed a bridge and saw the only one immediately available going up in smoke. In this crisis he turned to a special man, thirty-nine-year-old General Georges Mouton.

Napoleon had known Mouton since the first campaigns in Italy where Mouton had twice been wounded. He joked once: "My Mouton [French for sheep] is a lion."[28] He had promoted his "lion" to general and made him an imperial aide-de-camp in time for the Austerlitz campaign of 1805. During the following four years Mouton had rotated from staff to line positions, serving with great competence in the former and occasional brilliant distinction on the latter. To be an imperial aide meant one was at the apex of courage in an army full of brave men eager to distinguish themselves in front of the Emperor. Napoleon relied on that characteristic when he issued his order. Mouton had just returned from a mission when the Emperor spoke: "You come just in time; put yourself at the head of that column, and carry the town of Landshut."[29]

Mouton dismounted in front of the grenadiers of the third battalion of the Seventeenth Ligne. They quickly crossed to the island, which provided ample room to stage the assault's next phase (see Map 15). After pausing to reform, the column approached the second, longer bridge leading to the right bank. This bridge already was burning when Mouton raised his sword and pointed to the far shore. Looking ahead, it seemed a desperate thing to attempt. Gray-black smoke crowned the river bluffs above Landshut as Austrian artillery blasted away at the exposed French. The plunging fire kicked up spumes of spray when the shot and shell struck the water. Directly ahead stood a stone gate barricading the bridge's exit. From the windows and roofs of the town and from a church situated just behind the bridge came musket fire. Steady troops occupying such a position could have held indefinitely.

However, the cannons from the heights had a narrow target to fire at. The river swallowed up all misses, thus preventing the lethal richochets that occurred on land. The scattered popping of the uncoordinated musketry lacked the stopping power of controlled, massed volleys. As long as a column kept moving it would take some losses but could cross the fireswept danger zone in less than a minute. That is, a column could storm the bridge if the soldiers were willing to perform a naked bayonet charge. Mouton undoubtedly realized this when he spoke before the charge. His stentorian voice was renowned throughout the army; now his simple words carried above the noise of battle: "No firing. March!"[30]

Striding forward, Mouton also had to know that some enemy fire would hit home and that the men at the front would take the brunt of the losses. Sword in hand, Mouton's solitary figure led the way. Surging along behind came the grenadiers of the Seventeenth Ligne.

The wild Austrian fire struck a handful of grenadiers. Mouton and the rest reached the barricade. A section of especially big, strong men—sappers of the *tête de colonne*—strode up to the gate and began to deliver blows with their axes.[31] Soon the wood splintered and the grenadiers shouldered their way into Landshut. Behind them other Frenchmen forcibly employed Austrian prisoners to douse the smoldering bridge timbers.

Mouton rejoined Napoleon to resume a report on a mission he had accomplished prior to the charge. Strangely, during the conversation neither mentioned the bridge assault. After the campaign the Emperor acknowledged his aide's conduct when he presented him a magnificent painting depicting Mouton leading the attack over the bridge. Napoleon once commented that "Men are led with baubles." With this gift Napoleon showed he had the measure of his man. In the words of another aide: "This keepsake from Napoleon was worth more than the highest eulogies."[32]

After Mouton's initial success the French encountered stiffer resistance in

Landshut. Napoleon had ordered Morand to follow Mouton and seize Land-shut. Morand's Thirteenth Légère quickly passed over the bridge to support the victorious Seventeenth. The latter needed help because a battalion of the Austrian Klebeck Regiment positioned along the river bluffs and in the castle had opened a heavy fire. Furthermore, an Irish major in Hapsburg service led a splendid counterattack of the Kerpen infantry into the left-hand portion of the town and it required all of Morand's division to stabilize the situation. Only when a fresh French regiment entered the fray did the Austrians yield. The rear guard's tenacity gave the balance of Hiller's command enough time to form and retire toward Neumarkt. However, the French pursuit continued, slashing at the whitecoats' heels.

Meanwhile, the advance guard of Masséna's Fourth Corps remained mo-tionless as the noise of battle at Landshut swelled. Marulaz's cavalry had pursued Nordmann's men all the way from Moosburg. When they reached Landshut's southwest suburbs shortly before noon, a small detachment of Hapsburg infantry, the detail sent by Hiller for this express purpose blocked their further advance (see Map 15). Marulaz sent a messenger spurring back toward Moosburg to request assistance.

Help was surprisingly close at hand. A French infantry brigade com-manded by General Coehorn had managed to nearly keep up with the cavalry by jogging in quick step, a grueling 250 paces per minute.[33] Marulaz asked Coehorn to clear out the resistance so he could resume his advance. Coehorn was uncertain whether he should commit his men or wait for reinforcements. After all, the balance of the division was only a mile farther back.

Such indecision annoyed a French officer riding with the front ranks of Marulaz's cavalry. That officer, Major Karl de Sainte-Croix, rode off to find Coehorn's divisional commander. Sainte-Croix served as one of Masséna's aides-de-camp. A brilliant officer, Sainte-Croix's enormous talents would soon attract the favorable attention of Napoleon himself.[34] On this day what Sainte-Croix needed was greater powers of persuasion. He recognized the great opportunity presented by the bold French capture of the Moosburg bridge. If the French could only advance a little farther they would sever Hiller's line of retreat. Hiller's entire command would be caught between Masséna and Napoleon. It would have to surrender.

Sainte-Croix found the divisional commander, General Claparede, and explained the situation. Claparede stubbornly refused to accelerate his march. He claimed he could not authorize an advance without Masséna's direct order. Worse, he ordered Coehorn to halt his brigade as well! According to another of Masséna's aides: "Such circumspection probably saved Hiller."[35] Masséna himself arrived shortly after noon. He ordered Claparede to resume the advance. It was too late.[36]

By midafternoon Hiller's forces were well along the road leading to Neumarkt. Four grenadier battalions formed his rear guard. The ever-active Radetzky gathered the remnants of the Archduke Karl uhlans and the relatively intact Kienmayer Hussars to support the grenadiers. These men had fought and marched for three days, yet they held together and reached the Geisenhausen defile without loss.

The line of retreat entered rough, broken ground near the defile. Two companies of grenadiers from the Deutschmeister Regiment defended a small woodlot. They were the picked men from the elite regiment associated with the Teutonic Order. Upon receiving orders to continue the retreat, the companies emerged into the open. There on the plain they faced overwhelming numbers of French light cavalry. The French cavalry sighted the grenadiers from afar and charged. It appeared the grenadiers would be swallowed up by the enemy horse.

A solitary Austrian figure ran from the ranks toward the French. He paused next to an abandoned ammunition wagon, lit a torch, tossed it in the wagon, and ran. A violent explosion vaulted the grenadier into the air and threw him lifeless back onto the ground. The surprise explosion and resultant thick smoke provided a screen between the grenadiers and the charging cavalry. Temporarily stunned, the cavalry slowed, allowing the grenadiers just enough time to rejoin their unit without further loss. Even in retreat and defeat, the Hapsburg army was not without heroes.[37]

At dusk back in Landshut, one of Archduke Karl's aides-de-camp appeared along with a convoy he led that was carrying wounded to the hospitals. To his great surprise he fell into French hands. Only then did he learn that the Hapsburg army's vast magazine at Landshut had fallen to the French. Talking with French officers, the Austrian expressed amazement at how quickly the French had penetrated the Austrian rear. Even after it was explained to him, the aide could only begin to understand the whirlwind Napoleonic war of maneuver.

The Emperor Napoleon also rode into Landshut in the early evening of his third day of campaigning. He believed he had smashed Karl's army. Prisoners and captured equipment supported his view. Later tabulation would reveal that in the various combats around Landshut the Austrians suffered eleven officers and 639 men killed; twenty-nine and 2119 wounded; and twenty-one and 2313 captured. The French captured twenty-five artillery pieces and the pontoon train that had so helpfully blocked the defile leading to Landshut.[38] French losses had been light: 774 men killed, wounded, and missing.

The day's success put the Emperor in a good mood. He reviewed Morand's infantry and complimented them on their fine success in storming the Landshut bridge. Standing before the Thirteenth Légère he asked the colonel: "Who is the bravest man in the regiment?"

The colonel hesitated, so Napoleon repeated the question to the other officers. Silence. Finally the Emperor spied an elderly voltigeur captain: "Well, old fellow, who is the bravest soldier in the Thirteenth Regiment?"

"Sire," he replied, "it is the drum major. Everyone knows that."

Turning to the drum major, Napoleon said: "You have been designated the bravest of a brave regiment. I promote you to lieutenant and chevalier in the Legion of Honor."[39] The troops responded with predictable enthusiasm. In the next battle they would fight with the knowledge that extreme bravery could be rewarded.

A cavalry officer from the Second Chasseurs à Cheval approached the Emperor to present two flags his unit had captured when they overran a unit of Hungarian grenadiers. Blood dripped from his face where an Austrian saber had found its mark. After handing the trophies to Napoleon the Emperor asked his name. "Lion," the officer replied.

The Emperor exclaimed: "Lion! I will remember you and you will be grateful; you are well marked!"[40]

Later in the campaign when there was a vacancy in the Imperial Guard chasseurs à cheval, Berthier and the other marshals presented their preferred candidates for this exalted position. Napoleon examined the list and responded: "No, no. Bring me my Lion!"[41]

On the Austrian side there were neither reviews nor celebrations of valor. Serious as Hiller's losses were, they were by no means crippling. About 18 percent of Hiller's command had been lost on the twentieth, while during the debacle at Landshut a further 12 percent were subtracted from his muster rolls. However, the remaining troops were greatly dispirited and, more important, were led by a balky, incompetent general. Napoleon could safely ignore Hiller for the next few days if he so chose. Here lay the importance of the combats around Landshut. The French Emperor had sent one wing of the Austrian army reeling back toward the Inn, completely isolating it from Karl's command. He had achieved a central position between the isolated wings, although he did not yet realize it.

Nonetheless, he had already taken precautions to assist Davout. In the midst of the devastating pursuit of Hiller, when he saw Morand's division capture Landshut, he had ordered Gudin's division—marching behind Morand's—to halt and make camp. This placed them closer to Davout should that marshal require them. There were additional troops at hand: Vandamme had reported that his division of Württembergers had closed up, drawn rations, and was ready for orders.

It was good that the Württembergers were rested and fed, for they would soon call upon every reserve of stamina.

CHAPTER VIII

The Battle of Eckmühl

The art of war is like everything else that is beautiful and simple. The simplest moves are the best.

Two-A.M. Courage

The evening of 21 April found Archduke Karl in a complex situation fraught with both opportunity and peril. The opportunity lay in the fact that fewer than 35,000 French and Bavarians, the corps commanded by Davout and Lefebvre, confronted more than 50,000 Austrians. Furthermore, the Austrian Second Corps was crossing the Danube at Ratisbonne to reinforce Karl and would thus give the Archduke an even greater superiority. On the debit side, Karl had little news of events around Landshut and the whereabouts and status of Hiller's forces. By 10:00 P.M. Karl resolved to resume the offensive and destroy Davout's isolated force. He had had the same opportunity on the nineteenth and twenty-first and had bungled it. Whether a third chance would be the charm remained to be seen.

Karl planned a three-prong attack with the strongest effort involving Kollowrath's formidable Second Corps with some 27,000 men (see Map 16). They would march from Ratisbonne and reach Abbach at noon. On their left, 13,000 men led by Prince Johannes Liechtenstein would advance an hour later to attack between Peising and Dinzling. The leftmost column, commanded by Hohenzollern, would march at noon with 8000 men via Luckenpoint toward Peising. Rosenberg's Fourth Corps would hold its position around Laichling with Bieber's brigade detached from the Third Corps, providing flank support by guarding the Eckmühl defile (see Map 16). Over the Laber, another infantry brigade commanded by Vukassovich established outposts well out on

151

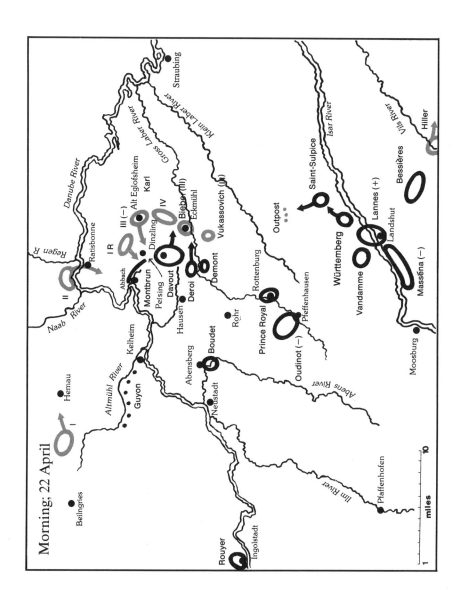

Morning; 22 April

the Landshut road. As usual, the grenadiers and cuirassiers of the reserve corps would stand in reserve. Karl calculated that his offensive could strike and destroy Davout before Napoleon could intervene, yet his plan did not call for any of his three offensive prongs to begin until noon. Apparently Karl believed he had ample time.

Twenty-three miles to the south, Napoleon spent the night of the twenty-first in Landshut's royal residence. It was an anxious time for everyone. Troubled by the failure of his main blow to connect with the Austrian main body, Napoleon's thoughts turned to developments elsewhere. He made life miserable for everyone, particularly the hapless Berthier. Where was Karl, he demanded? Why hadn't he heard from Davout? The Emperor's repeated questions failed to elicit satisfactory answers.

Finally, at 1:00 A.M., a courier from Davout arrived. Although a direct line from Davout to Napoleon was only a little over twenty miles, and General Piré, the courier, had departed at 7:00 P.M., the intervening no-man's-land made his journey difficult. Forced to detour frequently, Piré required six hours and had to travel nearly thirty-seven miles to reach Napoleon.

Piré's intelligence was a mixed bag. Davout's report described his continuing success in harrying Karl across the Bavarian countryside. However, for the first time Napoleon learned of the unfortunate Coutard's surrender at Ratisbonne. It could hardly have been worse news. Instead of confronting an Austrian army trapped against the angle of the Danube and Iser, he faced an enemy with a secure line of retreat. Worse, as Napoleon reflected on the situation and moved his pins around the map, Davout now stood in grave danger, supposing Karl resumed the offensive. Further information arrived: the report of an interrogation of a captured Austrian officer that contained only vague rumors and two spies' reports that Karl had his headquarters at Eckmühl. Armed with imprecise information, the Emperor relied on his map study. A flurry of couriers galloped away from imperial headquarters in the small hours of the morning as Napoleon recast his plans.

The Emperor sent Piré (French aides-de-camp were nothing if not hardworking) on the return trip to Davout. Piré carried a note informing the marshal that several infantry divisions and some cuirassiers were on their way to Eckmühl to assist him. Piré departed, and then a curious thing happened. Barely fifteen minutes passed, yet during those minutes Napoleon thoroughly reconsidered his strategy. He finally realized that the pursuit to Landshut had failed to knock out the Austrian army. Perhaps the situation offered a second chance. He wrote Davout again: "If the Archduke Karl remains today and his position is attackable, I hope to attack by 4 P.M. . . . It is necessary to exterminate the Austrians and avenge the regiment that has been captured."[1]

This succession of orders reveals the mind of one of history's Great Captains at work. In later life Napoleon expounded on "the courage of 2:00 A.M.," the extemporaneous courage that even in sudden emergencies "leaves one's freedom of mind, judgment, and decision completely unaffected."[2] He asserted that he possessed that 2:00 A.M. courage to a higher degree than any other man. From 2:00 to 4:00 A.M. on 22 April—the fourth day of a campaign that had seen him travel far, eat sparingly, sleep little, and exert a tremendous amount of physical and mental energy—he demonstrated what this special type of courage meant.

In a confused, fluid situation he completely changed his army's main line of operation within fifteen minutes of receiving some concrete information about his opponent. The fact that the information contradicted what Napoleon had heretofore supposed makes the change all the more remarkable. Scales cast from his eyes, the Emperor dictates an order to Davout that explains his new plan and, ever conscious of what motivates men, ends it with a sentence that is sure to put Davout on his mettle—a sentence that reminds the Iron Marshal that a French regiment under his command has surrendered and thus sullied the proud marshal's reputation; a sentence that ensures Davout will put forward his best effort.

A postscript to the message to Davout shows the further maturation of Napoleon's plans: "It is 4 A.M. I am resolved to begin the march personally, and I will be at Eckmühl at noon and prepared to vigorously attack the enemy at 3 P.M. I will have with me 40,000 men . . . I have decided to exterminate Archduke Karl's army, today or at the latest tomorrow."[3] If Davout was engaged, he was to notify the Emperor by firing a salvo of ten cannon shots at noon and on the hour thereafter. Above all, Davout was to stay in contact with Karl.

At 4:00 A.M. the Emperor stepped out onto his balcony. The mounted carabiniers detailed to guard headquarters recognized their leader. The courtyard echoed to cheers of "Vive l'Empereur!" Slumbering infantrymen awakened, placed their shakos atop their bayonets, and joined in the acclaim.[4] Undoubtedly satisfied with his men's fine fettle, Napoleon returned to his contemplation.

He decided he could safely ignore Hiller's beaten force. Marshal Bessières would continue to pursue Hiller with cavalry alone. Wrede's Bavarian infantry would support him. The rest of the army would march on Eckmühl. Having issued precise orders for his marshals, the Emperor turned his attention to the men in the ranks. Recognizing that they had to make a speed march on short rations and little sleep, he commanded that they be fortified for the trial with a triple ration of brandy. The Emperor caught a short hour of sleep, rose, and opened the window. The absence of cannon fire reassured him. All could proceed as planned. He drank a cup of warm milk to soothe a sore throat and headed down the highway toward Eckmühl.

He chose to travel by horseback rather than by carriage so he could better be seen by his soldiers along the way. They responded with characteristic zeal. The Emperor, in turn, saw all and attended to every detail. A group of horses mingled aimlessly by the roadside. Napoleon ordered them hitched to a captured pontoon train to speed its way along the poor country road. He planned to cross some rivers; they might be needed.

The scent of battle was upon Napoleon. Passing Marshal Masséna he beckoned. "Come. Every moment is precious, your presence is useless here; join the advance guard . . . I need a man who understands me; today's battle will be decisive."[5]

Along Marshal Davout's front the night of 21–22 April saw a large number of Austrian deserters enter French lines. Heretofore few Austrians had deserted. Davout's brigadiers believed the increased tempo of desertion presaged an Austrian stand. Nervous skirmish fire that erupted during the night reinforced the belief that battle was imminent.

Dawn came but did not bring the expected battle. The Austrians were not yet ready. Archduke Karl issued orders at 8:00 A.M. calling for the attack to begin between noon and one o'clock. Presumably he felt this delay would allow Kollowrath's Second Corps time to arrive from Ratisbonne seven miles away. Ponderously some forty-one Austrian battalions prepared to advance upon Davout's flank. Karl had targeted two of his three offensive wings against Peising, where he supposed Davout's main force was concentrated. In fact, the French force around the Peising plateau was merely a reinforced cavalry division commanded by General Montbrun (see Map 16).

That Montbrun could have fooled an experienced commander such as Karl into believing he commanded a much larger force is a great testament to Montbrun's skill. Like a matador waving his cape, Montbrun attracted Karl's attention by aggressive feints and maneuver. As had been the case for the three preceding days, Montbrun had the difficult assignment of keeping a vastly superior force in check while protecting Davout's open flank. His two light cavalry brigades and two attached battalions of the Seventh Légère remained stretched over a six-mile gap from the important Abbach defile on the Danube to Friant's outposts near Dinzling. The task could not have been entrusted to more capable hands.

While Karl's offensive wing prepared sluggishly to advance against the matador's cape, Prince Rosenberg's Fourth Corps stood facing Davout's main force. The prince's men lined a series of wooded ridgetops running from Eckmühl on the left to just outside Sanding on the right. It was an extensive front guarded by too few soldiers, yet all remained quiet until shortly before noon. At about that time, an Austrian front-line officer went seeking the prince and found him scouting French positions near Sanding.[6] He told Rosenberg what he had seen, and it was a strange tale.

On the plain near Schierling, over on the right flank, the officer reported seeing the French under Davout begin to maneuver, apparently to resist the Austrian attack from the northwest. But after changing front, the French had curiously paused, as if they were waiting for something. They remained in this position even now. In addition, Austrian officers remarked on the activity of their French counterparts. From the heights the Austrians saw French generals and their staffs constantly circulating among their front-line troops, pausing to study the Austrian position through their telescopes. Alarmed, Rosenberg returned to his field headquarters, where he found Karl's orders explaining the Fourth Corps' mission for the day.

These orders envisaged only a supporting role in the grand offensive. He was merely to hold his ground and occupy Davout's attention while Karl dealt the French the main blow. The prince dutifully obeyed. Around 1:00 P.M. the crackling of muskets could be heard off toward Dinzling on Rosenberg's right. Karl's advance guard had engaged, the Austrian offensive was under way. Then a courier from Vukassovich, on the opposite flank, brought frightening news: The French were advancing along the Landshut highway toward Eckmühl.

Initially Rosenberg hoped to maintain his position as ordered. Accordingly he commanded the reserve regiments stationed behind his left flank to extend the defense toward Eckmühl. Arriving at the dominating height behind Laichling, the Bettel Berg, the corps commander gazed south and realized this would not do. Across the Laber the slopes descending toward Eckmühl were solid with French troops. The hillside seemed alive with a massive dark shape flowing inexorably toward the river crossings.

The Hapsburg prince reacted swiftly. He directed his corps to retire off the heights west of Laichling and occupy a parallel rise east of the village. The new position offered favorable ground, although the Hapsburg army was never at its best changing positions under an imminent enemy threat. Several bare hilltops presented excellent fields of fire for the artillery while a series of small villages provided strong points for the infantry.

The Bellegarde and Reuss–Greitz Regiments garrisoned the twin village of Unter- and Ober-Laichling (see Map 17). In reserve were four squadrons of Vincent Chevaulégers commanded by Stutterheim supported by a two-tier earthwork defended by some Hungarian grenadiers. Three more infantry regiments stood in advance of this position in a woods that extended northward toward Karl and the main army. Anchoring the position's left flank was the Bettel Berg. Here stood an infantry regiment and two batteries of twelve-pound guns. Deployed in columns in close support were one-and-one-half regiments of cavalry.

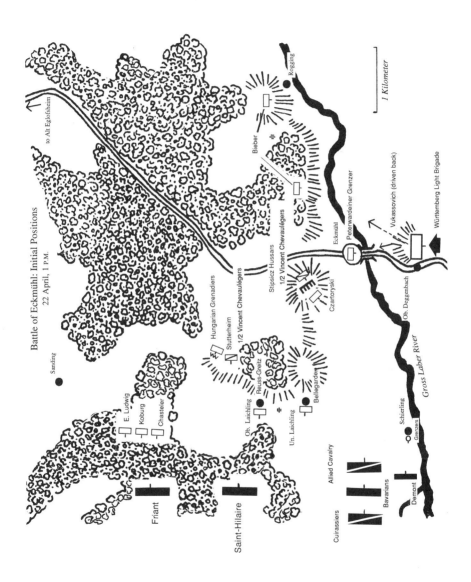

Battle of Eckmühl: Initial Positions
22 April, 1 P.M.

Rosenberg faced a near-impossible task. He had to maintain contact with Karl on his right flank, yet to hold his position he also had to defend the Laber crossings on his left. Failure to do so would allow the two wings of the French army under Davout and Napoleon to link up. To resist the combined assault of several French corps along this extended position the Fourth Corps fielded some 11,000 infantry and 1400 cavalry. The various formations supporting the Fourth Corps probably added another 4000 or 5000 men, yet because they belonged to three different divisions in two different corps, they caused a confusing command and control problem and exerted far less weight than their numbers warranted.[7]

Set-Piece Battle

Like Rosenberg, Marshal Davout had spent an uneasy morning. At first a thick fog obscured the ground. It did not begin to lift until eight o'clock. At this point the French, who had deployed parallel to the Austrian line, could gaze across the valley and look upward toward the Hapsburg position. It was apparent to all that a difficult task lay ahead. The Emperor's orders required Davout to assault the Austrian ridgeline position as soon he observed the arrival of the French flanking column. This pinning attack would prevent Rosenberg from shifting enough men to block the French assault over the Laber. By ten o'clock Davout had his forces ready. Joining the front-rank assault brigade he interrogated its leader, Colonel Berthezène, about the Austrian dispositions:

"How many men are in that village?"
"About two thousand."
"And on the flanks?"
"One thousand and five cannons."
"And in the woods on the heights?"
"I do not know; but I believe it is well defended: from here you can see abatis which cover their position."
"You see," replied Davout, "the clock tower on our right, that's Eckmühl! The Emperor will be there in one hour; when you see his advance guard engaged with the enemy, without waiting for orders, you will take that village and then the woods."
"With my lone regiment?" asked the stunned colonel.
"Of course," replied the Iron Marshal.[8]

It is difficult to imagine an Austrian corps commander relying upon a colonel's initiative to launch an important attack. Such communication and trust reveals an important underpinning of the French army.

Davout's estimate of the speed of Napoleon's approach was overly optimis-

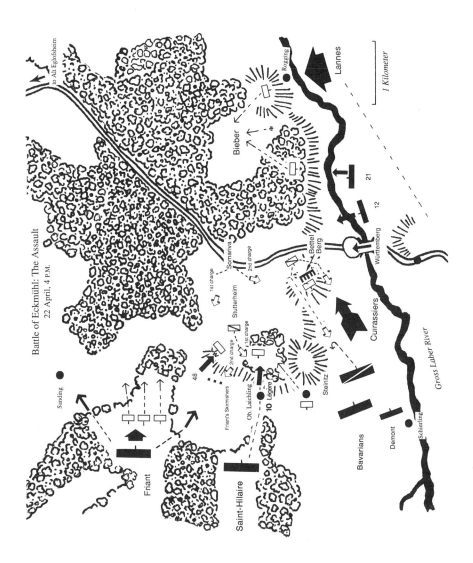

Battle of Eckmühl: The Assault
22 April, 4 P.M.

tic. For three hours Berthezène peered anxiously across the valley. Finally between 1:00 and 1:30 P.M. he saw the Austrians on the heights stir and begin to maneuver toward their left flank. Moments later the dull boom of cannon announced the arrival of the French emperor on the field. Berthezène ordered his Tenth Légère into the assault.

While the balance of Davout's corps launched a series of false attacks designed to tie down and confuse the defenders, the Tenth Légère went in hard against Laichling (see Map 18). Without pausing to fire, it stormed the twin village, overthrowing the feeble resistance provided by the Bellegarde and Reuss–Greitz regiments. Nearly 1500 demoralized defenders surrendered. The supporting Austrian battery fired several salvos and retired uphill.

As ordered, Berthezène next assaulted a small woodlot extending behind and upslope of the village. Here resistance was much more severe. Slowed by the line of felled trees, the Tenth Légère staggered beneath a hail of well-aimed musketry. The elite companies spearheading the charge were nearly wiped out; more than 600 men and twenty-eight officers in the regiment were killed or wounded in this assault. Yet the Tenth struggled on until it emerged into the open ground near the highway running toward Ratisbonne. However, it was a spent force, with the best soldiers down. The Hapsburg reserve line of cavalry and artillery stopped it in its tracks. An Austrian column massed to counterattack. The Tenth Légère's position seemed hopeless.

Suddenly General Compans, Davout's chief of staff, showing the same initiative here as he had displayed on the Teugen–Hausen ridge on the nineteenth, appeared through the trees leading two fresh French regiments. He hurled his men against the flank of the Austrian column and drove the Hapsburgs to the rear. The French skirmishers emerged from the copse toward the vital Eckmühl–Ratisbonne highway.

Backstopping the Austrian position was Stutterheim's cavalry. He launched his four squadrons of the Vincent Chevaulégers against the French and drove them back to the woods (see Map 18). An Austrian battery, on the verge of being captured, managed to withdraw under cover of Stutterheim's charge. Shielded by the cavalry advance, a trio of Austrian colonels rallied the infantry, ordered the drummers to beat the charge, and led a counterattack into the woodlot.

The Austrian infantry suffered severely. Yet the Bellegarde Regiment, inspired by the gallant front-line leadership of Captains Giletta and Herrmann, managed to reconquer a portion of the woodlot. Davout fed reinforcements into the wooded cauldron behind Laichling. On Davout's right a Bavarian division advanced and threatened to outflank the Hapsburg defenders. The Austrians could hold no longer. Rosenberg's center had been pierced.

Meanwhile, on the French left, Friant's division had begun to gain ground in the thick woods between Laichling and Sanding (see Map 18). Initially Friant's attack was designed to pin the Austrian right. Accordingly, when the division advanced out of the woods, it formed a line 500 yards from the Austrian position on the heights north of Laichling. Each French regiment sent forward its skirmishers to the foot of the ridgeline (see Map 18). They tried to shoot down the gunners on the heights, but before they accomplished much an Austrian cavalry charge (Stutterheim's chevaulégers again) drove them back on their supports.

The voltigeurs rallied and returned to the fray. This time Austrian infantry and artillery fire drove them back. Friant was not happy with this state of affairs. He also worried about his open left flank. Somewhere off to the north was Montbrun's cavalry division, perhaps even now being driven back by a superior Austrian host. Friant assigned two brigades the task of protecting the left, but he remained unsettled. Acutely aware of his division's isolation, Friant proceeded with caution against the enemy to his front.

Spearheaded by the 108th Ligne advancing in column, his men swarmed through the woods toward Sanding. French small-unit tactics were much superior to the Austrians in this broken wooded ground. Soon they cleared the forest and drove the defenders upon their cavalry support occupying the high ground along the highway. As had happened in the center, clouds of French skirmishers impetuously advanced into the open to cut the all-important Ratisbonne highway. Here also the Austrians received capable combat leadership. An advance-guard divisional commander with the warlike name of Hannibal, Graf Somariva skillfully led the tired four squadrons of Vincent Chevaulégers to another counterattack that drove the French back to the sheltering woods.

In response, Friant ordered Lieutenant Michel, commander of the Forty-eighth Ligne's voltigeurs, to climb a footpath, gain the heights, and hold his position at all costs (see Map 18). An infantry battalion would follow in the lieutenant's wake. Michel advanced under a hail of canister, yet his men suffered little. Scrambling up the ridge "like mountain goats,"[9] the French presented a dispersed, fast-moving target that the Austrians found hard to hit.

Near the crest the French struck a force of Hungarian grenadiers who manned a two-tier redoubt dug into the ridge. Under cover of the skirmish screen, the Austrians had no skirmishers along this portion of the front to oppose the French skirmishers, the French infantry massed and charged. They were led by a man eager to make a name for himself. General Barbanegre had only recently been promoted to the rank of general. He led his Forty-eighth Ligne with verve and passion to prove he merited his new rank. A brief but sharp firefight ensued. Friant's men gained the upper hand. They glided around the strong points in the Hapsburg defense and used the shelter of the numerous woodlots to penetrate the soft spots in the Austrian defense. Beset front and flank, the defenders yielded. Although intended as pinning attacks, Davout's assaults were splintering Rosenberg's position.

Only on the Hapsburg left did Rosenberg enjoy success. Here the Austrians faced two Bavarian infantry divisions formed in column who were screened by Bavarian and Württemberg cavalry (see Map 17). Along the Laber a third division, Demont's French conscripts, stood poised outside Schierling. In reserve was a cuirassier brigade belonging to Nansouty's division of heavy cavalry. The ground along the Laber was dead level and marshy in spots, and thus not particularly favorable for an attack. The French Marshal Lefebvre commanded this wing.

Confronting Lefebvre on the dominating height of the Bettel Berg were sixteen Austrian guns, including two twelve-pound batteries from the corps reserve capable of controlling the fields below. They were the linchpin of the defense because the Bettel Berg was where the Austrian line made a right-angle turn, the troops on the west slope facing Lefebvre and those on the south slope facing Napoleon. The Bettel Berg was ideally suited to defense; its summit provided a superb artillery position, while the smooth slope offered no concealed route to the top. The slopes were steep enough to give a downhill counterattack solid momentum but not too steep to interfere with maneuver. In addition to the guns, the Czartoryski Infantry Regiment and twelve light cavalry squadrons occupied the position (see Map 17). It was not a large force, in total perhaps 3000 men. Once the French cleared Eckmühl, the defenders would face substantial elements of two French corps. Yet the Bettel Berg was a position the Austrians had to hold.

From the Bettel Berg the Austrian line faced south to parallel the Laber. The pernicious Austrian habit of scattering brigades broadcast style meant that an isolated formation, Bieber's Brigade from Hohenzollern's Third Corps, continued the southward-facing defense from the Bettel Berg to the Rogging heights (see Map 17). Detached from its parent corps, Bieber could expect little cooperation from Rosenberg's corps once the battle began. Early in the battle the harried remnants of Vukassovich, after vainly trying to delay the Napoleon-inspired torrent that was descending on Eckmühl, joined Bieber. Together they manned a good ridgeline position. However, it was an overly long front for Bieber's and Vukassovich's fugitives to defend adequately. An exchange of fire between the Bavarian and Austrian guns began the combat for the Bettel Berg. Then the Bavarian cavalier general Steinitz boldly led his brigade to the assault (see Map 18). His troopers briefly overran an Austrian battery. Four squadrons of Vincent Chevaulégers and the Stipsicz Hussars, deployed to support the battery, countercharged with furious downhill speed and drove back the Bavarian horse. Deroi's Bavarian infantry division tried next. Deroi's assault lacked vigor from the start.[10] At the foot of the Bettel Berg a terrible fire swept through their ranks. Capitalizing on the artillery's effect, the Austrian troopers, having reformed from their cavalry combat, charged the struggling Bavarians. The Vincent Chevaulégers twice reached the Bavarian gun line, only to be thrown back by the well-served cannon and the countercharging Württemberg horse. One-and-one-half aggressive Hapsburg cavalry regiments, supported by good artillery, had fought Lefebvre's corps to a standstill.

Meanwhile, along the banks of the Laber, Demont's French conscripts advanced east through Schierling. Demont's horse was shot out from under him but the conscripts pressed on. The Austrians could not be strong everywhere, and here was a soft spot. Only a grenzer outpost manned the village.[11] The French seized Schierling and its all-important bridge over the Laber. While the defenders retired toward Eckmühl, one battalion of conscripts crossed the river to link up with the force commanded by Napoleon in person. In his early-morning orders Napoleon had foreseen the possibility that he might need assistance from Lefebvre to clear Eckmühl. This precaution proved unnecessary—the conscripts were not needed. They merely joined the already victorious French troops in the area. The fact that they were not needed to capture Eckmühl had much to do with the gallantry of the Württemberg light infantry.

The Württembergers had spearheaded the French advance from Landshut. Under way at 1:30 A.M., a bare half hour after Davout's courier arrived at Napoleon's headquarters and, in sharp contrast to Karl's offensive, which did not begin moving until noon, they struck the village of Ergoltsbach at 4:00 A.M. Here they bagged an unwary officer and forty hussars who had been on outpost duty for the Austrian general Vukassovich. Showing themselves capable of a Frenchlike speed march, they arrived at the next Austrian outpost at Buchhausen on the road to Eckmühl by two in the afternoon (see Map 16).[12] They proceeded to give a very professional demonstration of advance-guard tactics. They confronted elements of Vukassovich's advance guard division, including a cavalry battery backed by light infantry and some hussars. The Württemberg light infantry rapidly deployed into the woods left and right of the road. They advanced to gain ground for their own artillery to unlimber and open fire. A hundred paces to the rear, their light horse massed in columns by squadron. The three arms were in place for a combined-arms assault. After a brief softening-up by the skirmishers and artillery, the Württembergers stormed through the village and swept onward. The speed of their advance gave the Austrians little chance to prepare for Napoleon's unexpected flank movement. However, the narrow, muddy road forced the French to advance in a long, narrow column. If the massive road column met resistance it would be difficult and time-consuming to deploy.

The Württembergers reached Ober-Deggenbach, a small village over-looking Eckmühl, where—emboldened by their previous success—they charged again (see Map 17). Vukassovich's brigade repulsed them. Van-damme, an excellent combat general, rallied the Württembergers and brought up Morand's Frenchmen.[13] He extended the line to the right and at-tacked. Vukassovich conducted his defense ably. A spirited two-squadron cavalry charge led by Major Devay of the Ferdinand Hussars checked Mor-and's advance and forced Vandamme to commit Gudin's division. Gudin's battalion squares finally drove off the Austrian horse. Vukassovich had done his duty well and gained enough time to allow Rosenberg to redeploy his corps.

The Württembergers resumed the advance, seizing Lindach south of Eckmühl. Following closely behind came Napoleon. He ascended the recently conquered heights near Ober-Deggenbach, from which he could see the entire field. A martial amphitheater lay below him. In the middle of the Eckmühl Valley ran the serpentine outline of the Ratisbonne highway. To the assembled French staff, it pointed the way to Ratisbonne and victory. Immediately below, the tree-lined Laber wound its way through green pastures. In the mid-distance small villages dotted the countryside, which was bisected by streams and brooks and poplar-lined country roads. In the midst of this bucolic setting two armies, with all the panoply and terror of Napoleonic warfare, could clearly be seen:

> Davout and Lefebvre, their line formed at right angles to ours, ran along the serrated heights in front of Laichling; the mixture of French, allied, and Austrian troops combined to nonplus even the practiced eye. . . . One could easily untangle the white line of Rosenberg's corps, which stood out on the farmland of the Laichling valley, and which extended, like a ribbon, to the Laber, occupied Eckmühl, and turned toward the wooded Roking heights.[14]

After examining the Austrian positions, the Emperor snapped shut his telescope and seized Masséna by the arm: "You see that army deployed in a manner so imposing for us to look at, very good! We are going to defeat it and conquer Vienna at the same time. As a result of our attack, the Archduke will either give a second battle in front of Ratisbonne, and the war will be finished beneath its walls, or he will cross the Danube and we will head straight to Vienna."[15]

Immediately aides galloped off carrying attack orders: One group of heavy cavalry to cross the Laber at Schierling, link up with the Allied cavalry, and assault the Bettel Berg; another force of cuirassiers and Morand's infantry to advance straight through Eckmühl; Gudin to the right to assault the Rogging heights (see Map 18). The Emperor crossed the Laber at Schierling and coursed the field in front of Deroy's Bavarians, who received him with loud acclaim. On a low rise in front of Schierling he met with Davout to plan the battle's second phase.

Meanwhile, an intense combat enveloped Eckmühl. The French needed the village and its bridge over the Laber in order to assault the Bettel Berg. Defending were two tough Peterwardeiner Grenzer battalions. Vandamme's divisional battery swept the main street. The Twelfth and Twenty-first Ligne assaulted the right, where the defenders stood sheltered by a line of poplars along the far bank (see Map 18). The Württembergers charged straight over the Eckmühl bridge. In perhaps their greatest martial display of the entire Napoleonic wars, they captured the village house by house. Confronting stiff resistance at a farm, they set it afire and forced the Austrians back to the shelter of a small chateau in the village center. Soon the central square leading to the chateau lay covered with blue and brown shapes of the fallen Württembergers and grenzers. Undaunted, the Württembergers stormed the gate and then the door and, with blood lust roused, shot and bayoneted all the defenders.

The sound of thundering hooves reverberated off Eckmühl's cobblestone main street. Brigadier Clément, a one-armed officer known armywide for his front-line leadership, had formed his troopers in obedience to Napoleon's orders to storm through Eckmühl. He led a final saber-wielding charge by the French Fifth Cuirassier Regiment over the bridge and through the main street to seal victory.[16] The grenzers lost 400 casualties in the village. Only remnants dodged to safety.[17] The Württemberg assault opened the way for an attack on the Bettel Berg.[18]

Marshal Lannes joined Napoleon to report the success at Eckmühl. Seeing events proceeding as planned, the Emperor was in a buoyant mood. Referring to the Eckmühl combat, he chided Lannes: "It's about time you took that shanty." Wiping the sweat from his face, Lannes replied that the village had been "stuffed with infantry who had held onto it like ringworm."[19] More soberly, Lannes added that the assault had cost him his chief of staff, General Cervoni.

At 5:30 P.M. personal tragedy had struck the marshal. While examining his maps outside Eckmühl, a cannonball bounded through the headquarters group. Down went Cervoni, an old Corsican colleague from the glory days in Italy, who had arrived just the day before from his homeland, eager to make another campaign. Groaning with pain, he died. When Lannes relayed this news to Napoleon, the latter replied: "Poor Cervoni! It had been a very long time since he had seen bullets; he will not be forgotten."[20] Napoleon directed that the parson from Schierling take charge of the body and then returned to his planning for the battle's second phase. Dismissed, Cervoni's search for glory was slaked at last.[21]

Lannes returned to his infantry to oversee their assault against the Rogging heights (see Map 18). The defenders, Bieber's brigade from the Austrian Third Corps, fought a poor fight. They could not help but be concerned with the action to their right and rear. They could see the French and Bavarians massing for an attack against the Bettel Berg and were aware that more fighting was occurring along their line of communications, the Eckmühl–Ratisbonne road. With sweaty palms Bieber's men clenched their muskets and looked downslope.

They saw French skirmishers, Gudin's men, spearheading the assault. The skirmishers advanced to the banks of the Laber and halted to await the support from the balance of the division. Suddenly a mounted French officer appeared. He urged them forward, claiming that before them was the key to the Hapsburg position. This was not so, but neither the voltigeurs nor the officer, Captain Jean Pelet—an aide-de-camp to Masséna who had found himself at loose ends and was determined to join the combat—realized it. Led by Pelet, the skirmishers quickly gained the wooded heights, where they met repeated but half-hearted counterattacks from Bieber's brigade.

The situation was never serious. Morand's division, marching in Gudin's wake, never even had to deploy—it was not needed. There was also an abundance of French leadership for this secondary fight. At one point Marshal Berthier arrived to steady the troops and to ensure that Napoleon's master plan progressed. Had the Austrians held elsewhere, this attack that gradually turned the Hapsburg left flank would have eventually levered Rosenberg's corps from its position. But events on the Bettel Berg made all that took place at Rogging irrelevant.

In the fields below the Bettel Berg the Bavarian and Württemberg cavalry prepared to charge again. One in five Bavarian horsemen had already fallen before the Austrian guns and fierce cavalry countercharges. Yet when Davout saw the Württemberg attack against Eckmühl he ordered them in once more. Only three squadrons charged; the others could not be coaxed forward. The heavy Austrian guns on the Bettel Berg reduced this half-hearted effort to red ruin. Inspired by gallant front-line leadership, again the Austrian cavalry swept forward to clear its gun line. Halfway downslope it saw a new enemy force. Parting the wave of fleeing Bavarian cavalry, advancing with implacable fury, came the shock arm of the French army, the "men of iron," the cuirassiers (see Map 18).

The capture of the Laber crossing points at Schierling and Eckmühl had allowed the two wings of the French army to link up. On the marshy ground at the foot of the Bettel Berg, Saint-Sulpice's and Nansouty's heavy cavalry deployed; eight regiments of cuirassiers and two of elite carabiniers, a formidable force of nearly 8000 troopers. As a united mass on a two-regiment front they charged the Bettel Berg. At their head trotted the one-armed Clément. Stirred by the imposing assault of the metal-clad warriors, French and Allied enthusiasm crested. Cheers of "Hurrah the cuirassiers!" echoed across the field.[22]

Most of the cuirassiers had already marched more than eighteen miles from Landshut. Now they had to make an uphill charge against a formidable enemy artillery. A participant, Nansouty's aide-de-camp, describes advancing through the bombardment: "We crossed the field where grass grew to our horses' chests and large furrows caused by the roundshot impeded our progress, spattering us with mud as the shot passed beneath our feet."[23]

The leading squadrons absorbed all the Austrian fire. The clang of canister striking the cuirassiers' armored breastplates sounded above the roar of the cannon.[24] The French heavy cavalry did not falter. To their rear came successive untouched regimental waves. The French troopers urged their jaded horses upward.

Their officers constantly called out to them to maintain their ranks.[25] They were not permitted to advance at more than a trot. Their solid ranks shed the fleeing Bavarians, who were forced to escape around the cuirassiers' flanks. Then, looking upslope they saw the oncoming Austrian light horse.

The Austrians did not present as imposing an appearance as earlier in the day. They had suffered from their previous charges; now there were gaps in their ranks. Many of the most aggressive had fallen, some troopers and horses carried wounds, all were tired.

Just before impact, the French officers primed their men: "*En avant! Marche! Marche!*"[26] Without changing gait, the rank and file took up the cheer. The collision was violent and brief. The cuirassiers bowled over the Austrian horse and suddenly were in amid the Hapsburg guns. They scattered the brown-clad Austrian gunners and captured the same guns the Bavarians had briefly seized during an earlier charge. There were no Austrian reserves to salvage the situation. The cuirassiers' charge clinched victory.

This final French cavalry charge placed the Hapsburg battery commanded by Lieutenant Zadrazill in great peril. Caught in the midst of a confused cavalry melee, Zadrazill struggled to displace his guns. In the end, the cavalry battery's superior mobility allowed it to escape, though not before many gunners were cut down and the lieutenant himself received multiple saber wounds. The heavier, less-mobile twelve-pound position guns did not escape. The French captured twelve pieces atop the Bettel Berg.

News of the combat on the Bettel Berg quickly spread through the Austrian Fourth Corps. General Somariva, having just blunted the French advance from Laichling, made a soldierly decision. In spite of the perils to his immediate front, he sent his battered and just reformed cavalry at the trot to restore the left flank (see Map 18). As a backstop, in case they failed, he formed an infantry brigade in mass to block the Eckmühl–Ratisbonne highway.[27]

A swirling cavalry action proceeded along the highway between Eckmühl and the Hohenberg. The Austrian cavalry charged repeatedly to try to check the pursuit. But small-unit tactics were breaking down amid the strain of combat. A Hungarian lieutenant colonel, ordered to hold four hussar squadrons in reserve to cover the charging Vincent Chevaulégers and Stipsicz Hussars, disobeyed orders when he saw a mass of French cavalry advancing from Laichling. He led a brave but foolish counterattack that was ground up by overwhelming French numbers.

The Bavarian and Württemberg cavalry supported the French horse and charged again. This time they scattered the combat-worn Vincent and Stipcisz Regiments. Rosenberg and his officers, many covered with blood from their wounds or riding wounded horses, vainly tried to rally the Hapsburg horse. They failed. The three-hour battle of Eckmühl was over.

Meanwhile, on the opposite flank between Abbach and the Peising plateau, Karl's offensive had also ended. Before any of the three offensive columns came to grips with the French, Karl learned of Napoleon's maneuver against Eckmühl. Immediately he canceled his attack orders and commanded his men to retire. His abortive offensive had been a sad performance. Whether he could conduct a retreat in the face of the hard-charging, victorious French remained to be seen. For starters, he ordered Rosenberg to get out of his predicament as best he could, which was a shame, because the Fourth Corps deserved better support.

The corps had fought a hard battle against vastly superior enemy forces. It had been aided by favorable terrain that concealed the Austrian reserves. While in fact Rosenberg had been forced to commit his tactical reserves very early in the struggle, neither Davout nor his subordinates knew this. They worried that the wooded, hilly terrain concealed the bulk of Karl's army. This misapprehension induced caution and permitted the battered Fourth Corps to withdraw. During the battle it lost eleven officers and 415 men killed and fifty-six and 2457 wounded, respectively.[28]

On the French side many units had also fought well. The official battle report singled out only one regiment for special mention, Berthezène's Tenth Légère. It had, in the words of the army bulletin, "covered itself with glory."[29]

A battle had been won; the French pursuit remained.

CHAPTER IX

The Scale of Victory

The French soldier is indefatigable whenever he pursues a retreating enemy. He is capable of marching ten to twelve leagues a day and fighting for two or three hours in the evening.

Pursuit

The set-piece battle of Eckmühl ended when the French heavy cavalry penetrated the Austrian center on the Bettel Berg, Lannes turned its left at Rogging, and Davout outflanked its right along the Laichling heights. With only a few hours of daylight remaining, the task at hand for the French army was to see if it could convert an ordinary victory into something more. Organizing a victorious army for pursuit is a difficult military problem, perhaps exceeded only by the difficulties of organizing a vanquished army's rear guard. The French high command set to the former task with enthusiasm and skill; the latter task the Austrian command tackled out of dire need.

Napoleon improvised a simple plan for pursuit: The cavalry would attack along the Eckmühl road toward Ratisbonne; Lannes would advance along the east of the highway while Davout moved along its western side (see Map 19). The terrain favored the French. Once they traversed the wooded country in the immediate area of the battlefield fairly open terrain stretched all the way to Ratisbonne.

On the French right Lannes encountered the least opposition. Earlier the marshal's attack against the Rogging heights had enjoyed a considerable numerical advantage. Now, after piercing the crust of the Austrian defense, the French infantry formed column, Gudin still in the van, and chased

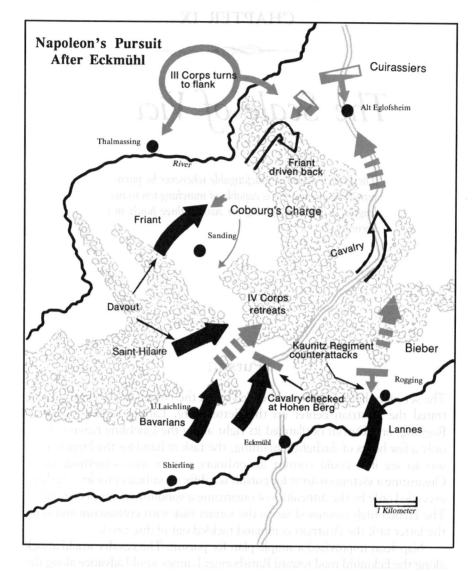

Napoleon's Pursuit After Eckmühl

III Corps turns to flank

Cuirassiers

Alt Eglofsheim

Thalmassing

River

Friant driven back

Cobourg's Charge

Friant

Sanding

Cavalry

Davout

IV Corps retreats

Saint-Hilaire

Kaunitz Regiment counterattacks

Bieber

Rogging

U.Laichling

Cavalry checked at Hohen Berg

Bavarians

Lannes

Eckmühl

Shierling

1 Kilometer

Bieber's brigade back toward Alt Eglofsheim. When the spirited Colonel Luxen's Kaunitz Infantry Regiment, the unit that had shown superb fighting zeal along the Teugen–Hausen ridge on the nineteenth, turned to face Gudin, the French received a brief check (see Map 19). The regiment's good service enabled the Hapsburgs to escape with only moderate loss. However, after besting the Kaunitz Regiment, the pursuit took on more of the character of a hunt than a contested rear-guard action. Morand's division never engaged; it merely continued to follow Gudin's warriors. During the advance Lannes' men collected small groups of dispirited Austrians, sending them to the rear to join the steadily mounting numbers of prisoners. The ease of the French advance along this front energized Lannes. Full of optimism, he departed to attend Napoleon's fateful council of war.

Meanwhile, in the center the French advance faced greater difficulties. Through his quick response to the French breakthrough on the Eckmühl–Ratisbonne highway, an unnamed Austrian battery commander created the first roadblock to Napoleon's plan. Riding with his guns for two miles along the main road, the artillery officer came to a place where the highway ascended steeply toward a forest. Climbing this road, he moved his unit to the left onto the heights of the Hohen Berg (see Map 19). The battery horses were unlimbered and retired behind the battery's position. Using handspikes and dragropes, the gunners feverishly strained to push the battery into firing position. The spongemen dipped sponges into buckets of water to swab out the barrels, begrimed by hard use on the Bettel Berg. The loaders hurried to place new rounds in the bores as the spongemen reversed their staffs to use the rammers to push the shot home. Simultaneously, the ventsmen cleared the vents, inserting firing tubes into the cartridges. Two men worked the levers in the trail to aim each piece at the approaching cavalry in the valley below. In less than a minute the battery opened fire, checking the immediate pursuit of the cavalry and in so doing allowing the Stipsicz Hussars and Vincent Chevaulégers to regroup. The first link in the chain of the Austrian rear guard had been forged.

Seeing the Hapsburg resistance begin to coalesce, Prince Rosenberg sent his chief of staff to direct the retiring infantry of the Fourth Corps through the woods behind the Hohen Berg toward Alt Eglofsheim and safety. The rallied cavalry marched along the side of the road. No wild rout here; instead the retreat began to assume form and purpose. Having permitted all of this, the heroic battery limbered up and retired to the next rear-guard position near Alt Eglofsheim.

The tired French horse continued the pursuit, their activity stimulated by the presence of the Emperor, who rode close to the van. The toiling foot soldiers marched in the cavalry's rear, collecting wounded and dazed Austrians unable to join the retreat. Eventually the French infantry would reach Alt Eglofsheim at 9:00 P.M., too late for the impending combat. When French scouts reported another Austrian line forming ahead, the cavalry rode forward to attack it alone.

Simultaneous with the advance of the right and center, the third and leftmost prong of Napoleon's pursuit, Davout's corps, set off. Having overcome stout opposition along the Laichling heights, the marshal quickly regrouped his weary men, directing them toward Luckenpoint and Thalmassing (see Map 19). By threatening the Austrian Third Corps' flank, Davout triggered one of a series of desperate countermeasures designed to seal off the French breakthrough before it could penetrate into the bowels of the Austrian army.

Prince Hohenzollern, commander of the Austrian Third Corps, had occupied the majority of the day in frustrating inactivity. Assigned the leftmost column in Karl's planned attack against Davout, Hohenzollern's troops had spent the day in light skirmishing. This no doubt disappointed the prince, whom Karl considered one of his better subordinates. His Third Corps faced west throughout the day until late in the afternoon the uproar to the south, around Eckmühl, became noticeable. Shortly thereafter, Hohenzollern learned that Karl had canceled all offensive plans until the situation clarified at Eckmühl. The prince grew increasingly apprehensive about his left flank as signs of a growing defeat became evident. First wagons and rear-area camp followers began their exodus from the battle front. Then walking wounded and ambulances carrying the badly injured hastened by. Soon the movement along his rear increased as entire battalions, batteries, and squadrons joined in the retreat toward Thalmassing, Alt Eglofsheim, and presumed safety. To Hohenzollern's trained eye, this movement indicated a considerable defeat. With several hours of daylight remaining and the left flank and rear endangered, the prince's task became one of extricating his men from the mounting disorder.

On his own initiative, Hohenzollern sent two battalions to occupy a dominating crestline in front of Thalmassing to protect the left flank in order to cover the withdrawal of the rest of his corps (see Map 19). This position overlooked the area of Davout's advancing French. Simultaneously, Austrian headquarters came alive to Davout's threat. It directed Prince Hohenzollern to send a brigade to occupy the woods between Alt Eglofsheim and Neu Eglofsheim. The brigade, accompanied by the Erzerhog Ferdinand hussars, would defend the highway leading to Alt Eglofsheim. However, the pace of events caught up with this commendable plan. Before the Austrians could take up their new positions, Friant's hard-fighting division appeared.

When Friant had captured the woods near Sanding he perceived he had outflanked the Austrian crestline position.[1] He received orders from Davout to pursue and to assist Montbrun around Sanding. The Bavarians could be trusted to protect his right in the Laichling area; any danger would come from the left. Consequently Friant carefully arranged his units: the light artillery at the front; the Thirty-third in column on the right; the Fifteenth deployed to attack a small copse near Sanding that apparently concealed two Austrian battalions; the Forty-eighth on the exposed left flank in square, the 111th in column to its rear; the 108th in column in the middle rear of the division; and the divisional battery behind the Fifteenth to support its attack. This was a judicious deployment, with particular weight on the left flank to face any unknown dangers.

Initially Friant gained ground easily, chasing the beleaguered Hapsburgs over a mile until reaching the extensive woods between Thalmassing and Alt Eglofsheim (see Map 19). Unknown to the French, this was the position the Austrian command had chosen to deploy the Third Corps as a rear guard, but it had not arrived yet. Shielded from French view, the rear-guard infantry brigade halted as it neared the woods. Its officers were dismayed to see enemy skirmishers nearing the key terrain. Without waiting for orders, Colonel Prince Cobourg formed four squadrons of the Erzerhog Ferdinand Hussars and charged the skirmishers. Typical of most Austrian cavalry actions during the campaign, the prince performed this maneuver on his own initiative. Less typically, it achieved a measure of success.

The sudden charge drove in the French voltigeurs. The brunt of the attack fell upon the Thirty-third and 111th as they emerged from the woods into a plain near Sanding (see Map 19). Warned by the skirmishers, the columns quickly formed square. Exhorted by its colonel, the Thirty-third prepared to receive the charge. As the French report of the next day was to say: "The same soldiers who had continually repulsed the Austrian infantry on the 19th and 21st received the cavalry with the calmness and character that assures success."[2] Waiting until the enemy drew within pistol range, the steady infantry began platoon volleys that forced the cavalry to retire at the gallop. Although repulsed, the hussars' impetuous charge gained badly needed time for the rear guard to complete its march into the woods and prepare a defense. Thus, by momentarily checking Friant's pursuit, Prince Cobourg performed a valuable service for the entire Austrian Third Corps. Another link in the growing chain of resistance had been forged.

As Friant's division toiled across the rolling terrain around Sanding, its sister division paralleled its advance. The difficult fighting along the Laichling heights had somewhat disorganized Saint-Hilaire's division. According to Saint-Hilaire, "the ardor of our troops augmented by the precipitous retreat of the enemy caused our regiments not to lack in vigor for the pursuit."[3] In fact, the French plunged out of control, with the voltigeur companies spearheading the chase. They paid for this behavior when four squadrons of Vincent chevaulégers (who had been steadily falling back from the French advance) counterattacked and sabered many of the scattered light infantry. The divisional commander, accompanied by his staff, hurried forward to the front ranks "to moderate the men's ardor and rally the regiments."[4] Having restored order, Saint-Hilaire formed the men into columns by regiment and set off to pursue again.

These new dispositions proved time-consuming, being hampered by the convergence of the division with other French and Bavarian troops advancing along the main highway. When Saint-Hilaire's division did resume its advance, a squadron of the Eighth Hussars supported by several Bavarian squadrons scouted in the van. This insufficient screen could not repel the aggressive enemy cavalry. The Austrians bluffed repeated charges, which forced the French to halt and form square. During one of these demonstrations Saint-Hilaire saw a menacing movement along the heights in front of his lead columns. In the growing shadows he rode forward to investigate and arrived to witness Prince Cobourg's previously described charge against Friant. Spurring his horse, the extremely competent Saint-Hilaire gave another demonstration of tactical ability that would soon earn him the promise of a marshal's baton from the Emperor.

After checking Friant, Cobourg had turned his attention to Saint-Hilaire (see Map 19). Cobourg's hussars charged and overwhelmed the outnumbered French hussars operating in Saint-Hilaire's van. Saint-Hilaire saw the French hussars ride back in disorder. He shouted to a horse artillery battery to gallop forward and deploy on a small rise. When the charging Hapsburgs closed to 200 paces, he ordered his infantry to deploy in line and advance while sounding the quick charge. The infantry ran the last few paces to the crestline, where they joined the horse guns. Together they confronted the Hapsburg hussars at point-blank range. The infantry's unorthodox maneuver caused the Austrian cavalry to halt in surprise. The shock of going from a victorious pursuit against scattered cavalry to facing a charging line of infantry proved too much. They wheeled to their right and galloped off toward Friant's division, accompanied by well-aimed shots from the French horse artillery. For the French, a potentially serious counterattack had been coolly dispatched.

Although Friant and Saint-Hilaire again advanced, progress was limited as their men continually halted to repel threatening cavalry. Nonetheless, Davout's men eventually managed to stumble through their fatigue to the outskirts of Thalmassing, where they camped for the night. Later, they learned that their persistent gallantry on this day and throughout the campaign had earned for their marshal the title Prince of Eckmühl. These and other honors were to come. On the night of the twenty-second, Friant's and Saint-Hilaire's men settled into weary bivouac, grateful to rest at last.

While the running skirmish between the Austrian horse and Davout occurred, Hohenzollern's Third Corps temporarily occupied the hill in front of Thalmassing. Seemingly secure on this front, Hohenzollern resolved to continue the Austrian defense along the Pfater Bach, a small stream north of Alt Eglofsheim that cut across the line of the French advance. Toward this end, he ordered the Austrian grenadiers to withdraw behind the stream. However, with French cavalry already hounding the heels of the Austrians who were retiring along the main Eckmühl–Ratisbonne highway, another rear-guard action would have to be fought to cover the establishment of the new defense position. The prince designated the cuirassier brigade of the Second Reserve

Corps for this task (see Map 19). Its deployment in front of the small village of Alt Eglofsheim precipitated the largest cavalry confrontation of the campaign.

Moonlit Combat

Alt Eglofsheim lay along one of a series of low ridges perpendicular to the Eckmühl–Ratisbonne highway. These gentle rises ran like steps from the village to the dominating terrain of the Hohen Berg. In front of the village on the eastern side of the highway, General Schneller deployed his cuirassiers in a position to challenge the French pursuit. Portions of the Fourth Corps infantry had already filed back along the road toward Ratisbonne in fair order when the ubiquitous Stutterheim, whose alert conduct had greatly aided the Austrian defense earlier in the day, appeared to add his light cavalry to the rear guard. While the cuirassiers had been only lightly engaged during the day, the arriving light cavalry was badly diminished from the furious fighting at Eckmühl. The Vincent Chevaulégers had already lost 150 men and nine officers. Nonetheless, the light cavalry dutifully deployed to support its heavy compatriots.

Theoretically, the Austrians should have numbered over 5000 sabers in some thirty squadrons, but the actual strength is estimated by Stutterheim to have totaled only 2000. Six squadrons of the Gottesheim Cuirassiers anchored the first line, while on their left stood eight squadrons of Stipsicz Hussars and two very weak squadrons of Ferdinand Hussars (see Map 20). Arrayed in a second supporting line ranked six squadrons of the Kaiser Cuirassiers next to eight of the Vincent Chevaulégers. To the right of this mass of horsemen stood at least twelve six-pound cavalry guns positioned to block the highway while another battery supported the left flank. Thus stood the mounted rear guard at 7:00 P.M. as the French pursuit began to debouch from the direction of Eckmühl.

Light from a rising moon reflected off the metal-encased Gallic warriors as two masses of French cavalry, who had advanced steadily up the highway since the roadblock on the Hohen Berg had been overcome, maneuvered to confront the Austrians. One column defiled from the main road near Hagerstadt; the other advanced along the open terrain to the right of the road (see Map 20). Where were the cavalry marshals to lead this host who were about to launch the most massive charge since Murat committed the cavalry reserve at Eylau in 1807? With Murat intriguing away in Naples and Bessières pursuing Hiller near Landshut the command devolved upon General Nansouty, and he welcomed the opportunity.

General Étienne-Marie-Antoine Champion, comte de Nansouty, had

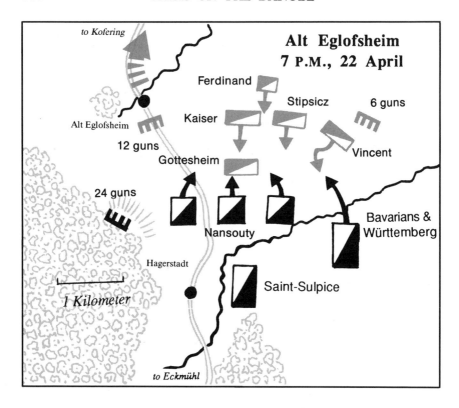

Alt Eglofsheim
7 P.M., 22 April

served in the French mounted arm since 1785. Promoted to general in 1799, he had led a cuirassier division since 1805, seeing action at Ulm, Austerlitz, Golymin, Eylau, and Friedland. A tough general who reputedly snapped at the meddling Emperor on another occasion "It is not your Majesty at any rate who can teach me to lead cavalry,"[5] he now led an independent command with the opportunity to make good his boast.

His force totaled some sixty-six squadrons with 6000 sabers. A regiment of carabiniers flanked by two of cuirassiers formed his first line with the remainder of his division providing a second, supporting line (see Map 20). All of these deployed in line while to their rear Saint-Sulpice's division stood in compact columns. German allied light cavalry supported the right, including six fresh Bavarian and about twenty jaded Bavarian and Württemberg squadrons. The horse artillery, three French and one Bavarian battery, trotted through the intervals, taking position on the forward slopes of the Eichel Berg.

Shortly after 7:00 P.M., in the growing darkness Austrian light artillery opened fire on the French cavalry masses as they completed their battle array. Nansouty's gunners returned the salute from the heights. Both engaged well within effective range: 700 yards for the French four-pounders, 500 for the lighter Austrian pieces. Working rapidly, the crews fired two rounds per minute. The rain-soaked earth greatly reduced the artillery's effectiveness by absorbing the impact of the round shot. When the French drew closer the Hapsburg gunners switched to canister while the French artillery fell silent, their target now masked. Nansouty's men braced for the expected continuous hail of canister, knowing if they continued into lethal short range they would suffer dearly. Instead the Austrian fire ceased. Rumbling through the gloom came Schneller's countercharging cuirassiers.

A single regiment advanced, the Gottesheim Cuirassiers led by Colonel Roussel (see Map 20). This brave French emigré officer sought to avenge his king, an activity assiduously pursued on numerous fields since 1793. Now, seeing the French still advancing at a walk (the French horses were badly tired from having covered over thirty miles since dawn) the colonel ordered his trumpeter to sound the charge. The Austrian troopers, many mounted on poorly trained horses, nervously strove to maintain formation as they spurred their chargers forward. The Gottesheims drew within a hundred yards, not failing to notice that the more numerous French overlapped their line on both flanks. Steeped in a long tradition of mounted-fire action, the opposing French center regiment of carabiniers aimed their carbines. At forty paces they fired a volley into the faces of the charging Hapsburg troopers. Replacing their firearms, the carabiniers drew swords and charged. Simultaneously, the order rang out to the French cuirassiers on either flank: "Squadron! Trot! March!"[6] The French line advanced. The physical pressure exerted by troopers riding knee-to-knee on giant Flemish and Norman horses ensured a proper alignment. The biggest troopers rode in the center. Only their superior strength, aided by high, stiff riding boots, kept them from being squeezed out of the formation. The supporting French second line conformed to the advance.

The Gottesheim Regiment, despite being stunned by the volley, closed impetuously. Galloping Austrian met trotting Frenchman with an impact heard across the field. When the two lines collided to a standstill all firing ceased. A French participant heard

the horrible working of *l'arme blanche*, its sabers echoing on the helmets and cuirasses like a hammer on an anvil, the shrill of the trumpets, the frightful cries of the combatants. . . . Iron clashed against iron, causing numerous sparks, which shone in the midst of the darkness. Soon the moon rose, lighting this terrible and imposing scene. The Austrian cuirassiers, protected only in front, received great losses yet all displayed the highest bravery. In this melee, where man fought against man, the Austrians received cruel wounds in the back and kidneys, without being able to avenge themselves; our cavalry, completely protected, could without fear deliver their blows. There was decided at last a question debated in the cavalry about the necessity of the double cuirass. [7]

As individual contests of sword-wielding skill continued, the opposing horseman's view narrowed to his immediate front. Adjacent events passed in a blur. Soon, however, Austrian troopers on the outside of the formation realized they faced multiple opponents, since the crescent-shaped French formation overlapped the Gottesheim's flanks. From outside the formation, single outnumbered Austrians fled. The contagion of defeat accelerated inward as, first by twos and threes and then by entire groups, the Gottesheim Regiment broke to the rear. Hapsburg gallantry and momentum proved less important than tactical finesse in this initial encounter. However, immediate help was at hand as reinforcements thundered to the fore.

Into the confused fighting charged the Kaiser cuirassier regiment, with the Stipsicz Hussars supporting its flank (see Map 20). The Austrian cuirassiers stabilized the situation along the front while the hussars gained some success when they momentarily chased down the disordered first rank of French troopers. Before the Austrians could further penetrate the French line, Nansouty's second line surged forward and the melee again became general. Meanwhile, the Vincent Chevaulégers calmly maneuvered to seek a flank position, hoping to take Nansouty's entire division along its vulnerable side. But the brash Frenchman had prepared for such a threat through his wise initial deployment. The Bavarian and Württemberg light cavalry counter-charged the chevaulégers, thus preserving Nansouty's threatened flank.

No fewer than seventy squadrons now engaged in a titanic moonlit combat. In the center, the second line of French cuirassiers drove their huge chargers into the intervals between the smaller Hapsburg horse. Each French swordsman could fight confident in the knowledge his sides and rear were protected by friends, while each outnumbered Austrian had to parry in all directions. Turning to confront one opponent, the Austrian troopers left an exposed back to a second enemy. In this unfortunate situation they paid the price for having only a front cuirass.

Seeing the fortunes of battle shifting against his compatriots, the Austrian major Devay (the same officer who, in late morning, had led the first cavalry charge at Ober-Deggenbach to start the battle) led the last reserve of two squadrons of Ferdinand Hussars into the fray (see Map 20). Protected by this final charge, the majority of the Austrians broke and ran. Amid indescribable confusion they galloped toward Alt Eglofsheim and the safety of the highway running back to Ratisbonne. Losing all cohesion in the jam-up on the highway, the Austrians dribbled casualties and prisoners. An Austrian eyewitness describes the scene: "Surrounding the Austrians on the road were the French cuirassiers; we gave blows with our sabers to the right and left, in front, and behind; the noise, the confusion, the disorder, were overwhelming."[8] Here General Schneller received a wound while General Stutterheim narrowly avoided capture when surrounded by French cuirassiers. His safety was due to the gallant Sergeant Petitipas of the Vincent Chevaulégers, who hewed an avenue of escape for his beleaguered leader.

Soon the Austrian's fresher horses outdistanced the blown French, and they escaped toward Kofering. The entire action ended before Saint-Sulpice's supporting cuirassier division engaged; thus the combat probably lasted less than ten minutes. The French claimed 300 prisoners taken on the field. Pelet, who watched the combat from the French artillery position, later wrote that the Austrians suffered thirteen and eight times more killed and wounded, respectively, than the French.

The Austrian choice of the Alt Eglofsheim position deserves censure. It provided few advantages and certainly was weaker than the Pfater Bach position only two miles farther back. Furthermore, the Austrians failed to incorporate all available cavalry units in the area into the rear guard. Schneller's piecemeal commitment of his regiments was a tactical error. Outnumbered as they were, the best Austrian chance was to charge with all units against the head of the French columns before they could deploy. Once this opportunity passed, a defensive stance waiting for the French to cross the intervening terrain offered the maximum advantage to the enfilading Hapsburg artillery. Schneller's actual tactical choice represents a third, and exceedingly poor, alternative. Nonetheless, although the Austrian horse was smashed on the battlefield, they succeeded in their goal of slowing the French pursuit. The majority of the army hurried onward to the comforting walls of Ratisbonne unhindered by further French charges.

Conference of War

At 9:00 P.M. an elated Napoleon arrived on the field at Alt Eglofsheim to review briefly the Württemberg light horse as it reorganized. Perhaps he reflected on how yet again his Germanic allies had performed valuable service. Perhaps he recalled Nansouty's bravado and how the cuirassier leader justified his lofty self-opinion with his flawless battlefield tactics. Much had been accomplished on this the fourth day of running battles. However, again Karl's main body eluded the Emperor's grasp. Although the compilation of reports and returns would show Eckmühl and the subsequent pursuit a notable French success, a realistic appraisal might indicate the French had merely, again, mauled an unsupported Austrian corps. Could something more be made of this victory? Napoleon prepared to consider this question.

First he completed the unfinished business with the Württemberg cavalry. Complimenting their behavior he dispatched them on a further nocturnal mission, their objective Straubing (see Map 16). Specifically they were to capture the bridge across the Danube at that town. Wishing to retain all options, the Emperor saw this bridge as a position to turn the presumed location of Karl's main body when it retired toward Ratisbonne. And so, having covered at least thirty-five miles already this day, the Württembergers set off to ride another twenty to the Danube bridge. They did not know the Austrian high command was also thinking of Straubing that night, having dispatched their own much-fresher cavalry to attend to it.

As the Württemberg light horse rode off into the darkness, Napoleon summoned his marshals for a conference. This action again subtly reveals he was not quite the man he had once been. Earlier in his career he met with his subordinates to tell them what he expected. At his other memorable campaigns—in Italy, Germany, and Poland—this man of action directed and shaped events, seldom if ever plagued by the self-doubt and indecisiveness that weakened others. Now, in the wake of his cavalry who had just overthrown the last apparent formed Hapsburg resistance, he gathered his marshals, not to dictate but to solicit their opinions as to what should be done next.

A glittering entourage of famous names and talents participated in the discussion, including the marshals Berthier, Lefebvre, Lannes, and Masséna. In a battlefield decision the opinion of the first of these mattered little. Although chief of staff and recent acting army commander, in the presence of the Emperor Berthier resumed the role he seemed born for and fulfilled so admirably, that of a clerk par excellence. Similarly, though for different reasons, the second marshal's views also were overshadowed. With his Corsican memory for past services, Napoleon continued to bestow honors upon Lefebvre. However, in Spain the year before the Marshal had given a vivid demonstration of his strategic incapacity. Lefebvre was a good comrade, but not the man to listen to when important decisions were at hand. Napoleon wished to hear the views of only two men: Lannes, the brilliant Gascon who was his friend, and Masséna, a general with whom the Emperor had experienced a rocky history but whose ability and judgment he respected.

The younger Lannes, having watched his corps chase the Austrians with relative ease for the last three days, arrived full of optimism. When Napoleon asked his advice, the ex-grenadier fervently counseled immediate continued pursuit. With the French cavalry spearheading the effort, Lannes proposed to advance all the way to the Danube that very evening. Such an action would capitalize on the Austrian disorder. Such an action would end the war beneath the walls of Ratisbonne. Having heard from the Gascon firebrand, the Emperor turned to listen to the wisdom of the older Masséna.

Masséna began by pointing out the extreme fatigue of the soldiers. They had marched more than twenty miles since dawn, fought a battle, then continued until nightfall. There had been little opportunity for rest during the past three days. In addition, a further advance would lead into the middle of an unknown Austrian host, since the victory today had involved only one wing of Karl's army. The Austrians had demonstrated an uncharacteristic persistence. Night combat was frought with hazard and uncertainty, the Duke of Rivoli emphasized, with gains seldom justified by losses incurred. Finally, he concluded, Ratisbonne offered shelter to the Austrians. A retreating army would gather behind its walls and rebuff any French pursuit. Berthier and Lefebvre seconded Masséna, stressing the army's exhaustion and hunger. The Emperor listened to these divergent opinions and decided on a course of action—or rather the course of inaction. The army would halt in place and camp for the night.

Across the span of history this decision can easily be criticized. One French commentator believed the French failure to continue the pursuit demonstrates the loss of stamina of the French army caused by its increasing dilution with conscripts. Another analyst defends Napoleon's decision on the basis that his troops were indeed extremely worn; neither Oudinot's nor Masséna's corps had reached the battle front; and 50,000 undefeated Austrians lay between the French and Ratisbonne. This line of reasoning certainly has merit, particularly advanced on the field by as able a general as Masséna. And yet one wonders when recalling the experience of the brief pursuit that did occur immediately following the French victory at Alt Eglofsheim. In defeat and retreat panic is infectious, but this panic was not fully promoted by aggressive French action.

Speculation aside, undoubtedly the French troops in the area of Alt Eglofsheim and Kofering greeted their leaders' decision with approbation. At last their needs for food and rest could be met. But, as always, the decisions by the high command required time to filter down to the rank and file most directly concerned. Thus for a while the pursuing French cavalry continued its chase along the Ratisbonne highway.

When the cavalry combat at Alt Eglofsheim began, the Austrian artillery, no longer able to contribute usefully, displaced and hurried down the highway toward Ratisbonne. There they encountered GM Kayser's Austrian brigade of the Third Corps retiring toward Kofering. News of the nearness of the French cavalry distressed Kayser's men, so they tried to accelerate their march. In the confusion, the brigade's artillery battery mistakenly entered a side road while fumbling about in the dark. It was later overrun by the French pursuit, losing four guns.

Thus unencumbered, Kayser reached the Kofering defile where he passed a Major Hager of the First Reserve Corps forming his grenadiers into square. His men were among the elite of the army but had yet to fire a shot in the campaign. As the infantry and artillery cleared his front, Hager heard the sounds of pounding hooves. The grenadiers presented arms in preparation when they saw cavalry rapidly advancing upon them. White coats, visible in the dark, identified the unit as friends. The routing cavalry passed by in small groups. They were Schneller's men, riding hard from Alt Eglofsheim, shouting that the French were close behind. Under cover of the flying Hapsburg horsemen, the French cavalry approached. Seeing the tightly formed mass of infantry, the French charged. One ineffectual volley from the grenadiers, greatly hindered since the target was intermixed with friendly riders, failed to arrest them. The French galloped the square, scattering the grenadiers into the darkness. They sabered some, took even more prisoners, and in total subtracted 200 men from the muster rolls of Major Hager's battalion.

Having crushed the Fourth Corps at Eckmühl, defeated the cavalry rear guard at Alt Eglofsheim, and now scattered the infantry rear guard at Kofering, the French pursuit threatened to sweep all the way to the gates of Ratisbonne. Fortunately for the Austrians, reinforcements arrived. The Austrian command clearly was not losing its head in the face of adversity, as so many of Napoleon's opponents were wont to do. The opportune arrival of fresh troops was a consequence of a far-sighted decision made hours earlier by the commander of the First Reserve Corps.

When Prince Johannes Liechtenstein canceled his offensive movement upon receipt of Karl's order, the veteran corps commander set his cavalry in motion toward the threatened sector near Eckmühl. This commendable battlefield reaction now bore fruit as his advanced riders spotted the pursuing French between Kofering and Ober-Traubling. Liechtenstein ordered the regiment at the head of the column, the Erzherzog Albert Cuirassiers, to deploy on some rising ground overlooking the Ratisbonne highway. Once deployed, the cuirassiers were to charge.

The strung-out, tired French horsemen saw the Austrians silhouetted against the skyline. They gamely tried to face the flank to confront this hostile mass but, despite hoarse cries from their officers, the French proved slow to form. The Austrian leader hurled the Erzherzog Albert Cuirassiers downslope. Facing fresh opponents who had materialized like an apparition on their flank, the French broke and ran. The pursuit ended. Full darkness arrived.

Although direct French pressure had ceased, confusion and near-panic continued in certain Austrian formations. This was illustrated by the nocturnal adventure of Colonel Gueheneux, one of Marshal Lannes' aides-de-camp. Carrying orders for the marshal, Gueheneux found himself surrounded by a regiment of Austrian infantry who had wandered into the middle of the French bivouacs. The Austrian colonel, fatigued by his struggle to lead his men to safety, said: "You were my prisoner, I am now yours."[9] Although no doubt surprised by the turn of events, the Frenchman proceeded to escort the Austrians to the rear, where they contributed to the swelling numbers of prisoners.

A final and altogether different testimony to Austrian behavior on this day is provided by the last actions of the Stipsicz and Ferdinand hussars. Although twice defeated and driven from the field during the day, Stutterheim managed to rally 500 men at Berg Weinting, north of Ober-Traubling. Here, on a third field, they stoutly joined other cavalry and prepared to check any further French pursuit. Shielded by this cavalry screen, Hapsburg infantry began to dribble in to join the ranks of the unbroken regiments. Even Bieber's isolated brigade, having faced Lannes single-handed at Rogging, managed to fight its way clear through the woods north of Eckmühl. Soon the entire mass stirred and trudged wearily back toward Ratisbonne.

Napoleon at Abensberg reviewing his German allies, 20 April.

French cuirassiers drive back Austrian cuirassiers at Alt Eglofsheim,
22 April.

Stone bridge at Ratisbonne. Note massive ice breakers at base of pier.

The Laber at Rottenberg. Here Vincent tried to delay the French pursuit on 21 April.

Mouton's bridge at Landshut. Austrian musketeers manned the buildings on far shore.

The hanging woods overlooking O. Laichling. The 10th Lègére's assault penetrated these woods.

Lannes seizes a scaling ladder for the assault on Ratisbonne as his aides hasten forward.

Marbot lends a hand to Labedoyere on the walls of Ratisbonne.

The Württemberg Light Infantry charged over this bridge at Eckmühl.

From Austrian position. Friant attacked through woods in distance, advanced across plain to O. Laichling in foreground.

View from Bettel Berg toward Eckmühl. Up this slope charged the cuirassiers.

CHAPTER X

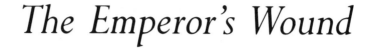

The Emperor's Wound

You know what words can do to soldiers.

To Cross the Danube

Despite Napoleon's decision to halt the army in place for the night there was one more night-time drama to be played out: the race to the Danube bridge at Straubing. The French entry, the Württemberg light cavalry (comprising four squadrons of the König and two of the Duc Louis chasseurs), departed Alt Eglofsheim at 9:00 P.M. They found the route to Straubing choked with Austrian stragglers and rear-element impedimenta. While these provided many tempting targets to cavalry assigned a pursuit role, the Württembergers had more serious business at hand: First, to determine if the Austrian army was retreating only on the route to Ratisbonne or was also using the road to Straubing; second, to determine the status of the Danube bridge at Straubing. The bridge provided a potential key to outflanking a fortified Hapsburg defense based on Ratisbonne. Furthermore, since the bridge lay between Ratisbonne and Vienna, the position offered the possibility of intercepting an Austrian retreat along the river's north bank. By advancing through Straubing, Napoleon could place his army between Karl and his capital.

Although the Württemberg brigadier general von Stettner, did not know it, the route to Straubing was clear of any formed enemy units. With the Hapsburg high command preoccupied directing the flood of troop movement on the Ratisbonne highway, little attention was given to the important Straubing road. Nonetheless, FZM Kollowrath dispatched a force to the town. Its

188

mission was to ensure the destruction of the bridge. Its composition: one squadron of the Riesch dragoons.

Closing in on the same objective, the rival cavalries experienced very different fates. Von Stettner led his troopers over the Pfater Bach toward Straubing. Although the men's extreme fatigue prevented them from reaching the town during the night, Stettner was able to inform the Emperor that the Archduke was not retiring in this direction. The hapless Austrian dragoons accomplished rather less. Stumbling about in the dark on rear-area roads filled with a constant stream of traffic heading toward Ratisbonne, they went astray. The dragoons eventually wandered into the midst of the French bivouacs, where they were taken prisoner.

While the Württemberg light horse scouted toward the Danube, Napoleon retired for the evening in Alt Eglofsheim. For the second time in three days he occupied quarters where the Archduke had slept the night before. How much rest he received is questionable; during the night a fire set by looters swept the village, forcing him to relocate to a tent in an adjacent field. The fire, coupled with the need to analyze reports and send orders, kept Napoleon awake most of the night. His army camped in a circle roughly centered on imperial headquarters. Three miles away Davout's men rested at Ober-Sanding (see Map 21). Four corps camped between Eckmühl and Alt Eglofsheim: Lefebvre's Bavarians, Lannes', and the hard-marching soldiers of Masséna's and Oudinot's, who arrived after midnight. The heavy cavalry massed along the Ratisbonne highway while the light cavalry extended toward Straubing. Montbrun remained around Abbach and Peising. Thus, with the exception of Bessières, who continued to pursue Hiller, the Emperor had a well-concentrated though tired force.

After receiving the report of General von Stettner about the open route to Straubing, Napoleon reviewed his outposts' reports to plan for the twenty-third. A report from Davout informed him that Karl seemed to be in full retreat on Davout's front. Scouts reported that, although the Austrians still lined the Pfater Bach, they would not hold there. Therefore Napoleon ordered everyone except Masséna to march directly on Ratisbonne. He assigned Masséna's corps the important task of seizing the Straubing bridge and intercepting Austrian baggage and troops who might retreat along either bank of the Danube. Marshal Bessières would continue his pursuit of Hiller. All would begin at daybreak. The Emperor planned to couple frontal pressure with Masséna's outflanking move. Whether Karl would hazard a battle at Ratisbonne remained to be seen.

The Archduke Karl reached Ratisbonne before midnight on the twenty-second. There he fell victim to one of the wild mood changes so characteristic of this man. Under the weight of profound depression, he contemplated the

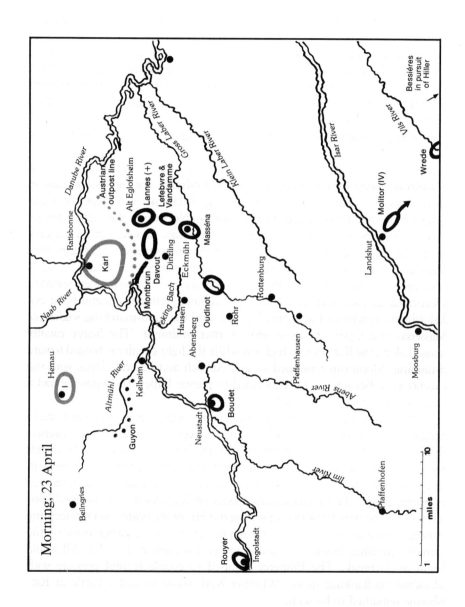

retreat of his entire army—or at least those portions he could still control, since Hiller was essentially on his own. Thinking it over, Karl favored a withdrawal into the fastness of Bohemia. To facilitate this maneuver he directed pioneers to construct a pontoon bridge near Ratisbonne at 2:00 A.M. on the twenty-third. Meanwhile, baggage and trains would cross the river on Ratisbonne's stone bridge, site of the gallant defense by the French Sixty-fifth Ligne three days earlier. With those orders issued, the dejected Karl caught what sleep he could.

News of the battle of Eckmühl, let alone Karl's preparations for retreat, did not reach Kaiser Franz at Scharding until 9:00 P.M. of the twenty-third. When information did arrive it proved misleadingly incomplete. Count d'Auersperg had ridden hard from Karl's headquarters on the battlefield in the late afternoon of the twenty-second. He coursed a circuitous route to avoid the intervening French army and did not arrive at Scharding until more than twenty-four hours later. Eager for news, the Austrian emperor immediately summoned Auersperg. The count reported that while the battle still raged, Karl's right had been gaining ground toward Abbach. The Austrian Third Corps similarly had been advancing against Luckenpoint. Admittedly, Eckmühl had fallen to troops apparently led by Napoleon himself, but all in all the outlook appeared favorable for Hapsburg interests when battle resumed on the twenty-third. Although Franz could only nervously ponder what might have transpired during the day since Auersperg departed, the count's report instilled confidence. What with Hiller's plan to turn and strike Bessières, the Corsican should be sent reeling across Bavaria by the Austrian double blow. The courtiers in attendance about Franz buzzed with optimism as Auersperg's news circulated and was published in the army bulletin and sent on to Vienna. Tomorrow would doubtless bring additional glad tidings.

Convergence on Ratisbonne

At daybreak on the twenty-third, some seventy miles distant from where the anxious Franz waited and some twelve from where the despondent Archduke Karl rose to breakfast, the victorious French army stirred around its campfires and prepared for another day of marching and combat. Once again a thick fog clung to the rolling terrain, which descended toward the Austrian outpost line along the Pfater Bach. Pickets reported they were still in contact with Austrian cavalry. An Austrian prisoner, bundled into French lines by an aggressive patrol, stated that the Archduke, reinforced by Bellegarde's First Corps, would contest the French advance somewhere in front of Ratisbonne. The combination of this intelligence and the reduced visibility necessitated a certain caution. The French commanders prepared accordingly.

The leftmost prong, under the masterful Montburn at Peising, exercised particular care. The winding river road leading from Peising to Ratisbonne passed in and out of many small copses. It had been here that Trobriand had lost his vital ammunition convoy on 20 April. With the possibility of ambush obvious, Montbrun organized a vanguard of hussars supported by the carabiniers of the Seventh Légère. These latter would proceed in skirmish order to scout any threatening position. The main body of the Seventh and the remainder of the cavalry followed, departing Peising at 6:00 A.M.

As the advance guard moved forward it picked up a local peasant who claimed that the Austrians were in full retreat. Consequently the march accelerated, until, about three miles outside Ratisbonne at a place the road passed through a narrow, rocky defile, scouts spotted formed opposition (see Map 22). If the Austrians had been retreating, they had apparently changed their mind and had chosen a good defensive position to demonstrate their new resolve. To dislodge the Hapsburgs, two foot-carabinier companies deployed to the left and right while a platoon of the Seventh Hussars, also in skirmish order, held the road. Advancing through this screen came an infantry battalion of the Seventh Légère. This battalion, with the help of the flanking pressure of the carabiniers, routed the Austrians out of the defile.

Immediately, Austrian uhlans charged in support but were driven back by a saber-wielding countercharge of a squadron of the French Fifth Hussars. With that, Montbrun pushed on through the defile, advancing to the plain in front of Ratisbonne while collecting 200 prisoners along the way. There on the right (the mist having dispersed by now) he could see a much larger cavalry action under way between the heavies of the French cavalry reserve and Hohenlohe's dragoons. Montbrun instantly sent Pajol's brigade of three regiments of light horse against the exposed Austrian flank (see Map 22).

The cavalry combat Pajol approached was the last in a series of charges and countercharges begun in the misty dawn. They came about because of the Archduke Karl's vacillation over the advisability of a general retreat. As Karl considered his army's next move after breakfast (he was still inclined to make that move to the rearward) the active Stutterheim gathered his cavalry screen along the Pfater Bach (see Map 21). The Austrian outpost line blocked the Ratisbonne highway. It comprised the Archduke Ferdinand and the Stipsicz Hussars supported by an infantry battalion of the brown-coated Archduke Karl Legion.

Rising in the predawn mist, the main Austrian army massed behind Stutterheim. By 4:00 A.M. the Third and Fourth Corps formed up along the Ratisbonne and Straubing roads. Intermixed between them were the First

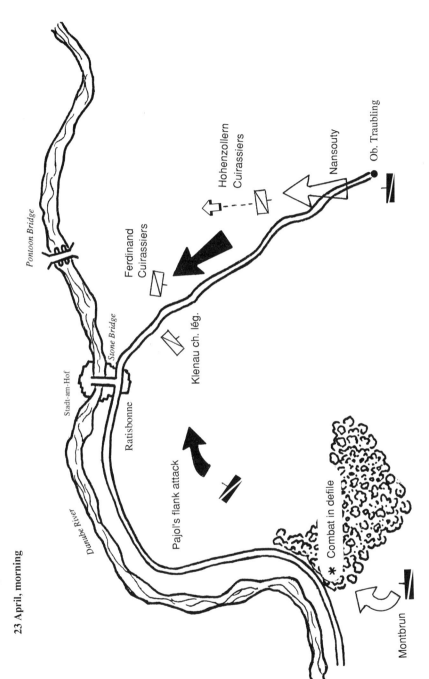

Austrian Rear-guard Action

23 April, morning

Pontoon Bridge

Stone Bridge

Stadt-am-Hof

Ratisbonne

Danube River

Hohenzollern Cuirassiers

Nansouty

Ob. Traubling

Ferdinand Cuirassiers

Klenau ch. lég.

Pajol's flank attack

Combat in defile

Montbrun

Reserve Corps and Lindenau's division of the Fifth Corps. Over along the Danube, on the Abbach-to-Ratisbonne road, massed the Second Corps, facing Montbrun's light cavalry. By 5:00 A.M. the army was under way, yet their march in multiple directions reveals the indecision in Karl's mind. The Third and Fourth Corps, followed by Lindenau's men, retired through Ratisbonne—men the Archduke felt were too badly battered to fight any more. Marching in the opposite direction went the cavalry of the First Reserve Corps with the assignment of relieving Stutterheim and covering the main army. The Second Corps would hold in place on the hilly terrain along the Austrian right. Simultaneously, a staff officer searched the area between Ratisbonne and Stutterheim's outposts, seeking a position that might be defended advantageously in case Karl decided to venture another battle in front of Ratisbonne.

The main body of the French army arose at the same time as the Austrians but set about with a great deal more purpose and unity of action. Two divisions of cuirassiers under Nansouty and Saint-Sulpice continued as an ad hoc cavalry reserve. They advanced through Kofering toward Ratisbonne. Lannes' two infantry divisions and the Bavarians followed as best they could. To their left, Davout marched along secondary roads toward Ratisbonne as well. Thus, Napoleon's planned frontal convergence began, using all available roads leading to the Danube.

Although somewhat hampered by the mist, which at times intensified to a thick fog, all French movements started well. The heavy cavalry hustled Stutterheim's overmatched lights out of their outpost line and crossed the Pfater Bach. A brief check occurred when six squadrons of the Merveldt Uhlan Regiment, ordered up to relieve Stutterheim, counterattacked. Recruited from Austrian Galicia, the uhlans comprised mostly Poles who demonstrated a particular facility with the lance. Nevertheless, they were swamped by the masses of French cuirassiers, a further example of the futility of unsupported single-regiment Austrian tactics. Advancing through Ober-Traubling, the French cavalry extended their front to the right to take advantage of the more open terrain and to cut the Ratisbonne–Straubing road.

Here they neared a sensitive Austrian position, the recently constructed pontoon bridge spanning the Danube (see Map 22). Hapsburg resistance stiffened accordingly. An attack by the Hohenzollern Cuirassier Regiment failed to stop the French. But through the initiative and dash of Prince Gustav Hessen-Homburg, the French advance toward the pontoons was blunted when the prince led the Ferdinand Cuirassiers against Nansouty's flank (see Map 22). The French recoiled from the pontoons and instead trotted off against the retiring Austrian light horse along the Ratisbonne highway.

On the outskirts of the city, the Austrian light cavalry received support from a fresh regiment, the Klenau Chevaulégers (see Map 22). The chevaulégers were achieving some success against the French cuirassiers when their officers spied a new threat advancing against the regiment's right flank. These were Pajol's men, sent as previously noted by Montbrun, and now thundering down from the rise along the Abbach road against the overextended Austrians. Austrian cavalry bugles sounded the retreat. They could do no more. The majority of the cavalry trotted over the pontoon bridge while some withdrew through the gates of Ratisbonne itself. Although committed in piecemeal fashion, the 4600 Austrian cavaliers had managed to protect the withdrawal of the infantry and remaining baggage. Yet their rear-guard charges lacked conviction, an understandable situation in view of the army's four consecutive days of defeat.[1] The French cavalry spearhead had also accomplished all it could. Its spirit wasn't lacking, just the means to successfully engage the enemy now holed up in isolated outbuildings in front of Ratisbonne. Several volleys from the sheltered Austrian infantry, particularly from a large building blocking the main highway, persuaded the French cavalry that here and behind, on the walls of Ratisbonne itself, were targets requiring infantry and artillery.

Soon infantry did appear—Gudin's men hurrying up the Ratisbonne highway. Riding with them came Napoleon himself, who now realized that the Austrians were not going to oppose him in front of Ratisbonne. In fact, at about 9:00 A.M. the Archduke Karl had finally determined upon a retreat. Following his early-morning letter- and order-writing, Karl had ridden out from the city to reconnoiter the situation personally. (His intervention had directed the Merveldt uhlans to Stutterheim's support.) Seeing the inability of his cavalry screen to block Nansouty and receiving no information from his staff officer regarding a favorable local defense position, Karl finalized the decision he had been leaning toward since the preceding evening. The army would retreat across the Danube, screened by a cavalry rear guard. Six battalions of infantry would man Ratisbonne's walls and gates to protect the retreat. They would be assisted by the artillery positioned on the far bank of the Danube. GM Folseis would hold hard until nightfall and then leave 300 men to maintain the pretense of resistance while the remainder abandoned the city. The forlorn 300 could surrender the following day. Having conceded the campaign, the Archduke rode back through the city and joined his troops streaming across the Danube bridges.

Before crossing, Karl paused to write another letter to his brother Franz, one that clearly demonstrates the badly frayed state of Karl's nerves. In it he informed Franz that having had his army severed by Napoleon's offensive, he had lost touch with Hiller and Louis and could only assume that they had been destroyed. Furthermore, although the main body had fought well the previous day at Eckmühl, they too had been severely mauled. Karl wrote that he therefore despaired of holding out in front of Ratisbonne. With luck the main body might escape into Bohemia. However, Franz should leave Scharding immediately, since the Archduke could no longer shield the road to Vienna. Finally, Franz should not depend on the Archduke's assistance in the immediate future; the army was too badly off to render useful aid.

This dismal letter does not reflect well upon Karl. While it was true he had lost contact with his left and only had vague reports about the retreat over the Isar, the army's current position at Ratisbonne had the advantage of being situated in closer contact with Bellegarde's First Corps. Here were 28,000 fresh men. Bellegarde had spent the preceding days searching ineffectually in the Hemau–Neumarkt area for the French line of communications (see Map 21). During the twenty-second, he re-established contact with the main army via the bridge at Abbach. Bellegarde then received orders to hasten to join Karl at Ratisbonne. Of the 66,000 effectives already concentrated at Ratisbonne, the Second, portions of the Third, and most of the First Reserve Corps had not participated in the previous day's defeat. These facts the Archduke could and should have comprehended. The inescapable conclusion is that on the morning of the twenty-third it was not the Austrian army who was defeated, but rather its leader.

Karl seems to have had some appreciation of what had gone awry during the abortive campaign. He dimly perceived there had been a lack of coordination among his army's various corps. His tacit recognition is shown by the orders he now drafted. Each corps received detailed instructions for the next five days specifying the route of march through Bohemia and the nightly objectives along the way. By issuing such inflexible orders, the Archduke seemed to be trying to grapple with the central problem in the Austrian army: how to maneuver its formidable mass, filled with soldiers of admirable fighting spirit, in a concerted, purposeful way. By trying to anticipate events for five days while his army was still in contact with a hard-pressing and victorious French army, Karl was feebly striving to exert order on what manifestly to date had been a disjointed Austrian effort.

Displays of Courage

As Karl wearily retired through the Ratisbonne gate, now feverishly being loopholed and barricaded by the Austrian defenders, Napoleon reached the rising ground overlooking the city. He saw Austrian baggage wagons to the rear of the field where the Ferdinand cuirassiers were attempting to block Nansouty's advance. Realizing that the thick line of wheeled transport converging on the Danube implied the existence of an Austrian pontoon bridge, the Emperor took steps to sever the Austrian escape route.

He directed the only available weapon against this vulnerable target. Several horse-artillery batteries galloped into position and began a rapid fire against the bridge and the Austrian cavalry jammed up near its approaches. The fire quickly had gratifying results as the Hapsburg masses accelerated their movement across the Danube. Apparently the artillery fire instilled a certain panic in the Austrian ranks. Almost before the last troops reached safety, Austrian pioneers cut the pontoon's thick mooring ropes. In their haste they bungled the job, allowing the majority of the pontoons to be carried by the current back to the opposite shore—where the French gratefully collected them. (This loss of the second and last Austrian bridging train would seriously impair future Austrian efforts in the battles around Vienna.) An auxiliary means for crossing the mighty Danube now lay in French hands. For the moment, though, Napoleon's attention centered on a more direct crossing point: the walled city of Ratisbonne and its massive stone bridge.

Ratisbonne lay encircled by a medieval wall supported by a high banquette (parapet with a firing step), with numerous angled turns offering enfilade fire. Stone towers flanked each gate. When originally built, these fortifications had protected the city against the ravages of the robber barons who fought up and down the Danube Valley. With peace and increasing prosperity, the burghers of Ratisbonne had allowed the fortifications to fall into crumbling disuse. Worse, the expanding city had built numerous suburbs and outbuildings along the exterior of the walls, thus restricting what should have been a clear field of fire. However, a deep dry moat fifty feet wide remained. Taking full advantage of this obstacle, the Austrian defenders had cast the small bridges and walkways spanning the moat into the bottom of the ditch.

As the Emperor and his aides examined Ratisbonne they could see the suburbs' numerous small gardens lined with whitecoated skirmishers. At 10:00 A.M. Lannes and Davout began to deploy their infantry 600 yards from these skirmishers. While formed troops spread out to encircle the city and artillery gathered to form a breaching battery, the French voltigeur companies went forward to clear the outlying Austrian-infested buildings.

The cumulative strain of the campaign hampered the French efforts. According to one of Napoleon's aides, "Everyone was so extremely fatigued, the Emperor among others, that everybody tried to catch some sleep, and those orders that were given were badly executed."[2] Over the next several hours the artillery began to fire against the walls, while the skirmishers kept up a popping fire at a range of 150 yards against the men sheltered behind the walls. French howitzers tried to clear the walls but their inaccurate fire merely succeeded in starting fires throughout the city. The field pieces proved similarly ineffectual. Both the balls of a Bavarian twelve-pound battery and those of eighteen French guns massed in front of Gudin's infantry harmlessly glanced off the medieval stone walls.

Next, in a series of disjointed assaults, the infantry tried to storm the gates. The Seventh Légère and Twelfth Ligne moved against the Straubing gate, but the defending infantry, first from the revetments along the moat and then from the crenellated walls themselves, repulsed this effort. The voltigeurs of the Thirteenth Légère fared no better against the Neustadt gate, where flanking fire from the towers stopped them cold. These desultory attempts might have continued indefinitely had not the Emperor bestirred himself.

Rising from his cape, on which he had been resting, Napoleon joined Marshal Lannes in a reconnaissance. In this action the Emperor reverted to the young artillery officer at the siege of Toulon. Faced with a campaign threatening siege (he did not know the Austrians merely planned a delaying action) Napoleon traversed the ground covered by Lannes' infantry. His attention soon focused on a three-story house built against the outside of the city's wall. Recognizing a weak link in Ratisbonne's defenses, the Emperor directed that a breach be created there. To this end an auxiliary arm of the French army entered the stage, the engineers and their chief, General Bertrand.

So far in this whirlwind campaign the services of the engineers had not been required. There had been neither fortifications to build nor fortresses to lay careful siege to. Now opportunity was at hand and Bertrand eagerly seized it to demonstrate his abilities and devotion to the Emperor. Ably seconded by the commander of the artillery reserve, General Songris, Bertrand gathered from the artillery park eight- and twelve-pound pieces and sited them against the overhanging house. Positioning the pieces with care and ordering each gun loaded with double the normal amount of powder to increase the impact, Bertrand commenced the bombardment. The first gun was aimed and fired by another of the Emperor's eager aides, the artillerist Lauriston. A second battery of six guns and four howitzers swept the area behind the intended breach. Next, the engineer had his sappers patrol the adjacent suburbs to gather materials to construct scaling ladders. Soon several carts filled with ladders arrived near the battery.

By 3:00 P.M. the house had been pulverized and the modest breach judged practicable. Bertrand directed the battery to switch fire in an attempt to neutralize any Austrian flanking fire. His job skillfully completed, he reported to Napoleon, who now arrived to supervise the assault personally. Advancing on foot accompanied only by his friend Lannes, the Emperor reached a small rise ten yards in front of the battery and began to inspect the breach through his glass. Suddenly the Emperor Napoleon I cried out in pain: The man whose unique will controlled the fate of nations had been shot. It was the first wound suffered by Napoleon since ascending the imperial throne.

In full view of thousands of French soldiers the Emperor was seen to lean heavily against Lannes. As aides hurriedly summoned a doctor, news of the event spread with electrifying suddenness throughout the army. Intense consternation and near-panic resulted. Thousands broke rank to hasten on foot or horse to the rear of the battery where Napoleon was surrounded by his aides. Surgeon Ivan, ashen-faced with the enormity of his responsibility, arrived to examine the wound.

Apparently he had been struck by a large-caliber ball from a Tyrolean rifle or a smallish round from a cannon. The blow hit the left foot at the joint of the big toe. This was not necessarily a trifling wound, since the shot of the period could and often did remove entire limbs. Furthermore, such blows often inflicted internal damage, sometimes leading to death, while leaving little outward signs of their damage. The distinguished surgeon Dominique Larrey, who normally attended in the Emperor's presence, was sick with typhus.[3] Thus it was a nervous assistant, Surgeon Ivan, who came forward to treat Napoleon. Although the shot did not penetrate the boot, once Ivan removed it he saw a nasty-looking, rapidly swelling contusion. Ivan applied a light wrap to dress the wound and implored Napoleon to retire to his carriage. Sensitive to the gathering disorder about him, though in considerable pain (the wound would take ten days to heal), the Emperor refused.

Hobbling to his horse, a beautiful white charger given him by the king of Bavaria, Napoleon mounted with difficulty. He commanded the drums and bugles to sound the recall ordering the troops to return to their standards. Aides coursed across the field to tell the troops that the Emperor's wound was not serious. The rank and file listened attentively. But more important than what they heard was what they saw.

Mounted amid a mass of men, Napoleon presented an unmistakable target. Austrian bullets whizzed by, prompting him to turn to his retinue and comment dryly: "Doesn't it seem that these bullets are reconnoitering us?"[4]

Then, in a thrilling display of personal courage and leadership, Napoleon spurred his mount in front of the French lines so the entire army could see he was unharmed. Immediately this spectacle was acclaimed by the deafening cries of "*Vive l'Empereur*" issuing from the throats of the emboldened soldiers.

The Emperor halted before his infantry to perform several gestures that would cement his unique relationship with his men and pass into Napoleonic legend. He solicited recommendations from the regimental officers, granting gratuities and decorations upon deserving soldiers. An old grognard, as was his right, personally asked him for the Cross of the Legion of Honor. The Emperor asked: "What have you done to deserve it?"

The veteran of Italy and Egypt replied: "It was I, Sire, who in the desert of Joppa gave you a watermelon."

"I thank you for it again," Napoleon said, "but the gift of a fruit is hardly worth the Cross."

The grognard, who had been calm to this point, lost his composure, shouting: "Well, and don't you reckon seven wounds received at the bridge of Arcola, at Lodi, and Castiglione, at the Pyramids, at Acre, Austerlitz, Friedland; eleven campaigns in Italy, Egypt, Austria, Prussian, Poland . . ."

The Emperor interrupted and, mimicking the soldier's excited manner, said: "There, there—how you work yourself up when you come to the essential point! . . . I make you a knight of the Empire, with a pension of twelve hundred francs. Does that satisfy you?

"But, your Majesty, I prefer the Cross."[5]

The veteran received both and Napoleon rode on to review other formations. He stopped before the Tenth Légère, complimenting it on the conspicuous display of gallantry the day before at Eckmühl. Before the assembled troops he clasped the shoulder of General Saint-Hilaire, loudly stating: "You have earned the marshal's baton; you will receive it!"[6]

He then asked the regimental officers who was the bravest man in the unit. When amid general acclaim the designated soldier stepped forward—an exceptionally small, pockmarked, red-faced sergeant-major—Napoleon with some mirth cried out: "You, the most brave! Well, since they all say you are, I make you a Baron with a four-thousand-franc pension."[7]

This pronouncement created an immediate sensation. Such an elevation to nobility had previously been the exclusive domain of high officers and generals. These dramas, enacted within range of Ratisbonne's walls, could not have occurred in any other army of the period. The egalitarian familiarity between the Emperor and his men was unique and gives an indication of why the French army, its conscripts leavened by devoted veterans, was able to achieve prodigies of valor. And now, having recovered from the stunning news of the Emperor's first wound and received homage from Napoleon himself, the army proceeded to give a further demonstration of its zeal.

The rubble from the house Bertrand's bombardment had pulverized had partially filled the moat beneath the city's walls. A three-yard gap extending from the top of the rubble to the top of the wall would have to be spanned by scaling ladders. Preferring as always to lead from the front, Marshal Lannes joined the men of Morand's division, who were sheltering behind a building near the breach. The marshal could see that the assault required crossing 200 paces of fire-swept open ground, descending into the ditch with the aid of the ladders, mounting the rubble pile, repositioning the ladders, climbing to the top of the ramparts, driving the defenders from the wall, and advancing to an adjacent gate to open it to the waiting masses of infantry. Lannes called for fifty volunteers; Morand's men responded with twice the number. Reducing the assault party to the required fifty while personally choosing officers to lead them, the marshal ordered the assault.

The fifty advanced with spirit, inspired by the recent display of their Emperor and the presence of the famous marshal. They had barely cleared the protection of the sheltering building when a storm of musketry assailed them. Only a few were unhit, but they courageously descended into the moat. Against the backdrop of a burning city, canister-firing artillery vomited death into their depleted ranks. The survivors fell back.

Lannes and Morand called for a renewed effort, to which fifty more volunteers responded. Seizing the ladders, the second group set off, but whatever advantage of surprise had aided the first attack was lost. The Austrians had the range and their fire nearly annihilated the attackers before they reached the moat. To stimulate a third effort, Lannes unpinned a medal from his breast, offering it to the first man to reach the top of the wall. In response volunteers again surged forward, only to be shattered by the intense musketry and canister. A call for a further effort failed.

An eyewitness recalls that had the marshal ordered another attack his orders would have met with compliance. However, Jean Lannes knew that, to succeed, the effort required the dash of volunteers. He eloquently beseeched the men, referring to them as the bravest of a brave division, reminding them that the eyes of the Emperor and the entire army were upon them. This appeal also met only a shuffling silence. Lannes' Gascon temperament overcame him: "Well, I will let you see that I was a grenadier before I was a marshal, and still am one!"[8]

He bent to lift a scaling ladder, hefted it, and set off toward the breach. Before he could move more than a few paces, his aides intervened. Lannes angrily ordered them out of the way but they wouldn't move. Marbot, while trying to wrestle the ladder from Lannes' grasp, said: "Monsieur le Maréchal, you would not wish us to be disgraced, and that we should be if you were to receive the slightest wound in carrying that ladder to the ramparts as long as one of your aides-de-camp was left alive."[9]

The sight of a Marshal of France disputing with his aides the right to lead the assault spurred the amazed bystanders into action. With shouts of enthusiasm officers and men alike rushed forward, jostling for possession of the now-sacred scaling ladders. As Marbot recounts: "If however we had given them up, we should seem to have played a comedy to stimulate the troops. The wine had been drawn, and we had to drink it."[10]

Marbot carefully organized the storming party. Rather than rush forward in an unwieldy mass, as had the prior assault groups, this time only parties of two, each man holding an end of a ladder, would advance. The subsequent pairs would follow at twenty-pace intervals. When the moat was reached, the ladders would be placed three paces apart to minimize confusion during the descent into the moat. Half the ladders would be left behind so supporting troops could climb down. The remainder would be carried up the rubble pile and placed next to each other (the limited space prohibited any other arrangement) to allow the attackers to scale the wall. In the optimistic words of Marbot, this placement would allow them to "reach the top rampart close together and push back the besieged when they tried to throw us down."

Marshal Lannes nodded approval to this sage plan: "Off with you, my boys, and Ratisbonne is taken"[11] echoed in the ears of the first party as Marbot and another aide, named de Viry, set off at a run.

Although the predictable storm of fire assaulted them and one bullet knocked a button off de Viry's pelisse, the rapidly moving, isolated targets proved difficult for the Austrians to hit. The first ladder parties reached the moat without loss and, as prearranged, moved down into the masonry-strewn ditch and up the precarious slope toward the breach. While the honor of first on the walls of Ratisbonne remained hotly disputed long past the dying days of the Napoleonic empire, two men, Marbot and Labedoyère, apparently reached the top simultaneously. The Austrian defenders balked before their intrepid charge, allowing the remainder of Lannes' staff with a small company of grenadiers to mass on the ramparts.

The group on the wall included an engineer, Captain Beaulieu, and a Bavarian noncommissioned officer who were familiar with the intricate labyrinth of the city's narrow streets. They led Marbot and his party toward the crucial gate. All was confusion as shots rained down on the storming party, some apparently fired by Ratisbonne's burghers themselves, outraged at the destructive French bombardment. With timbers from burning houses crashing all about, the French made their way to a small square near the Straubing gate. Here a defending Austrian battalion was taken by surprise in the rear. As the French demanded the Hapsburgs' surrender, the rival lines faced each other with leveled muskets at point-blank range. Before they could mutually annihilate one another, the sound of axes ringing against the outside of the gate told the Austrian major that he was surrounded, prompting him to order his battalion to lay down its arms. The gate swung open. With a rush a battalion of the Twenty-fifth Ligne swarmed into the streets of Ratisbonne, led by Marshal Lannes. Though restrained from participating in the assault on the walls, the Gascon couldn't be held back from leading the sappers against the gate.

While the Twenty-fifth collected the arms of the surrendered Austrians, engineers repaired the ramp leading to the gate. In ten minutes the job was done and more French infantry poured into the city. Austrian resistance continued sporadically throughout Ratisbonne. The Hapsburg units assigned to other gates didn't know their defense had been penetrated at the Straubing gate, thus they had to be rooted out separately. Small groups of soldiers continued to snipe from clock towers and second-story windows at the French columns marching through the streets below. Artillery fire from the far bank also impeded the French, particularly howitzer shells that extended the blazes already started by French fire. And, on the reverse side of the coin of martial glory, numerous units of the conquering army betook themselves of the ancient rights of the storming party. These undisciplined elements, who grew in number as the afternoon progressed, began to loot the houses of Ratisbonne. Although the city was substantially in French hands by four o'clock, order was not restored until late in the evening, when six grenadier companies halted the sack of Ratisbonne at the point of their bayonets. As one unsympathetic Frenchman said, recalling the civilian fire directed against his unit, the city paid the price for failing to demonstrate unswerving loyalty to the king of Bavaria. The combination of pillaging and shellfire destroyed over 150 houses this day.

These figures would become known as careful Germanic auditors counted the damage in the days to come. But now, as numerous soldiers broke ranks to begin looting, a solid core, led by Lannes' staff and an engineer officer specifically assigned the task, sought the important stone bridge across the Danube. They quickly became disoriented in the winding side streets of the medieval city. An unexpected guide appeared, a young Frenchwoman who had remained behind when the bulk of Davout's corps left the city four days before. As the frightened mademoiselle sought sanctuary with the first French troops she saw, she was quickly interrogated. Yes, she knew the way to the bridge. Sheltered behind a platoon of grenadiers, she somewhat unwillingly joined the van and led the way toward the bridge. Sporadic musketry continued. At one point a grenadier was hit in the arm, spewing blood over the Parisienne. Nonetheless she continued until reaching the bridge's approaches which were blocked by an iron gate. There, having found the sanctuary offered by Napoleon's grenadiers less than satisfactory, this unnamed heroine sought refuge in a nearby chapel.

The imposing presence of a chateau overlooking the Danube bridge caused the French to halt. Since it blocked access to the bridge and was occupied by Austrian infantry, an officer went in search of artillery. He returned with two twelve-pound pieces which commenced a short bombardment. A company of grenadiers hurled themselves against the chateau, overcame the resistance within, and continued onto the bridge. Fire from the high ground across the river in the Stadt-am-Hof suburb, the site of Colonel Coutard's defense on 19

April, stopped the French drive at a hastily erected Austrian barricade. The heavy fire dissuaded Lannes from trying to force the bridge. It was now 7:00 P.M., twenty-four hours after the cavalry action at Alt Eglofsheim. Just as an Austrian cavalry rear guard, although defeated, had prevented effective French pursuit then, so now an infantry rear guard, although similarly defeated, covered the unmolested withdrawal of the main body of the Hapsburg army.

Napoleon's bulletin typically inflated the magnitude of the Ratisbonne success. While claiming to have captured 8000 men, the bulletin chastised the Austrian high command for cruelly condemning the unsupported rear guard to certain annihilation. In fact, General Folseis' rear guard was far from destroyed. It lost some 2000 men in all, sixteen guns, and forty-four baggage wagons. French losses were about 700. The Emperor's fatigue, magnified by the pain of his wound, prevented him from issuing any further orders for the night.

He was aroused from his sleep to receive Masséna's report, dispatched at 9:00 P.M., describing the marshal's modestly successful drive against Straubing. After announcing the capture of eighty men and thirty baggage vehicles, Masséna reported that Straubing's two bridges were badly damaged. However, the town's carpenters, assisted by French sappers, would work all night to restore the bridge and by dawn at least one should be serviceable. He added a postscript reporting that a further 120 prisoners and thirty-seven baggage wagons had just been rounded up.

Similar glad tidings came from Marshal Bessières in Neumarkt, where he continued to chase Hiller's isolated command. In particular, Bessières spoke flatteringly of the conduct of the Hessian light dragoons. Although his report tended to minimize the severity of an Austrian counterstroke initiated by Hiller, and the situation around Munich remained vague, Napoleon could retire knowing all was in order with his detached commands.

Too tired to organize an effective nocturnal pursuit, the exhausted Emperor returned to bed, the solicitous Berthier fending off all who requested orders or would otherwise disturb the Emperor's slumber. The next morning Napoleon found time to express his sentiments in a proclamation to the army. In part it stated: "In less than a month, we will be in Vienna."[12]

CHAPTER XI

Conclusion

Everything on earth is soon forgotten, except the opinion
we leave imprinted on history.

Campaign's End

The capture of Ratisbonne and Karl's escape across the Danube mark the end of the Ratisbonne phase of the 1809 war. From the French perspective, much had been accomplished and much remained yet to do. Unquestionably, in the whirlwind five-day campaign Napoleon had dramatically retrieved French fortunes. Although he had failed in his major aim of destroying Karl's army, he had inflicted a heavy defeat and seized the initiative. From the Hapsburg viewpoint, the situation was bleak indeed. An offensive that had taken years to prepare had failed dismally. Napoleon's counterstroke dashed hopes of liberating Germany from the French yoke. The question now was whether the army could manage to defend the capital and somehow find a way to defeat Napoleon.

On 24 April Karl's army staggered into Cham on the edge of the Bohemian mountains. Recalling Bellegarde, Karl concentrated his shaken army. The Hapsburg Generalissimus believed his army comprised 50,000 men and so reported to the Kaiser. In fact, he had over 90,000. While straggling partially accounts for Karl's confusion, it was more due to his total demoralization over a campaign gone wrong. In a despairing letter he advised his brother Franz to sue for peace.

Five days later, while his army retreated deeper into Bohemia, Frederic Stadion arrived at Karl's headquarters. He brought the Kaiser's response to

Karl's suggestion. Franz's typically vacillating reply was open to several inter-
pretations. In essence, he seemed to authorize Karl to explore a negotiated
peace as long as it didn't compromise the Kaiser's dignity. A disclaimer such as
this was well designed to heap blame upon Karl should any undesirable
outcome stem from the negotiation. The choice of messengers was also note-
worthy. Frederic Stadion was a charter member of the war party, which had
guided Austria to war and prepared the best army the empire had ever fielded.
Sheltered from the shock of combat and the violence of Napoleon's counteroffensive, the war party found Karl's letter reporting disaster and suggesting
peace too incredible to accept. Only days earlier they had seen Karl invade
Bavaria and seemingly place the French in great peril. The most recent
message from the front had seemed to presage great things. Clearly, to the men
in the war party, something was radically wrong with Karl. They strongly
lobbied for his recall and, in order to stay on top of events, sent one of their
own to deliver Franz's message.

Karl must have been aware of this when Stadion visited. Nonetheless, the
Archduke and his trusted entourage set about to explore the possibility of
peace with France. Karl gave Grunne the task of writing to Napoleon.
Grunne's letter began by proposing an exchange of prisoners. Then he injected
a word of flattery: "I am proud, Sire, to fight against the greatest general of my
century."[1] He proceeded to write eloquently about the value of a durable peace
and stated how he would like to meet with Napoleon, bearing either "the
sword or the olive branch in hand."[2]

This remarkable appeal failed to elicit a response. Napoleon received it on
1 May. Characteristically the Emperor told his staff: "I will answer it when I
have time."[3] In its own way, his lack of time was an answer. All during the day
and into the evening a flurry of couriers set off from imperial headquarters
bearing orders for the army's future objectives. The orders directed all units to
move with haste, to march east, to march on Vienna.

On 13 May Napoleon entered Vienna for the second time. Two days later,
marching in retreat at a stout pace of over twelve miles per day, far in excess of
the rate the army had managed during its advance, Karl arrived across the
Danube from Vienna. There he rejoined, at last, the three corps commanded
by Hiller. Napoleon again sought to come to grips with Karl and a week later
launched an ill-advised attack over the river. A bloody two-day battle of
attrition around the villages of Aspern-Essling followed. It featured the isolation of the French army on the Austrian side of the Danube when flood-fed
waters severed the French bridge. The Austrians fought bravely, but it was the
river that forced Napoleon to retreat. Aspern-Essling was Napoleon's first
defeat.

For the next six weeks both sides summoned every available man, horse, and cannon to Vienna. Exercising meticulous care that had been so lacking at Aspern-Essling, Napoleon once more crossed the Danube and sought battle. On 5–6 July he narrowly defeated Karl at Wagram. Wagram was a colossal affair involving some 325,000 combatants, including 44,000 cavalry and 930 guns. In the armistice that followed Franz had to accept a costly, humiliating peace. Wagram was Napoleon's last great victory.

Assessment

During his Saint Helena exile Napoleon tried to make the case that he was a victim rather than an aggressor. In the 1809 war with Austria this is true. Napoleon's crisis on the Danube arose from his failed diplomacy in the years preceding the war. Salient among important decisions and encounters was the meeting between Napoleon and Czar Alexander at Erfurt, a pivotal event in European history. Erfurt sowed the fatal seeds that caused Napoleon to engage in two-front war, the strategic madness that led to the collapse of his empire. Never again would France be a dominant world force.

The outcome at Erfurt hinged on the Czar's determination not to fall again under Napoleon's spell. This thwarted the latter's grand strategy. Napoleon realized the Czar had changed but did not know why: "He came to Erfurt quite a different man from what he appeared to be at Tilsit. I noticed at Erfurt that he was defiant and unspeakably obstinate."[4] What he failed to notice was why. As we have seen, Alexander acted according to Talleyrand's instructions.

Napoleon never fully understood the depths of Talleyrand's betrayal. He did, however, comprehend the man. Two years into his Saint Helena exile he commented: "One may say that this man is immorality personified. I have never known a being more profoundly immoral."[5] One suspects Talleyrand would have been pleased with Napoleon's appreciation. Why did the Emperor entrust this devious minister with his plans? Quite simply, Napoleon was a superb judge of talent and in Talleyrand he recognized diplomatic genius. In Napoleon's words, "He is the most capable minister I ever had."[6]

Considering Talleyrand's persistent undermining of Napoleon's diplomatic goals, how could the Emperor fail to comprehend Talleyrand's betrayal? First, one must recognize that Talleyrand played an extremely able game. There is no doubt he badly fooled Napoleon.[7] Equally important, Napoleon knew—to the extent a supreme egotist can—that Talleyrand was indispensable.[8] The Emperor realized the danger of using Talleyrand but felt he could stay one step ahead of his minister. Like the moth drawn to the flame, Napoleon's attraction proved fatal. Six years after the 1809 War—during events preceding the battle of Waterloo—Napoleon tried and failed to woo Talleyrand to his cause. At that time Napoleon told a diplomat: "I've made two mistakes with Talleyrand—first, when I did not take his good advice, and second, because I did not have him hanged when I did not follow his ideas."[9]

Since 1805 Talleyrand had sought a Franco-Austrian alliance. He felt that only this alliance could give France a lasting peace. But Talleyrand confronted an unsolvable dilemma: Napoleon would not negotiate unless he held the upper hand. To gain the upper hand he sought battle, and on the battlefield he invariably triumphed. The Emperor firmly believed that the victor acquired rights.[10] This belief led him to impose terms that always inspired the vanquished to seek revenge. So it was with Austria, who fought and lost to France repeatedly until her final victory in 1814.

Without Talleyrand's counsel, Napoleon's diplomatic ineptness embroiled him in another war against a different power in 1812. While fleeing his army's destruction in the miserable Russian winter, the Emperor naively remarked to a traveling companion that Kaiser Franz and Metternich recognized that France's war against Russia was on behalf of all of Europe, including Austria. His companion responded with a fundamental truth that governed his enemy's behavior at Pressburg in 1805, Tilsit in 1807, Erfurt in 1808, and all of Europe in 1812: "As a matter of fact, it is Your Majesty they fear."[11]

Early in his career, while a mere general on his way up, Napoleon shared some youthful wisdom with Talleyrand. "All great events hang by a single thread," he wrote. "The clever man takes advantage of everything, neglects nothing that may give him some added opportunity; the less clever man, by neglecting one thing, sometimes misses everything."[12] In the events preceding the crisis on the Danube, Talleyrand showed he had taken this advice to heart, and in so doing demonstrated that in this instance, he was the more clever. Talleyrand took pride in having deceived Napoleon. Later in his career he boasted how his behind-the-scenes maneuvers at Erfurt had saved Europe. Napoleon had once told him that "true politics . . . is merely the calculus of combinations and of chances."[13] Talleyrand performed this calculus brilliantly.

However well Napoleon conducted the military aspects of the 1809 campaign, his diplomatic efforts proved disastrous. Partially this was due to his overweening self-confidence. He simply could not imagine that mere mortals could outwit him. This confidence was seconded by an extensive secret police who, he thought, gave him access to his enemies' plots. His postal interception office, the *cabinet noire*, did provide several timely intelligence coups, not the least of which was its interception of the letter to Murat preparing the marshal to be a successor to the throne. Napoleon boasted that although Talleyrand and Fouché did not commit their innermost thoughts to paper, their friends wrote many letters that the *cabinet noire* intercepted. These letters gave the

Emperor a window to observe Talleyrand's and Fouché's plans. Perhaps the tight control his secret police maintained contributed to Napoleon's overconfidence. Privy to a great deal his opponents thought was secret, he never knew as much as he thought he knew.

Of the trio of anti-Napoleon conspirators—Talleyrand, Metternich, and Fouché—the role of the latter remains the murkiest, a testament to the chief of police's skill at covering his tracks. However, an unlikely source provides an insight about the depth of Fouché's involvement with the Austrian court. When Kaiser Franz sent his daughter, Marie-Louise, to marry Napoleon in 1810, he told her to trust Fouché: "If you find yourself in any difficulty, take the advice of Fouché—he is the one who will be most useful to you."[14] A kaiser and a father as careful as Franz does not proffer such advice unless he is sure of his man. Clearly he based his confidence on a record of covert contacts that led him to believe that Fouché could betray Napoleon. At a minimum, Franz's remarks underscore that Fouché was playing both sides.

In 1812 Napoleon dismissed Fouché's importance, saying "The man is merely a schemer."[15] While he was manifestly a great deal more, the historian can only share Napoleon's conclusion: "Fouché needed intrigue like food. He intrigued always, everywhere, every way, with everybody."[16] He intrigued for several purposes, and this fact largely escaped Napoleon. Fouché wanted a stable, predictable political environment. But if the French ship of state suddenly veered, he wanted his own hand close to the tiller. In his own fashion he was a patriot—serving, in order, himself, France, and Napoleon.

As early as his first exile, on Elba, Napoleon well understood the pivotal role Metternich had played in his downfall. After noting Metternich's skill as a diplomat he added: "He has destroyed me systematically and I helped him with my mistakes."[17] Metternich wanted Austria to serve as the center of an anti-French movement and a source of German nationalism. Because of the reactionary fears of Austria's rulers, this wish only partially came about.

Although not a military man, Metternich hit upon an essential truth regarding the French empire. The empire was an unnatural collection of peoples having widely differing aspirations. It stayed together only because of the existence of the French army. When the French army became embroiled in the guerrilla war in the Peninsula, Metternich sent a solid strategic appraisal to Vienna: "The war against Spain divulges a great secret to us . . . Napoleon has only one army."[18] The army Metternich referred to, the Grande Armée, was scattered across the map of Europe in the months preceding the crisis on the Danube. The Emperor managed to concentrate enough of it to defeat the Austrians in Bavaria. Its valor propelled him to the gates of Vienna. There it died while winning Napoleon's last great victory.

Just as Napoleon seriously misestimated Talleyrand's behavior, so he under-estimated the rising tide of Germanic nationalism. It proved a second funda-mental cause of Napoleon's downfall. The French Revolution had released powerful human forces throughout Europe. It is surprising that a child of this revolution should have underestimated its impact. In 1807 the Emperor wrote a letter of advice to his brother Jerome, then king of Westphalia: "What the peoples of Germany desire most impatiently is that talented commoners should have the same right to your esteem and to public employments as the nobles."[19] He further explained that the genuine reforms of the Code Napoleon should satisfy the Germans. While the people of Europe did crave the elimination of the last vestiges of feudalism, more important was the freedom to express their own nationalism. This meant the removal of the hated French from their territories.

A year later the Emperor seemed to understand when he commented: "There are only two powers in the world—the sword and the spirit. By spirit I understand the civil and religious institutions. . . . In the long run, the sword is always beaten by the spirit."[20] In the long run, four years hence, events proved the accuracy of Napoleon's insight. But in 1809, for one last time, the French sword conquered.

Turning to military matters, strategically the timing of the 1809 war greatly harmed Napoleon's continental plans. Forced to return to Paris before the Spanish campaign ended, the Emperor left matters in the hands of his subordi-nates. While traveling he found time to write to his brothers and German allies that "It is all over in Spain; the Spanish armies are destroyed and the British forces thrown into the sea."[21] His assessment proved grievously incor-rect. He would never return to the Peninsula, while all too many Frenchmen never left. Recalled prematurely, Napoleon just missed a knockout blow against his enemies in the Peninsula. This failure was a huge factor in his eventual defeat. On Saint Helena he wrote: "No one can deny that if the Court of Austria, instead of declaring war, had allowed Napoleon to remain four months longer in Spain, all would have been over."[22]

From the Hapsburg perspective, overriding battlefield tactical and strategic considerations was the stifling defensive state of mind that pervaded the Austrian high command. Karl knew that his army was the cement binding the disparate peoples of the Austrian empire. The empire could not withstand its destruction. Accordingly, Karl believed he could not take large risks. To confront Napoleon with such an attitude meant Karl was half beaten before the war began.

Another major influence on Austrian military practice was her army's chronic state of unreadiness. Although the war party within the Austrian government had prepared for war against France ever since Austerlitz, the army was not ready when war began. This is most clearly shown by the problems associated with the formation of army corps. Leaving this task until February 1809 was a capital blunder. The need for strategic surprise mitigated against forming corps too early, yet waiting until February was simply too late. His commanders' inexperience with handling corps-sized units outweighed the mobility Karl hoped to gain by the corps structure. This inexperience manifested itself most clearly during the failed offensives of 19 and 22 April.

Karl realized that the Ratisbonne field test of his reforms showed the army lacking in many respects. He made major command and organizational changes before the fighting around Vienna. By the time of Wagram he had replaced three of his eight corps commanders. Gone was his young brother Louis, replaced by a more experienced soldier. Karl happily accepted Hiller's application for sick leave, thus finally ridding himself of an insubordinate corps commander. Karl also consolidated his two reserve corps to eliminate a corps command for the indifferent Kienmayer. Organizationally, Karl abandoned the advance-guard-division concept for the remainder of the campaign. These divisions had borne the brunt of the combat during the Ratisbonne campaign. Although they had fought gallantly, they had been consistently bested. Karl merged their units back into line formations and returned to the more orthodox formation of one advanced guard for the entire army.

Aside from an unwillingness to take risks and the teething problems of a new organization, Karl's army suffered a third affliction. The Austrian offensive into Bavaria suffered from the same problems that hampered earlier Hapsburg efforts against France. A British observer of the 1796–1797 campaign in Italy noted that the Austrian "mode of carrying on war was methodical and slow."[23] This contrasted with Bonaparte's "enterprising and violent" methods. Furthermore, "the Austrians persisted in dividing their forces and in making partial attacks."[24] Bonaparte preferred rapid concentration and mass. Thirteen years after the Italian campaign, the fundamental differences between the great rivals remained.

During the Ratisbonne campaign every Austrian offensive movement witnessed a steady depletion of mass as squadrons, battalions, regiments, and brigades were sent off on secondary missions. Every Austrian commander from Karl down seemed to have a fatal fascination with detaching forces to act as a flank guard or to garrison this or that key position. The closed terrain exacerbated this problem. Commanders seldom could see their entire force, let alone that of the enemy. They feared what might be concealed by the nearby ridgeline or forest. Such fears understandably instilled caution, a characteristic most Hapsburg generals did not need to have reinforced. Austrian generals would perform better in the plains around Vienna, where they could more clearly see French maneuvers. Around Ratisbonne, long-held Hapsburg habit coupled with the terrain meant that by the time a corps actually engaged it lacked a substantial part of its strength.

In contrast, Napoleon consistently maneuvered with masses. His emphasis on concentration allowed him to overcome his violation of other principles of war. Although on 20–21 April he mistakenly focused his attention on Land-shut, his advance carried an unstoppable mass. Its speed and violence over-threw all before it. Realizing in the early hours of 22 April that Karl's main body lay before Davout, he again reacted by placing himself at the front of a mass of 40,000 men and marching to Davout's assistance. The dispersed Austrian force could not stop him.

Napoleon arrived to find his forces extended along a wide front. He finished the campaign with his men in two compact masses. Karl, on the other hand, began the campaign with his army concentrated around Prague and never thereafter was able to act with unity of purpose using a massed force. The campaign ends with his main body conducting a demoralizing retreat after only a fraction has actually fought (and that fraction was defeated in detail) and Hiller's entire wing severed from Karl's army, out of contact, its status unknown to the Austrian commander in chief.

On Saint Helena Napoleon reflected that at the beginning of a campaign one had to carefully balance an offensive versus a defensive strategy. He went on to note that "once the offensive has been started, it must be sustained to the last extremity, for . . . retreats are always disastrous. They cost more lives and materiel than the bloodiest battles, with this additional difference, that in a battle the enemy loses approximately as much as you, while in a retreat you lose and he does not."[25] The basic premise underlying the Hapsburg decision for war was offensive. Karl consistently violated Napoleon's maxim regarding the need to sustain the offensive. On 19 April, when he decided against holding his ground and ordered Hohenzollern to retreat from the Teugen–Hausen position, he lost the initiative. On 21–22 April he had the chance to crush Davout and regain the initiative. Yet his offensive plans proved slow and ponderous, and Karl lacked the conviction to see them through to a conclusion.

Karl frittered away opportunity several times by failing to issue orders in a timely manner. In opposition, the French were led by a man who above all else recognized the value of time: "I may lose a battle, but I shall never lose a minute."[26] In a postwar analysis, Karl's chief of staff wrote admiringly about Napoleon's battlefield accomplishments in the forty-eight hours following his arrival at Abensberg.[27] The way Napoleon converted a dangerous Austrian offensive to a demoralizing retreat in two days of maneuver and combat awed the Austrian strategist. In fact, from the moment he departed Paris, Napoleon drove himself ruthlessly to make maximum use of every moment.

His activity contrasts dramatically with Karl's. It is extremely difficult to explicate Karl's behavior at crucial times during the campaign. Were his mistakes caused by intellectual confusion when confronting the fast-moving pace of events or were they caused by inopportune epileptic seizures? Up to 19 April Karl appears to have had full possession of his faculties. During this time he dispersed his forces and tolerated very slow advances. When combat is joined on 19 April he fails to commit his elite grenadiers while battle rages all about him. Did the stress of combat bring on a seizure? If such an embarrassing event occurred his staff most certainly would have tried to keep anyone from knowing. Karl sent an order (or was it sent in his name?) at 3:30 P.M. on the nineteenth, leading one to suppose that either he had not suffered a fit or had recovered by this time. The day's battle ended with the five-o'clock thunderstorm. That evening Karl could have rectified his failure to support the day's offensive by ordering his lieutenants to hold their ground and thus prevent Davout from rejoining Napoleon. Instead Karl chose retreat.

The next day, 20 April, there is no sign of Karl between eleven in the morning and early evening. During this period Hiller's wing is cut off from the main body. A German writer states that he had a seizure and locked himself in his room.[28] In all probability this is indeed what happened. Karl experienced another period of inactivity on 22 April. Having devised an offensive, he remains inert at headquarters until narrowly escaping the pursuing French cavalry in the twilight.

Across the span of time it is impossible to attribute selected periods of time to epileptic seizures. One must note the opinion of the most knowledgeable English-language historian on the Austrian army, Gunther Rothenberg: "Finally, I am not sure about Charles' epilepsy. The possibility that this is used as a cover for other causes remains strong."[29] What is clear is that the Hapsburg war leaders did not grossly miscalculate physical resources when planning the war against France. Rather, they "overestimated the capabilities of the man whom they placed in command."[30] Karl made many blunders while in full possession of his wits. Perhaps epilepsy contributed, but it does not explain all. Interestingly, some of the lower-ranking Austrian officers recognized their leaders' incapacity for high command. A French officer recalls a conversation with several captured officers shortly after the Ratisbonne campaign. The Austrians placed defeat squarely at the feet of the generals.[31]

The amazing reversal of fortune that took place after Napoleon arrived in Bavaria is a solid testament to the ability of one of history's greatest captains.

At his direction came order from disorder, concentration from dispersion. Once he seized the initiative he never let go. His massed corps pierced the Austrian center and pursued relentlessly across the bridge at Landshut. When he learned he was chasing only one wing of the Austrian army, the Emperor changed his line of operations ninety degrees to head for Eckmühl. Such strategic flexibility came from Napoleon's ability to improvise and the French army's ability to maneuver. The Jena campaign of 1806 had witnessed Napoleon's development of an army corps structure capable of rapid strategic movement to front or flank. Although markedly inferior to its predecessor, the French army of 1809 showed this same ability. No other contemporary army could have executed the complicated, improvisational maneuvers of the Ratisbonne campaign.

On Saint Helena Napoleon proclaimed: "The battle of Abensberg, the maneuver of Landshut and the battle of Eckmühl, were boldest, the finest, the most scientific Napoleon ever executed,"[32] an assertion history does not support. While any campaign is full of "the friction of war," the Ratisbonne campaign was fraught with French errors. It sees Napoleon making more strategic mistakes than ever before. Warned by Davout that the main body of the Hapsburg host was concentrating against the marshal, Napoleon instead set his forces on a drive toward Landshut. He erroneously believed that the major portion of the Austrian army was before him and clung to this belief until the facts could no longer support it. In this behavior one sees the growing self-delusion that foreshadowed his ultimate failure.

The Emperor's earliest orders to Masséna, ordering that marshal to march on Landshut, stem from Napoleon's fixation with capturing the enemy capital. Landshut lay on the road to Vienna. Its capture only had a secondary impact on what should have been the true objective, the destruction of Karl's army. When Masséna concentrated at Pfaffenhofen on the evening of 18 April, Napoleon had a formidable striking force of six infantry divisions well poised to march directly on Karl's left flank. If Masséna did this, he would bring his soldiers in closer contact with the balance of Napoleon's army. The French would be tightly concentrated and in good position to confront the unexpected. Instead, at noon on 19 April Napoleon sent Masséna off at a tangent by marching against Karl's line of communications through Landshut. Before he had completed a union of his three great masses—Davout, the Germans along the Abens, and Masséna—he again separated them. In so doing he sacrificed "the primary advantage of beating the Austrian army to the secondary one of seizing a bridge on the Isar" to cut Karl's communications.[33] Because of the Landshut maneuver, Napoleon was unable to force Karl to decisive combat before the Archduke escaped over the Danube.

If the drive on Landshut demonstrates Napoleon's growing self-delusion, overconfidence also revealed itself during the campaign. On the evening he recaptured Ratisbonne he believed the campaign was for all intents and purposes over. He had defeated Karl and sent him packing. All that remained, the Emperor believed, was to march on Vienna. Once in possession of the capital the enemy was certain to sue for terms. Consequently he failed to order an effective pursuit against Karl. Instead of hounding the dispirited Austrian army to exhaustion, Napoleon turned toward Vienna. A similar blind focus on Moscow during the 1812 campaign led the Grande Armée to disaster.

The Emperor also made a mistake when he failed to pursue with all-out vigor after thoroughly drubbing the Austrian Fourth Corps at Eckmühl. Uncharacteristically he called a council of war and then heeded the most cautious advice. Napoleon's behavior is reminiscent of another, later time at Borodino, when he again heeded the advice of one of his marshals. At Borodino Napoleon refused to employ his ultimate reserve, the Imperial Guard, and thus failed to deliver a knockout blow to the wavering Russian army. In 1812 Napoleon's cautious decision cost him the campaign and probably his throne. In 1809 it merely meant the war would continue.

Criticism aside, in the final analysis one realizes that the Austrian descent into Bavaria came as a strategic surprise to Napoleon. Yet twenty-seven days after departing Paris the Emperor entered Vienna at the head of a victorious army. Faced with a crisis, he improvised a series of winning maneuvers and exhibited martial skills that have not been seen since.

Throughout the campaign the French army's superiority in strategic movement stands out. More French soldiers could march a greater distance than the Austrians. The slow Austrian shift from Bohemia to Bavaria compromised Karl's plan. During this march the Austrian need to halt to allow the supply wagons to catch up stands in marked opposition to the French style of living off the land. Yet after being driven over the Danube at Ratisbonne, Karl's army moved fast for a prolonged period as it marched toward Vienna. When an army is slow in advance but fast in retreat something more than a sluggish supply train must be involved.

The French veterans' capacity for sustained marching and combat was remarkable. On 19 April Gudin's and Morand's divisions marched over eighteen miles on poor, water-soaked roads. The next day they marched and fought for fifteen hours and covered fourteen miles. On 21 April they marched seventeen miles to Landshut, Morand's division stormed the town, drove the Austrians from the heights on the far side of the Isar, and recrossed to the west bank. Starting out at 5:00 A.M. on 22 April, they marched until 9:00 P.M. with Gudin's men fighting up and over the Rogging heights near Eckmühl. They covered thirty miles. Rising at dawn on 23 April, they marched twelve miles to the walls of Ratisbonne, where Gudin's men stormed the town. During five days filled with frequent combats they marched over ninety miles. Such a performance must place them in the ranks of history's greatest warriors.

Napoleon worked hard to inspire such behavior. He would visit his soldiers and with "a word, a glance, inflame their spirit."[34] Seldom was a general better served by his men. However, back in France a war-weariness, first noticed in the lukewarm reaction to the triumphs of 1806, deepened and spread. The sharp-eyed Duchess of Abrantès wrote: "This campaign, however, was not like that of Austerlitz, crowned with laurels interspersed with flowers: mourning followed in the train of triumph, and every bulletin plunged a thousand families in tears."[35]

The campaign placed great emphasis on subordinate initiative. Turning to Napoleon's lieutenants, Marshal Davout's performance was nothing short of brilliant. Beginning with his acquisition of intelligence and concentration of his corps before war began, through his battlefield conduct during three days of lonely combat, Davout displayed martial genius. His divisional commanders, the three "immortals" Morand, Gudin, and Friant and the rapidly developing Saint-Hilaire as well as the masterful Montbrun, provided the Iron Marshal outstanding service. With one possible exception, the entire Third Corps lived up to its Grande Armée heritage.

Davout felt badly let down by his unfortunate cousin Coutard. Although the official French report of the battle issued on 24 April publicly exonerated his regiment, Coutard himself was severely reprimanded for his surrender at Ratisbonne.[36] Davout demanded his resignation. Not until 1811, when he became better acquainted with the facts, did the Iron Marshal forgive Coutard. However, some veterans never forgot that the surrender at Ratisbonne jeopardized Napoleon's entire campaign scheme and, furthermore, occurred during a period when French troops regularly performed prodigies against the contemptuous whitecoats. Writing almost forty years after the event, one of Masséna's staff officers observed that Coutard did not "live up to the high opinion he had earned by his firmness at the blockade of Genoa, and let slip the occasion to acquire immortal glory."[37]

Outside the Third Corps, Lannes and Nansouty provided stellar performances. Once Napoleon arrived, the French staff also operated relatively smoothly, and two high-ranking staff officers, Hervo and Cervoni, died on the field. This suggests that even among the staff, command was exercised at the front. Masséna's conduct was disappointing and foreshadowed his failures in the Peninsula.

On the next tier down the Army of Germany's chain of command, the brigadiers and colonels performed as a group exceedingly well. By and large they accepted the uncertainties of war, to which (as noted) the terrain contributed, and triumphed by dint of good reconnaissance and an aggressive willingness to take risks. Seruzier's conduct at Teugen, where he led his guns forward without support into the woods to achieve a flanking position, and Berthezene with the Tenth Légère at Eckmühl are just two examples of the frontline leadership that characterized the French army.

The Grande Armée formations had experienced junior officers. The new formations, on the other hand, relied on men who had little experience of war. This significant difference was less apparent than it might have been simply because the lower-ranking officers were not seriously tested in this campaign. Much of the combat involved meeting engagements in broken, wooded terrain, which exactly suited the peculiar genius of the French infantryman. The infantry won the battle before their officers had to make difficult decisions. Many of the combats featured the Austrian advance guard divisions versus French voltigeurs. While the jägers and grenzers fought well, they were usually bested by the French. Friant, whose division fought woodland brawls for three consecutive days, referred to the open-order training of his light troops when he wrote: "The voltigeur officers justified again and again the excellence of their institution."[38] He noted that his skirmishers constantly obtained tactical superiority over the Hapsburg light troops.

In a more traditional battle fought along fixed lines, where difficult changes of formation would take place under artillery bombardment and the threat of cavalry charge, the judgment of the captains and lieutenants would be much more severely tested. Many of the officers who performed well during the Ratisbonne campaign faltered under the different conditions during the battles near Vienna.

The veterans in the rank and file behaved as they had at Austerlitz, Jena, and Eylau. But the courageous and willing young soldiers who filled the new formations could not make up for their lack of military instruction. They maneuvered much less well than the veterans, a characteristic soon to be revealed in the battles around Vienna. Equally important, they were much less hardened to war. They were incapable of the long forced marches that Napoleon demanded and did not know how to feed themselves when the French supply train inevitably lagged far behind.[39] Exposure and privation hit them hard. Overall, the dilution of the army with young soldiers and German allies was causing a decline in the French army. The Ratisbonne campaign temporarily obscured this trend but could not reverse it.

French casualties had been remarkably low during the campaign, but hidden by the overall accounting was the fact that losses were heaviest among those hardest to replace. Davout's corps had borne the brunt of the fighting. A representative regiment, the Fifteenth Légère, entered the campaign with 2251 officers and men. One officer had been killed and thirteen wounded, seventy rank and file died and 580 received wounds.[40] In total, 29 percent of the unit were struck in eight days. In time some of the wounded would return, but the killed and wounded who did not represented irreplaceable losses. They were men of the Grande Armée: trained, confident veterans. Their presence stiffened the entire army. Their valor propelled Napoleon to victory even as their numbers diminished. The arithmetic was unavoidable; attrition promised that Napoleon's army would never perform as it had.

This quickly became apparent to keen observers. Savary, who accompanied Saint-Hilaire's division at Aspern-Essling a mere four weeks after the Ratisbonne campaign, wrote that the division maneuvered in dense columns and consequently took frightful losses from the Hapsburg artillery. He noted that if the division had comprised veterans from the camps of Boulogne instead of the young conscripts who replaced them, it would have been able to deploy under fire without risking falling into disorder. In his criticism Savary singled out the vaunted "Terrible 57th," the regiment that had maneuvered well under fire on the Teugen–Hausen ridge. Apparently even this regiment had declined noticeably as a result of the losses it had suffered during the Ratisbonne campaign.[41]

The French allies' performance clearly showed that they had improved since joining with France in 1806. Contact with French officers and reform based on French methods made them better. Vandamme raised his Württembergers to a new standard of excellence. The Bavarian Wrede fought an expert rear-guard action during the campaign's opening maneuvers and provided solid service throughout. Yet important differences remained and are shown by comparing a French and a Bavarian division who faced similar circumstances on 20 April. Both Gudin's French and the Prince Royal's Bavarians had orders to attack and pursue the enemy. Starting from adjacent position, Gudin's men routed all opposition and reached Rottenburg after a fourteen-mile advance, while the Bavarians caused little damage to the enemy and failed to even reach Rohr, a distance of seven miles, by nightfall.

Tactically, the campaign showed that the remnants of the Grande Armée remained without equal. French skirmish superiority, including the ability of entire infantry regiments to dissolve into loose knots of fast-moving marksmen, time and again tipped the scales in the hill- and wood-fighting characteristic of the campaign. The French also demonstrated a marked superiority in their mounted arm. French massed cavalry charges bowled over Austrian single-regiment charges. Artillery proved the least important of the three arms during the campaign. Rapid French movement provided little time for French gunners to arrive on the battlefield and contribute. Recall that Davout fought most of his memorable engagement around Teugen–Hausen with very little artillery support. Austrian artillerymen had greater opportunities than their

French counterparts. Massed Hapsburg batteries provided excellent service on the Bettel Berg, only retiring after being flanked on both sides. The well-served guns on the Hohen Berg helped prevent the defeat at Eckmühl from turning into a rout. Later in the day, however, the Austrian cavalry batteries at Alt Eglofsheim offered little assistance to the cavalry rear guard. Rather than aggressively supporting the cavalry, the gunners retired behind the cavalry screen.

The common Austrian soldier displayed an essential spirit that shone through the army's uneven performance. This is reflected by the way the Austrian landwehr responded to Vienna's appeal following Karl's retreat over the Danube. Men flocked to their banners and provided the Hapsburg army a nationalistic fervor it had never experienced. In the near future, at Aspern-Essling, would come the reward of a first victory over Napoleon.

Napoleon's own words show the extent of the Austrian improvement in battlefield prowess. Early in the campaign, before he had witnessed any encounter, the Emperor referred to the Austrians as "that scum." In later years, when a staff officer made a condescending remark about the Austrians, Napoleon corrected him, snapping "You were not at Wagram," the climactic battle of 1809.

The Danube River was the dominant terrain feature of the 1809 war. The stone bridge at Ratisbonne, in turn, played a key role. Writing with the clarity of hindsight, Savary mused about the possibility of destroying Karl's army if it had been unable to retreat over the Danube to safety. Noting that only sixty-six hours passed from the time Davout left until Napoleon returned, Savary speculates what might have happened had Davout detached an entire brigade, well stocked with ammunition, to defend the town. He believed that such a force could have held against all comers for the requisite sixty-six hours. An intriguing possibility, it is doubtful on two accounts. First, Davout had no ammunition to spare. He was separated from his trains and barely had enough ammunition to last for combat on 19 April. Second, a hypothetical brigade would have still had to defend from both north and south and would have been stretched very thin. The French success attacking from just one direction on 23 April makes it improbable that a French brigade could have held.

When the campaign reached Vienna, the mighty Danube continued to play a crucial part. A little-noticed consequence of the Ratisbonne campaign should therefore be emphasized. The Austrian army carried only two pontoon bridging trains. The French captured one during the pursuit through Landshut. The Austrians sacrificed the other to escape through Ratisbonne. The lack of pontoons severely hampered Karl's strategic options as the campaign moved on to Vienna.

Napoleon's crisis on the Danube reveals the qualities that rank him—

along with Alexander the Great and Genghis Khan—as one of history's Great Captains. It also shows the flaws that contributed to his downfall. What motivated Napoleon? What gave him an ambition, drive, and energy unlike almost any other person? A letter written two years before the 1809 campaign provides insight: "All my life I have sacrificed everything—comfort, self-interest, happiness—to my destiny."[42] Destiny, as he saw it, lay entwined with the fate of France. In 1809 he remarked: "I have only one passion, only one mistress, and that is France: I sleep with her. She has never failed me, she has lavished her blood and her treasures on me."[43]

France made enormous sacrifices for Napoleon and in the end he failed her.

APPENDIX I

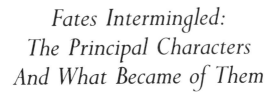

Fates Intermingled:
The Principal Characters
And What Became of Them

The Leaders

Napoleon

The war-ending Treaty of Vienna contained a secret clause betrothing the Arch-duchess Marie-Louise, Franz's daughter, to Napoleon. First he had to perform the disagreeable task of divorcing Josephine. In 1810 he remarried; two years later came the birth of a son. Superficially, 1810 saw the height of the Napoleonic empire. Only the war with England raged. Yet the decline in Franco-Russian relations had continued and worsened following Erfurt. Consequently, after a two-year absence from the field, Napoleon made the momentous decision to invade Russia. Although he received nominal help from his father-in-law's army, the 1812 campaign proved disastrous. Europe rose against the French occupier in 1813 as a wave of German nationalism even stronger than that of 1809 swept the continent. The pivotal event of the 1813 campaign was Austria's deliberation whether to enter the contest against France. Napoleon's stubborn unwillingness to compromise foiled Metternich's efforts for a Europeanwide peace. Once Austria declared against France, the balance fatally tilted. Napoleon still displayed moments of military genius. But the Allied decision to retreat when facing an army personally commanded by Napoleon while simultaneously advancing on all other fronts provided the key to a slow, grinding war of attrition that wore down the French. In 1814 the Allies occupied Paris and forced Napoleon into his first exile.

While welcoming peace, most of France did not embrace the return of a Bourbon king. His inept policies created a fertile soil for Napoleon to sow when he evaded his keepers and returned to France. The so-called Hundred Days followed, during which time Napoleon again failed to create a diplomatic basis to maintain his rule. Once more all Europe united against him. His gamble for power failed and France's fate was determined at the Battle of Waterloo. Defeat and exile followed. This time the Allies sent him to the remote South Atlantic island of Saint Helena, from where there was no escape. He spent six lonely years with little to engage his interest beyond dictating his memoirs. He died in 1821, at the age of fifty-two, an early death that may have been due to poison concocted by a royalist agent.

Czar Alexander

Economic and diplomatic tensions arising from Erfurt led to Napoleon's invasion of Russia in 1812. Alexander demonstrated great resolve when he refused to meet with Napoleon even after Moscow fell. He stubbornly held his position until Napoleon retreated and then allowed the Russian winter to complete the French army's destruction. He experienced a mystical religious transformation that saw him become a self-appointed champion of Europe. In this role he pursued relentless war against Napoleon, having the satisfaction of entering Paris in 1814 at the head of a victorious army. He then protected France from Prussia's vindictive postwar demands. He was a key participant at the Congress of Vienna, where—following the advice of his most trusted minister, Karl Nesselrode—he contested Metternich's balance of power vision. He withdrew to Russia, handed most of the decision-making duties to his ministers, and followed a bizarre religious life until dying four years after Napoleon—in 1825—at forty-eight.

Kaiser Franz

For three years following the marriage of his daughter to Napoleon, Franz remained a loyal ally. When the war party rose again on the heels of Napoleon's Russian disaster, he resisted popular passion and allowed Metternich to pursue complicated negotiations aimed at ending the conflict. Reluctantly he joined the Allies and followed, rather than led, them across Europe to Paris. He resisted Napoleon's efforts to place his son, Franz's grandson, in a French regency, preferring to have daughter and boy return to Austria, where they passed into insignificance. His fears concerning the spark of nationalism proved well-founded in the postwar years, when he twice had to crush revolts. Indecisive and reactionary to the end, he died in 1835 at the age of sixty-seven.

The Diplomats

Metternich

Metternich hoped he had created a special relationship with France when he arranged the marriage of Napoleon to Marie-Louise. The Russian campaign changed everything. Foiled in his attempt to forge a comprehensive peace, he reluctantly (he feared

Russian expansion absent French influence) advised Franz to declare war on France in 1813. Following the Allied triumph he staged the Congress of Vienna, a gathering of diplomats from all European powers. Proposing ideas that anticipated the European Community and the United Nations by about 150 years, he vainly struggled to create a lasting peace. The Congress succumbed to the narrow, nationalistic views of its participants. After the Hundred Days he served as the virtual master of Austria for thirty-four years. He was the dominant figure in Europe for this period, the arbiter of all important European relationships. Prominent in crushing revolutionary nationalism externally and promoting absolutism within the Hapsburg empire, his system worked until 1848. In that "year of revolutions" he misjudged the strength of liberal feeling and was forced to resign. A short exile followed, and then he returned to his estates to lead a retiring life until dying in 1859 at the age of eighty-six. Then and now Metternich is rightfully considered the unsurpassed diplomatic genius of his era and one of the great leaders of history.

Talleyrand

Following his dismissal in 1809 he remained out of power until Napoleon fell. Having secretly opened negotiations with the Allies in 1814, he found himself again conducting French foreign policy when the Bourbon king Louis XVIII returned. At the Congress of Vienna he brilliantly parlayed an empty hand into a prominent role in determining Europe's future. He remained in Vienna when Napoleon returned from exile, resisted Napoleon's pleas to return to the fold, and equally resisted Louis' appeals to join the royalist government in exile. He preferred to sit on the fence until the situation clarified. Important in his decision to stay in Vienna was the presence of a woman. With the intensity of an aging man's final passion he had fallen hopelessly in love with a much younger woman. She was the Duchess of Courland's daughter: Dorothée, the woman Talleyrand had secured to marry his son in return for the "diplomatic favors" he had given the Czar at Erfurt. Over the years Talleyrand had grown to appreciate the bright and lovely daughter-in-law and sometime at the Congress of Vienna his appreciation had become something much more. When she eventually left him, he fell into "a mental and physical dejection impossible to describe."[1] Even in the throes of love he continued to display his customary shrewdness. When one of Fouché's agents arrived to ask point-blank about an alternative candidate to Napoleon and Louis XVIII, Talleyrand said: "That door is not yet open, but if it ever came to the point of opening, I would see no necessity for slamming it shut."[2] While the people orbiting about him changed, Talleyrand always navigated with care. The Bourbons restricted his activity, yet he worked to good effect in secondary assignments until his death at the age of eighty-four in 1838.

Fouché

Napoleon dismissed Fouché in 1810 for intriguing with the Bourbons. He remained out of power during Louis XVIII's return, but maintained good relations with the Bourbons while keeping clandestine links with Napoleon. During the Hundred Days Napoleon appointed him, inevitably, minister of the police. Sensing that the Allied powers would combine again to crush Napoleon, yet disliking the unpopular king, Fouché examined alternatives and tried to enlist Talleyrand's help. So feared was his intelligence network that following Waterloo Louis XVIII appointed him to a key post. In a general purge of anyone connected with Napoleon, he was dismissed for a final time in 1816. A true survivor, he moved to Prague and then Trieste, living out his days in great comfort thanks to the riches amassed during his various appointments. He died at sixty-one in 1820.

The Warriors

Archduke Karl

Karl led his army to Austria's greatest victory over Napoleon, the two-day battle of Aspern-Essling on 21–22 May 1809. Six weeks later he displayed front-line courage, taking a bullet wound to the shoulder while rallying some troops, yet suffered a resounding defeat at Wagram, the last battle he ever fought. For the remainder of the Napoleonic wars Austria trusted her fortunes on the battlefield to Prince Schwarzenberg. After 1809 Karl lived in relative obscurity until his death in 1847 at the age of seventy-six.

Berthier

Continuing in his familiar role as chief of staff, he served brilliantly, overseeing complex logistics for the Danube crossing preceding Wagram. This performance earned him the title Prince of Wagram. He acted as chief of staff through Russia but became increasingly war-weary. Wounded in France in 1814, he joined a mutinous group of marshals who forced Napoleon to abdicate. He backed Louis XVIII when Napoleon returned from exile and saw his name struck from the list of marshals. Two weeks before Waterloo he was either murdered or committed suicide at age sixty-two. Of all Napoleon's marshals, Berthier—because of his ability to translate Napoleon's concepts into clear operational orders—was indispensable.

Bessières

Defeated by Hiller's surprise counteroffensive at Neumarkt on 24 April, he redeemed himself on the bloody field of Aspern-Essling. After distinguishing himself on the first day, he had to be physically separated from Lannes when the two nearly began a duel over a point of honor. The next day he led the Imperial Guard cavalry in a sacrificial assault to cover Lannes' retreat. He showed great courage steadying his men under a withering artillery barrage. Serving in Spain in 1811 he again quarreled with a fellow marshal, Masséna this time, and thus failed to support him at a potentially decisive battle against the British. At the head of the Guard cavalry at Borodino in 1812 he advised Napoleon not to commit the Guard to battle, advice Napoleon heeded to his profound detriment. In 1813 a cannonball killed him while he was conducting a reconnaissance. Marshal Ney gazed at his body and said "It was a good death, our kind of death!" The second marshal to fall in combat, he died at the age of forty-five.

Davout

At Wagram Davout commanded the decisive flanking attack and was rewarded for both this and his earlier performance during the Ratisbonne campaign with the title Prince of Eckmühl. His corps, renumbered the First Corps, again garrisoned Germany until the invasion of Russia. In 1812 he commanded the largest corps, a sure sign of Napoleon's trust, and was wounded at Borodino. His reputation was slightly tarnished during the winter retreat, but he rebounded to defend Hamburg for nearly a year, refusing to yield until receiving a direct order from Louis XVIII a month after Napoleon's abdication. He served as minister of war during the Hundred Days and saw no field action. Exiled for a time, he regained favor in 1819. He died of consumption in 1823, at fifty-three. Although never friendly with Napoleon, Davout was extremely loyal and the Emperor's most able marshal. On Saint Helena Napoleon called him "one of the purest glories of France." He was never defeated in battle.

Friant

Gravely wounded at Wagram, he recovered to lead a division under Davout into Russia. Wounded at Smolensk and twice at Borodino, he survived to become Napoleon's chamberlain, a position of great trust and honor. He commanded Guard formations in battles from 1813 to 1815 and was again wounded when leading the final, disastrous attack at Waterloo. He retired from service in 1815 and lived for fourteen more years until his death at the age of seventy-one.

Gudin

Davout's favorite divisional commander, Gudin was wounded four times at Wagram. He recovered to lead a division in Davout's corps into Russia but died at forty-four of wounds received at Valutina.

Hiller

Showing surprising energy, Hiller gathered his forces and attacked Bessières on 24 April, winning a small victory. He abjectly failed to defend a strong position at Ebelsberg (in the words of one observer, "a man who could fail so hopelessly in such a position . . . is not worthy of the name of a general").[3] At Aspern-Essling he led his corps with firmness; four times it captured Aspern, only to be driven out by French counterattack. He resigned his command, pleading illness, before Wagram. In 1813–

1814, again operating in his cherished role as an independent commander, he achieved some success on secondary fronts in Dalmatia and Italy. He died at age sixty-five in 1819.

Lannes

On 21 May he led his men over the Danube onto the field of Aspern-Essling. Fighting with his back to the river, Lannes typically exhibited superb tactical skill in an exceedingly difficult situation. He had to rely upon Bessières to extricate him, which led to a bitter quarrel that night. The next day featured more grim combat as he tenaciously held onto a key village in the face of overwhelming assault. Toward evening a cannonball struck down a dear comrade (reminiscent of Cervoni's death at Eckmühl) and he sat down to mourn. Another cannonball from the same battery smashed both his legs. Nine days later gangrene killed him at age forty. Mourned by Napoleon and the whole army, thus died the first Napoleonic marshal and one of the Emperor's few true friends.

Masséna

At Aspern-Essling he held the Aspern sector with great aplomb and then covered the retreat. His intercession kept Bessières and Lannes from dueling. Unable to ride due to injury, he conveyed himself about the battlefield of Wagram in a carriage pulled in prominent display by white horses. Rewarded with the title Prince of Essling, he unwillingly went to Spain to lead an army against Wellington. Returning to the lax habits displayed on the road to Landshut, he was defeated and disgraced in 1811. That ended his active service although he rallied, with a distinct lack of enthusiasm, to Napoleon during the Hundred Days. He died at fifty-nine in 1817. Considered one of Napoleon's most able marshals, his great days were behind him by the time of the 1809 war.

Montbrun

Napoleon showed his great satisfaction with Montbrun's conduct during the Ratisbonne campaign by giving his light cavalry a place of honor during a grand review staged the following month in Vienna. He went to Spain as head of Masséna's cavalry, distinguished himself in many actions and beat the British at the combat of El Bodon. Recalled for the Russian campaign, he died at Borodino at age forty-two.

Morand

Like Gudin and Friant, he was wounded at Wagram (thus of Davout's four divisional commanders, one died and three were wounded in the grim fighting around Vienna). Morand served under Davout in Russia and received a grave wound at Borodino. He survived to fight the 1813–1814 campaigns with distinction. He rallied to Napoleon during the Hundred Days, serving as aide and leading the Imperial Guard against Placenoit on the field of Waterloo. Forced into exile when Louis XVIII returned, he was later permitted to come back to France and to lead an honored life. He died in 1835 at the age of sixty-four.

Mouton

The hero of Landshut distinguished himself again during a desperate moment at Aspern-Essling. At a time of crisis Napoleon sent him to lead units of the Imperial Guard in a counterattack against Essling. As at Landshut, he led his men in column in a bayonet assault that cleared the village. Rewarded with the title Count Lobau, he fought at Wagram, performed senior staff duty in Russia, and was one of a select few to accompany Napoleon back to France. He led major units in the 1813 campaign. Now referred to as Lobau, he commanded a corps in Napoleon's army that went to Waterloo and was wounded and taken prisoner at Placenoit. He entered liberal politics, putting down a revolt of Bonapartist rioters in 1831—which earned him the final step that Napoleon (for all his respect of the man) had denied: promotion to marshal. He died seven years later, at sixty-eight, when an old wound reopened.

Nansouty

Nansouty led his cuirassiers with distinction at Aspern-Essling and Wagram. Promoted, he commanded an entire cavalry corps during the Russian campaign and like so many others was wounded at Borodino. He commanded the Imperial Guard cavalry during the 1813–1814 campaigns, suffering another wound. He died at age forty-seven, shortly before the Hundred Days, in 1815.

Radetzky

In 1813 Radetzky served as chief of staff to Schwarzenberg when Austria joined the Allied fight against Napoleon. He contributed his share of wild schemes during the numerous councils of war that characterized Allied war planning in 1813. Following the Napoleonic wars he tried unsuccessfully to reform the Austrian army and was retired for his efforts. Recalled to service for a last time at age eighty-two, he defended Northern Italy during the 1848 Italian war of independence. He conducted a brilliant offensive-defensive campaign worthy of Napoleon himself, culminating in the victory at Novara. Venerated by the rank and file, he served as governor of Lombardy-Venetia until 1857 and died in January 1858.

Saint-Hilaire

Promised a marshal's baton on the field at Ratisbonne, Saint-Hilaire did not live to receive it. At Aspern-Essling his left foot was shot away, a wound differing only slightly in aim and velocity from Napoleon's wound at Ratisbonne. Two weeks later gangrene killed him at age forty-three.

Schwarzenberg

Schwarzenberg departed his St. Petersburg embassy in time to join the army and lead a cavalry brigade at Wagram. Following the 1809 war he was transferred to Paris, where he participated in negotiations over Napoleon's marriage to Marie-Louise. He commanded the Austrian corps in Napoleon's invasion of Russia and skillfully managed to avoid any serious fighting. When Austria declared war on France in 1813 he became Generalissimus of all Allied armies. Here he acted in an Eisenhower-type role by forwarding grand strategy amid the squabble of rival national goals. He commanded at the great Allied triumph at Leipzig—"the Battle of Nations"—and led the invasion of France. In 1815 he led the Austrian army toward the Rhine, but news of Waterloo forestalled him. Stricken by paralysis in 1817, he died at the age of forty-nine in 1820.

The "Terrible Fifty-seventh"

At Aspern-Essling the Fifty-seventh spearheaded the major French attack. It breached the Austrian defense and captured hundreds of defenders and six guns. Lacking sufficient support, its attack degenerated into a costly musketry duel. At Wagram the regiment again distinguished itself by defeating two Austrian regiments defending a key village and then standing firm in the face of near-overwhelming counterattack. It accompanied Davout to Russia. Only a few veterans survived.

The Tenth Légère

Advancing near the Fifty-seventh at Wagram, the Tenth took four colors and 2000 prisoners. It continued and ruptured the Austrian position behind the Russbach. Karl personally led a cavalry counterattack that broke before the Tenth's squares. Taking a bullet probably fired by someone in the Tenth, Karl rallied his troopers for a renewed effort that eventually forced the Tenth into a sullen withdrawal.

APPENDIX II

Order of Battle

der k.k. Hauptarmee as of 20 March 1809†

Generalissimus: FM Erzherzog Karl
Generaladjutanten: Phillipp Grunne
Staff troops: one dragoon squadron; two infantry companies
Technical troops: three pontonier companies with 145 pontoons; 1st and 4th Sapper
Companies, one boat handler company

I ArmeeKorps GdK Heinrich Graf Bellegarde
(27,653 and 62 guns)

Staff troops: one-half dragoon squadron; one infantry company
Technical troops: two pioneer companies

Division FML Vogelsang		*(battalions/squadrons)*
Brigade GM Henneberg	Erzherzog Johann IR#35	(3 guns)
	Erbach IR#42	(3)
	6lb brigade baty	(8 guns)
Brigade GM Am Ende	Reuss-Plauen IR#17	(3)
	Kollowrat IR#36	(3)
	6lb brigade baty	(8 guns)
	6lb position baty	(6 guns)

Division FML Ulm		*(battalions/squadrons)*
Brigade GM Wacquant	Anton Mittrowsky IR#10	(3)
	Erzherzog Rainter IR#11	(3)
	Vogelsang IR#47	(3)
	6lb brigade baty	(8 guns)
Division FML Fresnel		
Brigade GM Nostitz	Mahr Freiwilliger Jager	(1)
	2d Jäger Battalion	(1)
	4th Jäger Battalion	(1)
	Schwarzenberg Uhlans #2	(8)
	3lb brigade baty	(8 guns)
Brigade GM Wintzingerode	Mahr Freiwilliger Jager	(1)
	1st Jäger Battalion	(1)
	3d Jäger Battalion	(1)
	Blankenstein Hussars #6	(8)
	6lb cavalry baty	(6 guns)
Reserve Artillery:		
two 12lb position baty		(12 guns)
one 6lb position baty		(6 guns)

II ArmeeKorps FZM Karl Kolowrath-Krakowsky
(28,168 and 68 guns)

Staff troops: one-half dragoon squadron; one infantry company
Technical troops: two pioneer companies

Division FML Brady		
Brigade GM Greifenbach	Zach IR#15	(3)
	Joseph Colloredo IR#57	(3)
	6lb brigade baty	(8 guns)
Brigade GM Folseis	Zedtwitz IR#25	(3)
	Froon IR#54	(3)
	6lb brigade baty	(8 guns)
	6lb position baty	(6 guns)
Division FML Treunenfels		
Brigade GM Wied-Runkel	Stuart IR#18	(3)
	Rohan IR#21	(3)
	Frelich IR#28	(3)
	6lb brigade baty	(8 guns)
	6lb position baty	(6 guns)
Division FML Klenau		
Brigade GM Vecsey	2d Bat. E. Karl Legion	(1)
	7th Jäger Battalion	(1)

		(*battalions/squadrons*)
	8th Jäger Battalion	(1)
	Klenau Chevaulégers #5	(8)
	3lb brigade baty	(8 guns)

Division FML Klenau

Brigade GM Crenneville	4th Bat. E. Karl Legion	(1)
	5th Jäger Battalion	(1)
	6 Jäger Battalion	(1)
	Merveldt Uhlans #1	(8)
	6lb cavalry baty	(6 guns)

Reserve Artillery:

two 12lb position baty	(12 guns)
one 6lb position baty	(6 guns)

III ArmeeKorps FML Friedrich Hohenzollern-Hechingen
(29,360 and 96 guns)

Staff troops: one-half dragoon squadron; one infantry company
Technical troops: two pioneer companies

Division FML Lusignan

Brigade GM Kayser	Wenzel Colloredo IR#56	(3)
	Karl Schroder IR#7	(3)
	6lb brigade baty	(8 guns)
Brigade GM Thierry	Kaiser IR#1	(3)
	Lindenau IR#29	(3)
	6lb brigade baty	(8 guns)
	6lb position baty	(6 guns)

Division FML Saint Julien

Brigade GM A. Liechtenstein	Manfredini IR#12	(3)
	Wurzburg IR#23	(3)
	6lb brigade baty	(8 guns)
Brigade GM Bieber	Kaunitz IR#20	(3)
	Wurttemberg IR#38	(3)
	6lb brigade baty	(8 guns)
	6lb position baty	(6 guns)

Division FML Vukassovich

Brigade GM M. Liechtenstein	1st Bat. E. Karl Legion	(1)
	3d Bat. E. Karl Legion	(1)
	E. Ferdinand Hussars #3	(8)
	3lb brigade baty	(8 guns)
Brigade GM Pfanzelter	Peterwardeiner Grenz #9	(2)
	Hessen-Homburg Hussars	(8)

		(*battalions/squadrons*)
	3lb Grenz baty	(8 guns)
	6lb cavalry baty	(6 guns)
Reserve Artillery:		
three 12lb position baty		(18 guns)
one 6lb position baty		(6 guns)

IV ArmeeKorps FML Franz Rosenberg
(27,800 and 60 guns)

Staff troops: one-half dragoon squadron; one infantry company
Technical troops: two pioneer companies

Division FML Dedovich

Brigade GM Grill	Erzherzog Louis IR#8	(3)
	Koburg IR#22	(3)
	6lb brigade baty	(8 guns)
Brigade GM Neustadter	Czartoryski IR#9	(3)
	Reuss-Greitz IR#55	(3)
	6lb brigade baty	(8 guns)
	6lb position baty	(6 guns)

Division FML Bartenstein

Brigade GM Riese	Josef Mittrowsky IR#40	(3)
	Bellegarde IR#44	(3)
	Chasteler IR#46	(3)
	6lb brigade baty	(8 guns)
Brigade GM Waldegg	5th Bat. E. Karl Legion	(1)
	6th Bat. E. Karl Legion	(1)
	6lb position baty	(6 guns)

Division FML Somariva

Brigade GM Stutterheim	Deutsch-Banater Grenz	(2)
	Vincent Chevaulégers #4	(8)
	3lb Grenz baty	(8 guns)
Brigade GM Radivojevich	Walachish-Illyr. Grenz	(2)
	Stipsicz Hussars #10	(8)
	6lb cavalry baty	(6 guns)
Reserve Artillery:		
two 12lb position baty		(12 guns)
one 6lb cavalry baty		(6 guns)

V ArmeeKorps FML Erzherzog Louis
(32,266 and 68 guns)

Staff troops: one-half dragoon squadron; one infantry company
Technical troops: two pioneer companies

Division FML Lindenau		(*battalions/squadrons*)
Brigade GM Mayer	Erzherzog Karl IR#3	(3)
	Stain IR#50	(3)
	6lb brigade baty	(8 guns)
Brigade GM Berenburg	Hiller IR#2	(3)
	Sztarrai IR#33	(3)
	6lb brigade baty	(8 guns)
	6lb position baty	(6 guns)

Division FML Reuss-Plauen		
Brigade GM Bianchi	Duka IR#39	(3)
	Gyulai IR#60	(3)
	6lb brigade baty	(8 guns)
Brigade GM Rothacker	1st Bat. Vienna Freiwill.	(1)
	2d Bat. Vienna Freiwill.	(1)
	3d Bat. Vienna Freiwill.	(1)
	6lb position baty	(6 guns)

Division FML Schustekh		
Brigade GM Mesko	Broder Grenz	(2)
	Kienmayer Hussars #8	(8)
	3lb Grenz baty	(8 guns)
Brigade GM Radetzky	Gradiskaner Grenz	(2)
	E. Karl Uhlans #3	(8)
	6lb cavalry baty	(6 guns)

Reserve Artillery:		
two 12lb position baty		(12 guns)
one 6lb cavalry baty		(6 guns)

VI ArmeeKorps FML Johann Hiller
(35,639 and 96 guns)

Staff troops: one-half dragoon squadron; one infantry company
Technical troops: two pioneer companies

Division FML Kottulinsky		
Brigade GM Hohenfeld	Klebek IR#14	(3)
	Jordis IR#59	(3)
	6lb brigade baty	(8 guns)
Brigade GM Weissenwolff	Deutschmeister IR#4	(3)
	Kerpen IR#49	(3)
	6lb brigade baty	(8 guns)
	6lb position baty	(6 guns)

Division FML Jellacic		*(battalions/squadrons)*
Brigade GM Hoffeneck	Benjowsky IR#31	(3)
	Spleny IR#51	(3)
	6lb brigade baty	(8 guns)
Brigade GM Ettingshausen	Esterhazy IR#32	(3)
	de Vaux IR#45	(3)
	6lb brigade baty	(8 guns)
	6lb position baty	(6 guns)

Division FML Vincent		
Brigade GM Provencheres	4th Bat. Vienna Freiwill.	(1)
	5th Bat. Vienna Freiwill.	(1)
	6th Bat. Vienna Freiwill.	(1)
	Warasdin-Kreuzer Grenz	(2)
	O'Reilly Chevaulégers #3	(8)
	3lb brigade baty	(8 guns)
	6lb cavalry baty	(6 guns)
Brigade GM Nordmann	Warasdin-St. George Grenz	(2)
	Liechtenstein Hussars #7	(8)
	Rosenberg Chevaulégers #8	(8)
	3lb Grenz baty	(8 guns)
	6lb cavalry baty	(6 guns)

Reserve Artillery:
   three 12lb position baty   (18 guns)
   one 6lb cavalry baty   (6 guns)

1 Reservekorps GdK Johannes Liechtenstein
(18,063 and 34 guns)

Brigade GM Rohan	Grenadier Bat. Mayblumel	(1)
	Grenadier Bat. Leiningen	(1)
	Grenadier Bat. Hohenlohe	(1)
	Grenadier Bat. Hauger	(1)
	Grenadier Bat. Cappy	(1)
	Grenadier Bat. Peccaduc	(1)
	Grenadier Bat. Wieniawsky	(1)
	Grenadier Bat. Nissel	(1)
	Grenadier Bat. Stark	(1)
	Grenadier Bat. Georgy	(1)
	Grenadier Bat. Bissingen	(1)
	Grenadier Bat. Hahn	(1)
	two 6lb brigade baty (16 guns)	

		(*battalions/squadrons*)
Brigade GM Siegenthal	E. Albert Cuirassiers	(6)
	E. Franz Cuirassiers	(6)
	6lb cavalry baty	(6 guns)
Brigade GM Lederer	E. Ferdinand Cuirassiers	(6)
	Hohenzollern Cuirassiers	(6)
	6lb cavalry baty	(6 guns)
Brigade Rottermund	Riesch Dragoons	(6)
	E. Johann Dragoons	(6)
	6lb cavalry baty	(6 guns)

2 Reservekorps FML Michael Kienmayer
(7,975 and 20 guns)

Brigade GM d'Aspre	Grenadier Bat. Puteani	(1)
	Gren. Bat. Brezeczinsky	(1)
	Grenadier Bat. Scovaud	(1)
	Gren. Bat. Kirchenbetter	(1)
	Grenadier Bat. Scharlach	(1)
	6lb brigade baty	(8 guns)
Brigade GM Schneller	Kaiser Cuirassiers	(6)
	Gottesheim Cuirassiers	(6)
	6lb cavalry baty	(6 guns)
Brigade GM Clary	Levenehr Dragoons	(6)
	Württemberg Dragoons	(6)
	6lb cavalry baty	(6 guns)

Summary:

	btns.	sqds.	guns	inf.	cav.	total[*]
I Armeekorps	27	16	62	25,487	2,166	27,653
II Armeekorps	27	16	68	26,099	2,069	28,168
III Armeekorps	28	16	96	27,483	1,877	29,360
IV Armeekorps	27	16	60	25,600	2,200	27,800
V Armeekorps	28	16	68	30,048	2,218	32,266
VI Armeekorps	31	24	96	33,576	2,063	35,639
I Reservekorps	12	36	34	13,904	4,159	18,063
II Reservekorps	5	24	20	4,960	3,015	7,975
total	185	164	504	187,157	19,767	206,924

† From official Kriegsarchiv returns. When returns noted the exclusion of certain units, those units' estimated strengths were added in.

[*] Does not include artillerists and technical troops.

L'Armée d'Allemagne as of 16 April 1809#

La Majeste L'Empereur Napoleon
Chef d'état-major du Armée d'Allemagne: Maréchal Berthier
Staff troops: about 300 officers and aides

II Corps General de Division Nicolas Oudinot
(21,298 and 42 guns)

1st Division Tharreau		*(battalions/squadrons)*
Brigade Conroux	6 Légère	(1)
	24 Légère	(1)
1st Division Tharreau		
	25 Légère	(1)
	9 Légère	(1)
	16 Légère	(1)
	27 Légère	(1)
Brigade Albert	18 Ligne	(1)
	24 Ligne	(1)
	45 Ligne	(1)
	94 Ligne	(1)
	95 Ligne	(1)
	96 Ligne	(1)
Brigade Jarry	4 Ligne	(1)
	18 Ligne	(1)
	54 Ligne	(1)
	63 Ligne	(1)
	baty (two 8lb, six 4lb)	(8 guns)

2d Division Claparede		
Brigade Coehorn	17 Légère	(1)
	21 Légère	(1)
	28 Légère	(1)
	28 Légère	(1)
	Tirailleurs du Po	(1)
	Tirailleurs Corses	(1)
Brigade Lesuire	27 Ligne	(1)
	39 Ligne	(1)
	59 Ligne	(1)
	69 Ligne	(1)
	76 Ligne	(1)

		(*battalions/squadrons*)
Brigade Ficatier	40 Ligne	(1)
	88 Ligne	(1)
	64 Ligne	(1)
	100 Ligne	(1)
	103 Ligne	(1)
	4lb baty	(8 guns)
Brigade Colbert	9 Hussars	(3)
	7 Chasseurs à cheval	(3)
	20 Chasseurs à cheval	(3)

3d Heavy Cavalry Division d'Espagne

Brigade Raynaud	4 Cuirassiers	(4)
	6 Cuirassiers	(4)
Brigade Fouler	7 Cuirassiers	(4)
	8 Cuirassiers	(4)
	two 8lb horse baty	(12 guns)

Corps Reserve Artillery	12lb baty	(6 guns)
	8lb baty	(8 guns)
	three sapper/engineer companies	

III Corps Maréchal Louis Davout, Duc de Auerstadt
(60,597 and 65 guns)

1st Division Morand

Brigade Lacour	13 Légère	(3)
	17 Ligne	(3)
	30 Ligne	(3)
Brigade l'Huillier	61 Ligne	(3)
	65 Ligne	(3)
	8lb baty	(8 guns)
	4lb horse baty	(4 guns)

2d Division Friant

Brigade Gilly	15 Légère	(3)
	33 Ligne	(3)
Brigade Grandeau	108 Ligne	(3)
	111 Ligne	(3)
Brigade Barbanegre	48 Ligne	(3)
	8lb baty	(8 guns)

3d Division Gudin		(*battalions/squadrons*)
Brigade Petit	7 Légère	(3)
Brigade Boyer	12 Ligne	(3)
	21 Ligne	(3)
Brigade Duppelin	25 Ligne	(3)
	85 Ligne	(3)
	8lb baty	(6 guns)
	4lb horse baty	(6 guns)
4th Division Saint-Hilaire		
Brigade Lorencez	10 Légère	(3)
	3 Ligne	(3)
	57 Ligne	(3)
4th Division Saint-Hilaire		
Brigade Destabenrath	72 Ligne	(3)
	105 Ligne	(3)
	8lb baty	(8 guns)
	6lb horse baty	(7 guns)
Reserve Division Demont		
1st Brigade	17 Ligne	(1)
	30 Ligne	(1)
	61 Ligne	(1)
	65 Ligne	(1)
2d Brigade	33 Ligne	(1)
	111 Ligne	(1)
3d Brigade	7 Légère	(1)
	21 Ligne	(1)
	12 Ligne	(1)
	85 Ligne	(1)
2d Heavy Cavalry Division Saint-Sulpice		
Brigade Clement	1 Cuirassiers	(4)
	5 Cuirassiers	(4)
Brigade Guiton	10 Cuirassiers	(4)
	11 Cuirassiers	(4)
	8lb horse baty	(6 guns)

Light Cavalry Division Montbrun		(*battalions/squadrons*)
Brigade Pajol	5 Hussars	(3)
	7 Hussars	(3)
	11 Chasseurs à cheval	(3)
Brigade Piré	8 Hussars	(3)
	16 Chasseurs à cheval	(3)
Brigade Jacquinot	1 Chasseurs à cheval	(3)
	2 Chasseurs à cheval	(3)
Corps Reserve Artillery	two 12lb baty	(12 guns)
	four sapper battalions	
	one pontoniers company	

IV Corps Maréchal André Masséna, Duc de Rivoli
(37,570 and 67 guns)

1st Division Legrand		
Brigade Ledru	26 Légère	(3)
1st Division Legrand		
	18 Ligne	(3)
Baden Brigade	Leib Regiment	(2)
	Grossherzog Regiment	(2)
	Erbgrossherzog Regiment	(2)
	Jäger battalion Lingg	(1)
	6lb baty	(8 guns)
	6lb horse baty	(6 guns)
	Baden 6lb baty	(8 guns)
	½ Baden 6lb horse baty	(4 guns)
2d Division Carra Saint-Cyr		
Brigade Cosson	24 Légère	(3)
Brigade Dalesme	4 Ligne	(3)
	46 Ligne	(3)
Hesse-Darmstadt Brigade	Leib Garde	(2)
	Leib Garde Fusilier battalion	(1)
	Hesse-Darmstadt Fusiliers	(1)
	Hesse-Darmstadt Musketeers	(1)
	6lb baty	(8 guns)
	6lb horse baty	(6 guns)
	Hesse-Darm. 6lb baty	(7 guns)

3d Division Molitor   (*battalions/squadrons*)

Brigade Leguay	2 Ligne	(2)
	16 Ligne	(3)
Brigade Viviez	37 Ligne	(3)
	67 Ligne	(2)
	6lb baty	(6 guns)

4th Division Boudet

Brigade Fririon	3 Légère	(2)
Brigade Valory	56 Ligne	(3)
	93 Ligne	(2)
	6lb baty	(6 guns)

Light Cavalry Division Marulaz

1st Brigade	19 Chasseurs à cheval	(3)
	23 Chasseurs à cheval	(3)
Brigade Castex	3 Chasseurs à cheval	(2)
	14 Chasseurs à cheval	(3)
3d Brigade	Baden Light Dragoons	(4)
	Hesse-Darmstadt Chevaulégers	(3)
Corps Reserve Artillery	12lb baty	(8 guns)
	three sapper companies	
	one pontoniers company	

VII Corps (Bavarian) Maréchal François Lefebvre, Duc de Dantzig
(27,603 and 72 guns)

1st Division Prince Royal

Brigade Rechberg	1 Light battalion Habermann	(1)
	Leib Regiment	(2)
	2 Regiment Prince Royal	(2)
Brigade Stengel	4 Regiment Salern	(2)
	8 Regiment Duc Pius	(2)
Cavalry Brigade Zandt	Minuzzi Dragoons	(2)
	Prince Royal Chevaulégers	(4)
	two 6lb baty	(12 guns)
	6lb horse baty	(6 guns)
	staff escort infantry company	
	staff reserve cavalry squadron	

2d Division Wrede		*(battalions/squadrons)*
Brigade Minuzzi	6 Light battalion Laroche	(1)
	3 Regiment Prince Karl	(2)
	13 Regiment	(2)
Brigade Beckers	6 Regiment Duc Wilhelm	(2)
	7 Regiment Lowenstein	(2)
Cavalry Brigade Preysing	Konig Chevaulégers	(4)
	Leiningen Chevaulégers	(4)
	two 6lb baty	(12 guns)
	6lb horse baty	(6 guns)
	staff escort infantry company	
	staff reserve ½ cavalry squadron	

3d Division Deroi		
Brigade Siebein	5 Light battalion Buttler	(1)
	9 Regiment Isenburg	(2)
	10 Regiment Juncker	(2)
Brigade Vincenti	7 Light battalion Gunter	(1)
	5 Regiment von Preysing	(2)
	14 Regiment	(2)
Calvary Brigade Seydewitz	Taxis Dragoons	(4)
	Bubenhoven Chevaulégers	(4)
	two 6lb baty	(12 guns)
	6lb horse baty	(6 guns)
	staff escort infantry company	
	staff reserve ½ cavalry squadron	

Corps Reserve Artillery	three 12lb baty	(18 guns)

Württemberg Corps General de Division Vandamme
(12,242 and 22 guns)

Infantry Division Neubronn		
Brigade Franquemont	Regiment Prince Royal	(2)
	Regiment Duc Wilhelm	(2)
	Fusilier Regiment Neubronn	(1)
Brigade Scharfenstein	Regiment Phull	(2)
	Regiment Camrer	(2)
	Fusilier Regiment Neubronn	(1)

		(*battalions/squadrons*)
Light Brigade Hugel	Jäger battalion König	(1)
	1 Light battalion Wolff	(1)
	2 Light battalion Bruselle	(1)
Cavalry Division Wollwarth		
Brigade Roeder	König Chevaulégers	(4)
	Duc Henry Chevaulégers	(4)
Brigade Stettner	Konig Chasseurs à cheval	(4)
	Duc Louis Chasseurs à cheval	(4)
Corps Artillery	6lb company	(10 guns)
	two 6lb horse baty	(12 guns)

Unattached Troops

Reserve Division Dupas
(6,091 and 12 guns)

Brigade Gency	5 Légère	(2)
	19 Ligne	(3)
Cavalry Brigade Bruyer	13 Chasseurs à cheval	(3)
	24 Chasseurs à cheval	(2)
	two baty	(12 guns)

1st Heavy Cavalry Division Nansouty
(5,085 and 12 guns)

Brigade Defrance	1 Carabiniers	(4)
	2 Carabiniers	(4)
Brigade Doumerc	2 Cuirassiers	(4)
	9 Cuirassiers	(4)
Brigade Saint Germain	3 Cuirassiers	(4)
	12 Cuirassiers	(4)
	two 8lb horse baty	(12 guns)

Rhinebund Division Rouyer
(3,820)

	2 Nassau Regiment	(1)
	Nassau contingent	(1)
	Anhalt Lippe Regiment #5	(2)
	Saxon Regiment #4	(3)
	Waldeck Regiment #6	(2)

Summary (based on "present under arms" on 15 April 1809):

	btns.	sqds.	guns	inf.[*]	cav.[†]	total
II Corps	32	23	42	16,005	5,293	21,298
III Corps	70	37	65	51,968	8,629	60,597
IV Corps	43	18	67	34,805	2,765	37,570
VII Corps	28	22	72	24,334	3,269	27,603
Württemberg Corps	13	16	22	10,028	2,214	12,242
Dupas	5	5	12	4,713	1,378	6,091
Nansouty		24	12		5,085	5,085
Rouyer	8			3,820		3,820
total	199	145	292	145,673	28,633	174,306

† Includes field artillery, parks, and engineers.
* Includes horse artillery.
# From Pelet; Bowden and Tarbox; Petre; and Saski II.

APPENDIX III

Command and Control

The confused ridgeline and woods fighting that took place along a broad front put heavy demands upon the rival commanders. Napoleon (and Karl) absolutely depended upon the timely arrival of information from their subordinates. Thus it is of special interest to consider data on how much time a message required to pass from one headquarters to another.

Normally Napoleon's staff kept careful track of the flow of orders: when sent, when received, duplicate copy to file. The beginning of the 1809 war saw the staff not yet fully assembled. Consequently, improvisation ruled. Even so, most messages to and from imperial headquarters began with words like "I have just received yours of 6 P.M." so that both parties clearly understood what information they were discussing. Much could go wrong. On the night of 20 April Lefebvre wrote the Emperor that he had just received his first communication from Davout, a matter of critical importance since everyone worried about what had happened to the isolated Third Corps. The message carried the postmark *Teschen*. Lefebvre lamented that he could not find this village on his map. In fact, Davout's staff had erred. The postmark should have read *Teugen*.

Transit times:

17 April: *Napoleon (Donauworth) to Masséna (Augsburg); sent 1 P.M., arrived 7 P.M. All secure roads, distance 25 miles. Rate: 4.2 miles per hour (mph).*

17 April: *Berthier (Donauworth) to Masséna (Augsburg); sent 7 P.M., arrived 2:30 A.M. All secure roads, distance 25 miles. Rate: 3.3 mph.*

19 April: *Lefebvre (Neustadt) to Napoleon (Ingolstadt); sent 6 P.M., arrived 3 A.M. (20th). All secure roads, distance 17 miles. Rate: 1.9 mph.*

19 April: *Masséna (Pfaffenhofen) to Napoleon (Ingolstadt)*; sent 9 A.M., arrived 11:30 A.M. *All secure roads, distance 20 miles. Rate: 8 mph.*

19 April: *Savary (Teugen) carries dispatches and personal report to Napoleon (Neuburg)*; departs 7 P.M., arrived 2 A.M. (20th). *Travels along unsecured roads, distance 40 miles. Rate: 5.7 mph.*

20 April: *Berthier (Vohburg) to Lefebvre (Abensberg)*; sent 3 A.M., arrived 6 A.M. *Against the grain of French communications, distance 12 miles. Rate: 4 mph.*

20 April: *Berthier (Vohburg) to Masséna (Pfaffenhofen)*; sent midnight, arrived 6:45 A.M., *distance 18 miles. Rate: 2.7 mph.*

20 April: *Berthier (Vohburg) to Masséna (Pfaffenhofen)*; sent 3 A.M., arrived 10 A.M., *distance 18 miles. Rate: 2.6 mph.*

20 April: *Davout (Teugen) to Napoleon (en route Bachel)*; sent 4:30 A.M., arrived 5 P.M. *Imperial headquarters moving forward during the day, distance 10 miles. Rate: 0.8 mph.*

21 April: *Napoleon (Bachel) to Davout (Teugen)*; sent 8 P.M. (20th) arrived 4:30 A.M. *Courier riding mostly on secure roads but across some recently cleared area, distance 10 miles. Rate: 1.2 mph.*

It is difficult to generalize from a small sample, yet clearly the average transmission of messages required longer than the five to ten miles per hour claimed by some. Variables slowing speed of transmission included the presence of the enemy, the type of road net, and darkness. Moreover, the exchange of information was not merely a matter of how fast a courier moved. Army headquarters staff had to digest the information and decide what to do (a paralyzing problem when Karl fell prey to epileptic seizures). A corps headquarters receiving an order had to disseminate the order down the chain of command. All of this took time and helps explain why commanders often failed to take advantage of many opportunities clearly apparent long after the event.

APPENDIX IV

The 1809 Campaign as a War Game

Take away the differences between Napoleon and Karl, and the forces contesting the fate of Europe during the Ratisbonne campaign were extremely evenly matched. It was a dynamic war of maneuver through the rolling, wooded terrain of the Bavarian countryside. These features make a fine campaign for the historical war-gamer. One can refight actual historical encounters; the skirmish-gamer can refight Meda's reconnaissance (recounted in Chapter IV, Part 1) or the assault over the Landshut bridge, the tactical commander the fight along the Teugen–Hausen ridge or the cavalry combat at Alt Eglofsheim, the grand-tactical gamer Karl's offensive against Davout or the Battle of Eckmühl. Alternatively, one can design original games based on historical forces and terrain or, better yet, games that result from map movement over the historical terrain. Based on my six years of research I have come to certain opinions regarding the characteristics of the rival forces. Others may differ, but the following provides a synthesis that can assist the wargamer in designing games using his favorite rules set.

Leadership

Leadership (called initiative in some rules) is a measurement of a general's ability to respond to orders, to recognize a situation not covered by his orders, and to exercise independent action. It is on a scale of 1 to 10 with 1 equaling little ability and 10 equaling total prescience.

French

II Corps   Oudinot 5; Claparede, Tharreau, d'Espagne 4

III Corps   Davout 9; Friant, Gudin, Saint-Hilaire, Montbrun 7; Gudin, Saint-Sulpice 6; Demont 3

IV Corps   Masséna 6; all divisional commanders 5

VII Corps   Lefebvre, Wrede 5; Deroi 4; Prince Royal 3

Württemberg Corps   Vandamme 6; Neubronn 5; Wollwarth 4

Attached   Nansouty 7; Dupas 3; Rouyer 2

Austrians

I Corps   Bellegarde 4; Fresnel 3; Vogelsang, Ulm 2

II Corps   Kollowrath 3; Klenau 4; Brady, Treunenfels 2

III Corps   Hohenzollern 6; Vukassovich 5; Saint-Julien, Lusignan 2

IV Corps   Rosenberg, Somariva 5; Dedovich, Bartenstein 2

V Corps   Louis, Reuss-Plauen Lindenau; Schustekh 4

VI Corps   Hiller 4; Vincent 6; Kottulinsky, Jellacic 2

I Reserve   Liechtenstein 3

II Reserve   Kienmayer 2

Unit Ratings

Unit ratings are Elite, Veteran, Regular, and Militia. These ratings indicate how much a unit can endure before it must check morale. As a general point of reference, *Regular* indicates a professional military formation accustomed to the rigors of the battlefield.

Most Austrian formations should be rated as such. They include line infantry, artillery, jägers, grenzers, and most light cavalry. Grenadiers, cuirassiers, Vincent Chevaulégers, Stipsicz Hussars, and the Deutschmeister Regiment deserve a *Veteran* rating. All Friewilligers (landwehr) are rated *Militia*. Unlike other European powers, the Austrian army had no elites.

Absent the Imperial Guard, the French army likewise has no elites. The Second Corps conscripts and Demont are rated *Militia*. Davout's other four divisions and artillery, all heavy cavalry, Montbrun's division, and Colbert's cavalry brigade ("Infernal Brigade") must have the exalted *Veteran* status. All other French and French-allied units are rated *Regular*.

Morale

Morale is on a scale of 1 (cowardly) to 10 (heroic). Unless otherwise noted, Militia-status units have a morale of 6, Regular 7, and Veteran 8.

Numerous exceptions reflect the personality of individual units. For such a subjective decision I suggest that readers should make their own designations. For example, in this campaign a Bavarian regular was not quite the equal of his French counterpart. Reflect this by giving the Bavarians a 6 morale. Oudinot's conscripts went to war with a high morale; give them a 7. If you fight the entire campaign, adjust a unit's morale based upon its battlefield experience. If it performs gallantly, promote it. A tabulation of such adjustments provides a fine diary of past battles when weary war-gamers gather around a glass of brandy to discuss the action at campaign's end.

Staff

Staffwork played an important role in the campaign. The French functioned relatively smoothly, although not without occasional errors, while slow transmittal of and response to orders plagued the Austrians. I suggest calculating fifteen minutes of real time for the French and thirty minutes for the Austrians for the passage of orders through each level in the chain of command. If one wants to incorporate Karl's presumed epilepsy (and face a real gaming challenge), roll a six-sided die every hour. On a roll of one, Karl falls prey to a fit and all subsequent orders for the day emanating from his headquarters require sixty minutes for the headquarters staff to prepare.

Provide for Napoleon's ability to "commit" one his aides (Mouton, Savary) to battle. A unit led by an aide should have enhanced morale.

Weather

The rainy April weather and the characteristic ground mist in this part of Bavaria influenced military events. Morning and evening should have restricted visibility. During the day there should be a good chance of periodic showers and the occasional thunderstorm like the one that put an end to the battle along the Teugen–Hausen ridge.

Forced Marches

The French showed much better marching ability. If you make strategic map moves before your tabletop encounters this ability should be included.

Terrain

If fighting historical encounters, extract the terrain features from the battle maps. If fighting imaginary encounters, remember that the rolling Bavarian countryside invariably provided defenders a good ridgeline position. Both defender and attacker should be able to conceal reserves behind elevations and in the numerous forests and woodlots common to this part of Bavaria. Open areas are cultivated, planted to potatoes, beets, and grains. Unlike most places in Europe, the woods are thick enough to preclude passage by cavalry and artillery. If incorporating one of the rivers, remember that they are narrow indeed, generally fordable to infantry but impassable in most places to cavalry and artillery due to their high banks. Villages tend to be small with a handful of stout stone and timber farms surrounded by wooden dwellings. The village center is dominated by a stone church with an onion dome.

The Teugen–Hausen Fight

Here is how I make out the order of appearance for Davout's fight along the Teugen–Hausen ridge:

Turn	French	Austrian
1	3d (2033)	Kayser's Bde (6000) 1 cav. reg.; 12 guns
2	57th (1934)	
4	7th Légère (2894)	Liechtenstein's Bde (4309); Vukassovich (1665)
5	10th Légère, 72d, 105th (6590); 30 guns	56 guns
7	Friant's Div (11,032)	
9		Bieber's Bde
10	Gudin's Div (11,071)	
12	12th (2085)	Grenadier Btn

APPENDIX V

The Battlefield Today

The tourist searching for a historical excursion off the beaten path will find a trip to the part of Bavaria featured in this book quite rewarding. But do not expect a clearly delineated, signposted tour; this is not the European way. Take battle maps with you, as you will have to work out the maneuvers for yourself. Sometimes frustrating, this has the advantage of offering the opportunity for real insight into the events of 1809.

Many tourists will arrive at the hub airport of Frankfurt. Drive south and follow the Romantische Strasse (Romantic Way) to one of the delightful medieval walled villages that dot the route to our theater of operations. Consult your guidebook, find lodgings, and relax as you recover from jet lag.

Refreshed, continue on to Ingolstadt. Napoleon arrived here on the eighteenth, the eve of Davout's fight along the Teugen–Hausen ridge. You should allocate time to visit the excellent Bavarian Army Museum (Bayerisches Armeemuseum, Schloss, Paradeplatz 4; take the Schloss exit and park; as of 1988 it was closed Mondays), where fine Napoleonic uniforms on display include three worn by Lefebvre's Bavarian divisional commanders. Be sure to ascend the stairways to the top, where there are some superb Seven Years' War dioramas using flats, including a huge Leuthen.

Proceed to Abensberg, where I suggest you establish headquarters for at least two days. It is a quiet, charming town centrally located for battlefield-touring purposes. In 1988 the Hotel Zum Kuchlbauer offered nice rooms at a reasonable price. The dining room was friendly (offering my wife bottomless cups of coffee while she awaited my return from a dawn reconnaissance) and the upstairs writing desks inspire. Eat one evening at d'Latern, where the cheese spatzle and mushroom dishes are extremely good. Here as elsewhere, avoid the German red wines and drink the *trocken* (dry) white wines.

251

Throughout the battlefield area, dirt paths cross the farmers' fields and woods. These paths are frequented by the hiking public, so feel no guilt about trespassing as long as you take care not to trample the crops.

On the first day drive to Saal and follow the river road to Bad Abbach. You pass through the Saal defile and realize how terribly vulnerable Davout's position was. A small Austrian force could easily have blocked him here. At Bad Abbach you can double back to Teugen or continue on toward Regensburg (Ratisbonne). Regensburg has sprawled well beyond its 1809 borders, but you can visit the town center and lose your way quite as easily as the French assault columns in the narrow, charming streets. The stone ice guards of the Danube bridge remain and a quick sortie over the river to Stadt-am-Hof reveals the problems of a cross-Danube assault.

The area around Teugen–Hausen should be your primary focus. Very little has changed. Walking the steep ridges while deploying the defending lines and batteries in one's mind teaches much about Davout's epic fight. A cross-country hike from Paring toward Eckmühl along one of the numerous walking paths allows you to follow Davout's progress on the twentieth. Return to Abensberg via Schierling and you will have covered the ground half the French participants traversed as they concentrated prior to the Battle of Eckmühl.

Begin day two of your tour by driving along the Abens to Siegenburg and return via the opposite bank. This covers the ground of Ludwig's fight against Lefebvre and the Württembergers. Now you should follow the advance to Landshut, choosing either Lannes' route or that of the Bavarians. Your goal is Landshut for lunch. Stops along the way can include Bachel, Rohr, and Rottemburg. Note the many excellent rear-guard positions that Hiller declined to use. In Landshut walk the bridge over which the majority of Karl's army passed on the sixteenth and Mouton led his assault column on the twentieth. Many of the buildings lining the river can be recognized from Mersent's presentation painting commissioned by the Emperor as a gift to his gallant aide.

Suitably refreshed (possibly with some of the fine Bavarian beer), follow Napoleon to Eckmühl via Route 15. You will arrive at Napoleon's first vantage point near Lindach and be able to survey a battlefield little changed from that memorable day in 1809. Below you lies the panoramic view described by Pelet (Chapter VIII). If you have time, turn to the northeast for a quick visit to Rogging. Lannes' attack followed the country lane leading to that small village. Returning to Lindach, descend to cross the Laber over the bridge where the Württemberg light infantry charged. The chateau has unfortunately been converted to a hospital; the remaining Napoleonic-era buildings are easily distinguished from more recent construction. Park and climb up the Bettel Berg. Its steepness will surprise. From its commanding summit, survey the field from the vantage point of an Austrian artilleryman. Return to your car and drive to the twin villages of Laichling, being sure to note the hanging woods on your right just before reaching the village. This is the woods that gave the Tenth Légère such difficulty. Take as much time as you can afford exploring the field, but leave a little in reserve to follow the French pursuit along Route 15. You will easily make out the hill (the Hohen Berg) between Eckmühl and Alt Eglofsheim used by that dauntless Hapsburg battery commander to delay the French. Arrive near dusk on the ground of the great cavalry combat at Alt Eglofsheim. It took place along the slopes just before the village. The village itself has a new housing development that encroaches on the battlefield.

This completes your tour. If you return via Frankfurt, try to detour to Rastatt, a town south of Karlsruhe. It houses the Wehrgeschichtliches Museum, in my opinion one of the three best repositories of Napoleonic uniforms on the Continent. Be sure to find the Württemberg light infantry uniform worn by Napoleon's gallant allies on their great day in 1809.

If in your travels you should turn west to visit the Paris area, you will of course want to see the Musée d'Armée. In addition, go to the Musée Napoleon in Fontainebleau. Here you will find many fine French uniforms and Napoleon's hat left on the ground when he was wounded at Ratisbonne. An aide named L'Monnier picked it up (the Mameluke Rouston fetched the Emperor another after Ivan treated the wound) and later left a certified note testifying that this is indeed the Ratisbonne hat! Alternatively, if your travels take you east toward Vienna (and its excellent Heeregeschtliches Museum) you can tour Aspern-Essling and Wagram . . . but that is the subject for a different book.

Notes

Chapter I

1. Christopher Duffy, *Austerlitz 1805* (London, 1977), p. 162.
2. The loss of prestige and power would be recognized formally the next year when Napoleon dissolved the Holy Roman Empire and Franz would be forced to change his title from Franz II of Germany to Franz I of Austria.
3. Clemens Metternich-Winneburg, *Memoirs of Prince Metternich* (New York, 1881), p. 367.
4. Ibid., p. 385.
5. Pasquier wrote in 1829: "I am convinced that the battle of Eylau had led M. de Talleyrand to reflect very seriously upon the weakness of a regime based solely on a life that was so often risked in the most dangerous enterprises." See Etienne-Denis Pasquier, *The Memoirs of Chancellor Pasquier* (Cranbury, N.J., 1968), p. 75.
6. *Memoirs Related to Fouché* (New York, 1912), p. 256. Although ghosted by another French writer, this account is guardedly reliable.
7. Ibid.
8. Metternich, p. 403.
9. Cited in Alan Palmer, *Metternich: Councillor of Europe* (London, 1972), p. 58.
10. Metternich, p. 409.
11. Ibid., p. 408.
12. Ibid., p. 416.
13. Ibid., p. 418.
14. Ibid., pp. 430–431.

15. Walter Langsam, *The Napoleonic Wars and German Nationalism in Austria* (New York, 1930), p. 72.
16. Metternich, p. 449.
17. John G. Gallagher, *The Iron Marshal: A Biography of Louis N. Davout* (London, 1976), pp. 163–164.
18. Ibid., p. 164.
19. Metternich, p. 451.
20. Ibid., p. 454.
21. Ibid., p. 458.
22. Jack F. Bernard, *Talleyrand: A Biography* (New York, 1973), p. 291.
23. Duff Cooper, *Talleyrand* (Stanford, Calif., 1967), p. 175.
24. Bernard, p. 192.
25. Ibid.
26. Ibid., p. 293.
27. J. Christopher Herold (ed.), *The Mind of Napoleon: A Selection from His Written and Spoken Words* (New York, 1955), p. 173.
28. Bernard, p. 295.
29. Ibid., p. 294.
30. Ibid., p. 296.
31. For further examples of this type of oratory see Langsam, p. 68.
32. Ibid., p. 115.
33. Pasquier, p. 77.
34. Metternich, p. 508.
35. Thiebault describes passing Napoleon on the road in Spain: "I was passed by Savary at full gallop and the Emperor, who was furiously whipping the hind quarters of his aide-de-camp's horse and spurring on his own." It is impossible to imagine any other head of state acting with such urgency.
36. Metternich, *Memoirs of Prince Metternich*, p. 511.
37. Hubert Cole, *Fouché: The Unprincipled Patriot* (New York, 1971), p. 183.
38. Bernard, p. 301.
39. Ibid., p. 301.
40. Ibid.
41. Ludwig, Comte de Lebzeltern, *Mémoires et Papiers de Lebzeltern, un Collaborateur de Metternich* (Paris, 1949), p. 69.
42. Metternich, p. 518.
43. Pierre-Marie Desmarest, *Quinze ans de haute police sous le consulat et l'empire* (Paris, 1900), p. 185.
44. Emile Dard, *Napoleon and Talleyrand* (New York, 1937), p. 205.
45. Ibid.
46. Herold, p. 159.

Chapter II

1. Otto von Pivka, *Armies of the Napoleonic Era* (New York, 1979), p. 60.
2. Austrian and French drill specified march and attack rates of 70 to 140 paces per minute, a pace equaling 22 inches. However, these rates presume peacetime passage over flat terrain. My time estimate is based on a battalion line charge over unequal, but not rough, terrain.
3. The influence of an army's recent past is great. Doctrine and drill come from earlier, often marginally relevant experience. To understand the influence of the Fredrickian period see Christopher Duffy, *The Army of Maria Theresa* (New York, 1977).
4. Gunther Rothenberg, *Napoleon's Great Adversaries* (Bloomington, Ind., 1982), p. 107.
5. David Chandler, *Dictionary of the Napoleonic Wars* (New York, 1979), p. 105.
6. This skirmish role during the battle was not according to doctrine. It is, however, what usually occurred during the Ratisbonne phase of the 1809 campaign.
7. General Karl Mack, cited in Rothenberg, p. 85.
8. Grunne's views are contained in an interesting analysis written after the war. See Edouard Gachot, *1809 Napoleon en Allemagne* (Paris, 1913), Appendix J.
9. Cited in Rothenberg, p. 130.
10. Charles Parquin, *Military Memoirs* (London, 1969), p. 90.
11. From the report of the French ambassador in Vienna; Dodun to Champagny, 13 April, 1809. Cited in Walter Langsam, *German Nationalism in Austria* (New York, 1930), p. 64.
12. Saint-Hilaire to Davout, 15 April 1809; in C.G.L. Saski, *La campagne de 1809* (Paris, 1899–1900), II, p. 184.
13. Rouguet notes that the third rank could fire to the right only with great difficulty (because of the limited traverse of the lead, left arm), while to the left they could fire at up to a 45-degree angle. See C. M. Rouguet, *L'officeur d'infanterie en campagne* (Paris, 1846), p. 11.
14. In many details the Austrian system was inferior to the French. Certain important evolutions, such as forming column from line, took longer to execute than comparable French maneuvers.
15. Another innovation, the battalion mass, had no utility in the rolling Bavarian countryside where the Ratisbonne campaign took place.
16. In theory the third rank of the line battalion could skirmish, but there is little evidence they did so during the Ratisbonne campaign.
17. A French test conducted under near-perfect conditions showed that at 100- to 400-meter increments, the carbine hit 40, 20, 1, and 0 percent of the time. See Rouguet, p. 10.
18. See General Stutterheim, *La Guerre de l'An 1809* (Vienna, 1811), p. xxvii.
19. Rothenberg, p. 113. Professor Rothenberg is the first modern historian to write in English about this very important omission in the Austrian drill.

20. Terrance Wise, *Artillery Equipment of the Napoleonic Wars* (London, 1979), p. 27.
21. For a full discussion of Napoleonic artillery see Wise's excellent work.
22. Rothenberg, p. 113.
23. J. Christopher Herold (ed.), *The Mind of Napoleon* (New York, 1955), p. 218.
24. Savary remarks that the heavy losses in the battles around Vienna were in part due to the fact the men were no longer those of the Grande Armée. Instead they maneuvered in heavier formations and consequently took much heavier losses from enemy artillery. See General A. Savary, *Mémoire sur l'Empire* (8 vols.; Paris, 1828 et. seq.).
25. Even the grenadiers for the newly created fourth battalions had to have served in two out of the four campaigns of Ulm, Austerlitz, Jena, and Friedland.
26. The status of the fourth battalions varied among the different French corps. In Davout's corps, before the 1808 reorganization each division had five regiments. Napoleon believed that twenty battalions would be too much for a divisional general to control. Therefore he ordered Davout's fourth battalions to form a so-called reserve division commanded by Demont.
27. Writing on leadership, Napoleon said "It is preferable to have much character and little intellect" as opposed to the reverse. Thus he made marshals out of such dull-witted but full-character men as Bessieres and Macdonald.
28. David Chandler, *The Campaigns of Napoleon* (New York, 1966), p. 370.
29. Napoleon to Berthier, 9 April 1809; Saski, II, pp. 36–39.
30. Even in 1807, one department in France found that over half its 2332 conscripts had to be exempted because of disabled limbs, deficiencies in sight or hearing, and tuberculosis. See René Boudard, "La Conscription Militaire et ses Problemes dans le Departement de la Creuse" in *Revue de L'Institut Napoleonic*, No. 145 (Paris: 1985/2), pp. 23–57.
31. See Maurice Hewson, *Escape from the French: Captain Hewson's Narrative* (Exeter, 1981), p. 100.
32. Petre notes the difficulty of calculating how many conscripts entered the ranks. See F. L. Petre, *Napoleon and the Archduke Charles* (London, 1976), pp. 21–22.
33. Meda to Friant, 13 April 1809; Saski, II, pp. 140–142.
34. Victor Dupuy, *Souvenirs Militaires* (Paris, 1892), p. 112.
35. See *Empires, Eagles, and Lions*, 70 (1 March 1983): 38–39.
36. Bavarian performance in 1812, a faraway campaign they had little reason to support, has obscured their solid performance in 1809.
37. Berthier to Lefebvre, 21 April 1809; Saski, II, p. 302.

Chapter III

1. Wrede to Oudinot, 7 April; in C.G.L. Saski, *La campagne de 1809* (Paris, 1899–1900), II, pp. 85–86.
2. See Saski, I, p. 401.
3. Maurice Hewson, *Escape from the French* (Exeter, 1981), p. 152. Hewson also comments on Austrian attitudes: Although border officials had preemptory orders

to return British escapees to France, he told Hewson that he always let them find asylum.

4. The term *order of battle* denotes an army organizational structure: who commands which units of what strength.

5. Andreossy to Ministre des Relations, 3 March 1809; Saski, I, pp. 258–259.

6. For example, in the Austrian Second Corps the French believed the Archduke Charles Legion had three battalions while in fact it had one; the other two battalions present belonged to jäger units.

7. The French summary is in Saski, I, p. 336. The modern source used was Scott Bowden and Charlie Tarbox, *Armies of the Danube 1809* (Arlington, Tex., 1980), p. 73.

8. Vincent J. Esposito and John Robert Elting, *A Military History and Atlas of the Napoleonic Wars* (New York, 1964), p. 93.

9. In 1808 Archduke Charles ordered the testing of an experimental telegraph intended to link the empire, using Vienna as a central hub. Based on a different design than Chappe's, it used flags and large wooden paddles, the system was not in place in time for the 1809 war. Had the system been finished it might have prevented some of the Hapsburg mistakes. See Ray Johnson, "Field Telegraphy in the Austrian Army" in *Empires, Eagles, and Lions*, 83 (October 1984).

10. Davout to Napoleon, 3 April 1809; Saski, II, p. 11.

11. Napoleon to Berthier, 10 April; Saski, II, pp. 122–23.

12. Unlike other historians of this campaign, particularly Bonnal and Petre, I feel Berthier was more sinned against than sinner. However, an indication of his lack of firm leadership during the crisis is provided in a letter written on 14 April to Davout. Asked for advice, Berthier responds: "I cannot give you any since I am not aware of your situation, after all of the marches and countermarches you have made."

13. Berthier to Napoleon, 14 April 1809; Saski, II, pp. 162–63.

Chapter IV

1. Gunther Rothenberg, *Napoleon's Great Adversaries* (Bloomington, Ind., 1982), p. 131.

2. Nearly every French diarist billeted in Germany comments on the comfortable life. For Davout's men during this period see Victor Dupuy, *Souvenirs Militaires* (Paris, 1892), p. 111.

3. Napoleon had also hand-picked an aide to establish an intelligence-gathering net at Passau. He even gave the aide specific instructions about what to do should Passau be besieged.

4. Edouard Gachot, *1809 Napoleon en Allemagne* (Paris, 1913) p. 43.

5. Napoleon completed the Paris-to-Strasbourg trip in fifty hours; Berthier, who departed Paris at 8:00 P.M., 31 March, required seventy-nine hours to complete the same journey. No continental general or statesman traveled like Napoleon.

6. Gachot, p. 49. Prince Louis commanded one of the three Bavarian divisions in Lefebvre's corps.
7. General Comte de Ségur, *Histoire et Mémoires* (Paris, 1873), III, p. 322.
8. Napoleon to Davout, Donauwerth, 17 April, 10:00 A.M.; in C. G. L. Saski, La campagne de 1809 (Paris, 1899–1900) II, p. 199.
9. For example, see Gachot, pp. 49–50.
10. Ibid., p. 57.
11. Wrede commanded the Austrian rear guard following the Battle of Hohenlinden, 3 December 1800.
12. F.L. Petre, *Napoleon and the Archduke Charles* (London, 1976), p. 88.
13. Ibid., p. 89.
14. Napoleon to Lefebvre, 18 April, 4:00 A.M.; Saski, II, p. 247.
15. Exchanging Hoffmeister's brigade for Dollmayer's brigade belonging to Vincent's division. For details see *Empires, Eagles, and Lions*, #85 (January 1985): p. 40.
16. J. Christopher Herold (ed.), *The Mind of Napoleon* (New York, 1955), p. 217.
17. Vincent J. Esposito and John Robert Elting, *A Military History and Atlas of the Napoleonic Wars* (New York, 1964), p. 95.
18. Napoleon to Masséna, Donauwerth, 18 April; Saski, II, pp. 241–242.
19. Ibid., p. 242.

Chapter V

1. John G. Gallagher, *The Iron Marshal* (London, 1976), p. 213.
2. From the Austrian gun line, the first French-held crestline appears uphill and blocks line of sight. Only the spires of Teugen can be seen; everything else behind the first crestline is hidden.
3. P. Berthezène, *Souvenirs Militaires* (Paris, 1855), Vol. III, p. 196.
4. Edouard Gachot, *1809 Napoleon en Allemagne* (Paris, 1913), p. 70.
5. For Lefebvre's digest of these interrogations see Lefebvre to Napoleon, 9:00 A.M., 19 April; in C.G.L. Saski, *La campagne de 1809* (Paris, 1899–1900), II, p. 267.
6. The Major General to the Duke of Danzig, 1:00 P.M., 19 April; Saski, II, p. 268.
7. Duke of Danzig to the Emperor, 10:00 P.M., 19 April; Saski, II, p. 270.
8. General Stutterheim, *La Guerre de l'An 1809* (Vienna, 1811), p. 167.
9. General Koch, *Mémoires de Masséna* (Paris, 1850), Vol. VI, p. 135.
10. Marcel Doher, *Charles de La Bedoyère, Aide-de-Camp de l'Empereur* (Paris, n.d.), p. 45.
11. French accounts greatly exaggerate this force. Koch speaks of a full division, commanded by a general, that boldly attacks Oudinot's advanced guard. A Major Scheibler actually commanded the outpost.
12. For this particular division, the next battle would be the absolute charnelhouse at Ebelsberg on 3 May where it would lose 25 percent of its men.
13. Napoleon to Masséna, Ingolstadt, 19 April, noon. Saski, II, pp. 250–251.

14. Ibid., p. 251.
15. General compte de Ségur, *Histoire et Mémoires* (Vol. III, Paris, 1873), p. 325 and duc de Rovigo, *Mémoires du Duc de Rovigo* (Vol. III, Paris, 1901), p. 66.
16. Rovigo, p. 64.

Chapter VI

1. C.G.L. Saski, *La campagne de 1809* (Paris, 1899–1900), II; p. 287. The importance of soldiers' loyalty to their regiment is seen in the grave reference to a consequence of defeat: dissolution of the regiment.
2. Baron de Marbot, *Memoirs of Baron Marbot* (London, 1892), Vol. I, p. 445.
3. Nominally, Vincent commanded the advance guard division. The command he took to Rohr comprised two line brigades from two separate Sixth Corps divisions, another example of the amazing muddle the Austrians could work themselves into even during an unopposed march.
4. General Stutterheim, *La Guerre de l'An 1809* (Vienna, 1811), p. 184.
5. Edouard Gachot, *1809 Napoleon en Allemagne* (Paris, 1913), p. 81.
6. Ibid., p. 80.
7. Ibid.
8. J.J. Pelet, *Mémoires sur la Guerre de 1809* (Paris, 1824), Vol. II, p. 10.
9. Montbrun to Davout, 21 April, 6:00 A.M.; Saski, II, p. 307.
10. Coutard to Davout, 20 April, 10:00 P.M.; Saski, II, p. 306.
11. Pelet, Vol. II, p. 21.
12. Stutterheim, pp. 197–198.

Chapter VII

1. Berthier to Lefebvre, Rohr, 21 April, 5:00 A.M.; in C.G.L. Saski, *La campagne de 1809* (Paris, 1899–1900), p. 302.
2. Napoleon to Davout, Rohr, 21 April, 5:00 A.M., Saski, II, pp. 304–305.
3. Departing Vohburg at 11:00 A.M., the trains reached Langquaid at 2:00 A.M., 22 April, an impressive twenty-five miles in fifteen hours.
4. Davout had Friant (minus one battalion on the Altmühl), Saint-Hilaire, four squadrons of light cavalry from Montbrun, and eight squadrons of cuirassiers versus Hohenzollern (minus Thierry) and Vukassovich and Rosenberg. An Austrian battalion was considerably larger than a French one.
5. Lefebvre to Napoleon, Langquaid, 9:00 A.M.; Saski, II, p. 319. Thus Lefebvre provided independent confirmation of Davout's claims that the French Third Corps faced the bulk of the Austrian army.
6. Louis Friant, *Vie Militaire* (Paris, 1857), p. 167.
7. An odd characteristic of this day's combat was that at the point of attack both sides seemed to feel the enemy had artillery superiority.
8. General Stutterheim, *La Guerre de l'An 1809* (Vienna, 1811), p. 219.

9. Napoleon to Davout, 21 April 1809; Saski, II, p. 304.

10. Ibid.

11. Montbrun to Davout, 21 April, 6:00 A.M.; Saski, II, pp. 306–307.

12. Montbrun to Davout, in front of Dinzling, 3:30 P.M.; Saski, II, p. 310.

13. Minus the two voltigéur companies on the Altmühl, thirteen French voltigéur companies—say 1500 men—versus four Grenzer battalions probably in excess of 2000 men. The ease of the French success is striking.

14. *Rapport Historique des Operation du 3e Corps de l'Armée d'Allemagne;* Saski, II, p. 312.

15. Stutterheim (pp. 221–222) makes the French 32,000; I calculate it closer to 34,000.

16. *Lettres du Commandant Coudreux à son Frère* (Paris, 1908), p. 148.

17. Friant, p. 167.

18. While Davout calls them Hungarians, no such units were in the Austrian Fourth Corps. Probably they were grenzers, some of whom also wore blue pants. In their skirmish role, grenzers would be more likely to be out in front.

19. Davout actually wrote his analysis on the back of originals sent from Montbrun to Davout.

20. Davout to Napoleon, 21 April, between 10:00 and 11:00 A.M.; Saski, II, p. 308.

21. Davout to Napoleon, Paring, 21 April; Saski, II, p. 309. The report does not include a dispatch time but seems to have been sent between 2:00 and 3:00 P.M.

22. Friant's report written from the bivouacs near Ober-Sanding, 22 April 1809; Saski, II, p. 317.

23. Edouard Gachot, *1809 Napoleon en Allemagne* (Paris 1913), p. 84.

24. Nowhere did the tremendous bulk of the Hapsburg supply train harm the army more than here. Each line regiment carried thirteen four-horse wagons and twenty-six pack animals for their food alone. Add the vehicles and horses for the regiments' ammunition as well as the requirements for the artillery and cavalry and the tremendous size of the jam-up at Landshut becomes apparent. For information on the Austrian train see Scott Bowden and Charlie Tarbox, *Armies on the Danube* (Arlington, Tex., 1980), p. 11–12.

25. General compte de Ségur, *Histoire et Mémoires* (Paris, 1873), Vol. III, p. 326.

26. Stutterheim, p. 205.

27. Victor Dupuy, *Souvenirs Militaires* (Paris, 1892), p. 115.

28. F.L. Petre, *Napoleon and the Archduke Charles* (London, 1976), p. 152.

29. Baron de Marbot, *Memoirs of Baron de Marbot* (London, 1892), Vol. I, p. 371.

30. Charles Thoumas, *Le Maréchal Lannes* (Paris, 1891), p. 284.

31. In the 1808 reorganization Napoleon first acknowledged the position of the sappers as an integral part of the head of the infantry columns. Every battalion was to have four, commanded by a sapper corporal. They were to clear hedges, fences, gates, and the like to permit the column to advance.

32. Marbot, I, p. 372. Mouton continued to distinguish himself in the campaign around Vienna, where he was wounded again and elevated to the imperial nobility.

33. The *pas de course*.
34. During the campaign around Vienna Napoleon said of Sainte-Croix: "I have never . . . met a more capable officer, nor one who understood my thought quicker and executed it better." See Marbot, II, p. 5.
35. General Koch, *Mémoires de Masséna* (Paris, 1850), Vol. VI, p. 159.
36. Clapardes' failure on this day may explain the suicidal fervor with which he launched his troops into the caldron at Ebelsberg on 3 May. At Ebelsberg his division suffered 25 percent losses.
37. This account is from Stutterheim, pp. 208–209. Information on the Deutchmeister regiment is from Bowden and Tarbox, p. 24.
38. These figures are according to Stutterheim. The First Bulletin of the Army of Germany claimed thirty cannon and 9000 prisoners (undoubtedly an exaggeration), while Saski notes thirteen cannon abandoned in Landshut.
39. Victor Dupuy, *Souvenirs Militaires* (Paris, 1892), pp. 115–116.
40. Ibid., pp. 112–113.
41. Ibid., p. 113.

Chapter VIII

1. Napoleon to Davout, Landshut, 22 April 1809; in C.G.L. Saski, *La campagne de 1809* (Paris, 1899–1900), II, pp. 335–336.
2. J. Christopher Herold (ed.), *The Mind of Napoleon* (New York, 1955), p. 220.
3. Napoleon to Davout, Landshut, 22 April; Saski, II, pp. 336–337.
4. *Les Mémoires de Jef Abbeel* (Brussels, 1971), p. 84. He was a carabinier present in the courtyard.
5. General Koch, *Mémoires de Masséna* (Paris 1850), Vol. VI, p. 166.
6. The officer is unnamed undoubtedly because this incident later became a sore subject. It was probably Stutterheim or a fellow officer in the advance guard division.
7. Vukassovich's men included elements of Moritz Liechtenstein's and Pfanzelter's brigades. They had fought continuously since the nineteenth and were greatly depleted. Bieber's brigade of the Third Corps was largely intact, while the Hungarian grenadiers had not yet engaged.
8. Pierre Berthezène, *Souvenirs Militaires* (Paris, 1855), Vol. III, p. 206. He commanded the Tenth Légère at this time.
9. Friant uses the term to describe his men's advance. See Compte Louis Friant, *Vie Militaire* (Paris, 1857), p. 172.
10. As opposed to the Bavarian cavalry, which fought well and suffered moderate losses, 194 out of about 1000; the infantry lost only slightly more than 600 out of 7000.
11. Schierling had remained a no-man's-land following the combat the previous evening.
12. On the twenty-first and twenty-second, they marched about fifty miles.
13. Koch mentions that shortly thereafter Masséna rode forward to join Vandamme.

Because of Vandamme's tactical skill the marshal quickly realized he was not needed on this front and rode elsewhere. See Koch, p. 169.

14. J.J. Pelet, *Mémoires sur la Guerre de 1809* (Paris, 1824), Vol. II, pp. 78–79. Pelet was present at this sight.

15. Koch, p. 167.

16. Rovigo remarks that "he should have been killed a thousand times, yet had only lost an arm." See Rovigo, *Mémoires du Duc de Rovigo* (Paris, 1901), Vol. III, p. 72.

17. The regiment suffered so severely that it was apparently not reformed for the later campaign around Vienna.

18. French participants and some authors variously describe the final assault as an all-French charge or as led by French officers. I believe this is rampant nationalism and have relied upon Gachot and the Württemberger's battle report for my version. For the entire day the Württemberg light infantry brigade suffered 177 casualties, a figure indicative of serious but not desperate combat. See Edouard Gachot, *1809 Napoleon en Allemagne* (Paris, 1913), p. 99.

19. General compte de Ségur, *Histoires et Mémoires* (Paris, 1873), Vol. III, p. 327.

20. Ibid.

21. Certain authors have Cervoni dying in the Emperor's arms. This is propaganda. Ségur and Marbot, both present, agree on the facts as presented.

22. Pelet, p. 84.

23. Saski, II, p. 345.

24. Several spectators mention this ringing noise.

25. For a detailed account of this charge see Saski, II, p. 354.

26. Ibid. Their cheers are recalled by a Württemberg squadron leader who observed the charge.

27. This is the only mention in Stutterheim's account of the use of the battalion mass formation. See General Stutterheim, *La Guerre de l'An 1809* (Vienna, 1811), p. 253.

28. The losses are taken from ibid., p. 231.

29. "Premier Bulletin de L'Armée D'Allemagne," in Saski, II, p. 342.

Chapter IX

1. Friant believed that his maneuver forced the Austrians to retreat from the Eckmühl position. Actually, it was the capture of the Bettel Berg that precipitated the Austrian withdrawal. See Compte Louis Friant, *Vie Militaire* (Paris, 1857), pp. 172–173.

2. In C.G.L. Saski, *La campagne de 1809* (Paris, 1899–1900), II, p. 348. Friant's after-action report is provided in full.

3. Ibid., p. 345. Saint-Hilaire's aide-de-camp's report is provided in full. Saint-Hilaire died at Aspern–Essling and thus never wrote an after-action report.

4. Ibid., p. 346.

5. Charles A., Thoumas, *Les Grands Cavaliers du Premier Empire* (Paris, 1892), II, p. 37.

6. Saski, II, p. 356.
7. J.J. Pelet, *Mémoires sur la Guerre de 1809* (Paris, 1824), II, p. 92.
8. General Stutterheim, *La Guerre de l'An 1809* (Vienna, 1811), p. 263.
9. Pelet, p. 97.

Chapter X

1. The Austrian decline in morale is evidenced by the experience of Saint-Sulpice's cuirassier division. The division was barely engaged during the twenty-third even though it marched in direct support of Nansouty's spearhead. If Nansouty's 4000 or so men could thrash Stutterheim's screen and then push back the fresh cavalry of the Austrian reserve corps without calling on the assistance of Saint-Sulpice, the Austrians must have fought with somewhat less than their usual èlan.
2. Duc de Rovigo, *Mémoires du Duc de Rovigo* (Paris, 1901), Vol. III, p. 75.
3. It is a significant indication of the ravages of disease during the Napoleonic wars that here, during a springtime war of maneuver—one of the healthiest types of campaign—the highest-ranking French medical officer should have contracted typhus.
4. J.J. Pelet, *Mémoires sur la Guerre de 1809* (Paris, 1824), II, p. 106.
5. Baron de Marbot, *Memoirs of Baron de Marbot* (London, 1892), Vol. I; p. 383.
6. P. Berthezène, *Souvenirs Militaires* (Paris, 1855), Vol. II, p. 212.
7. General compte de Ségur, *Histoire et Mémoires* (Paris, 1873), Vol. III, pp. 329–330.
8. Marbot, p. 385.
9. Ibid.
10. Ibid.
11. Ibid., p. 386.
12. In C.G.L. Saski, *La campagne de 1809* (Paris, 1899–1900), II, p. 375.

Chapter XI

1. Grunne's entire letter is contained in Edouard Gachot, *1809 Napoleon en Allemagne* (Paris, 1913), appendix J, p. 429.
2. Ibid.
3. F.L. Petre, *Napoleon and the Archduke Charles* (London, 1976), p. 227.
4. Armand de Caulaincourt, *With Napoleon in Russia* (New York, 1935), p. 376.
5. J. Christopher Herold (ed.), *The Mind of Napoleon* (New York, 1955), p. 175.
6. Ibid.
7. Talking to Caulaincourt in 1813, Napoleon addressed the failure at Erfurt and attributed it to betrayal by Marshal Lannes. He had no idea it was Talleyrand. See Caulaincourt, pp. 376–380.
8. In 1813 Napoleon commented "My affairs always prospered when Talleyrand was handling them. . . . Better than anyone else, he understood France and Europe." See Jack F. Bernard, *Talleyrand* (New York, 1973), p. 280.

9. Dorothy Gies McGuigan, *Metternich and the Duchess: The Public and Private Lives at the Congress of Vienna* (New York, 1975), p. 462.

10. In 1805, when Talleyrand attempted to negotiate peace after Austerlitz, he proposed terms similar to those discussed before the battle. Napoleon responded that the terms offered before a battle can't be offered after a victory.

11. Caulaincourt, p. 278.

12. Herold, p. 42.

13. Ibid., p. 159.

14. Hubert Cole, *Fouché* (New York, 1971), p. 200.

15. Caulaincourt, p. 340.

16. Herold, p. 175.

17. McGuigan, p. 270.

18. Josephine B. Stearns, *The Role of Metternich in Undermining Napoleon* (Urbana, Ill., 1948), papière I-2, p. 247.

19. Herold, p. 74.

20. Ibid., p. 76.

21. Henry Lachouque, *Napoleon's Battles* (New York, 1967), p. 220.

22. *Napoleon's Own Memoirs* (London, 1823), p. 89.

23. General Thomas Graham, *The History of the Campaign of 1796 in Germany and Italy* (London, 1800); Vol. I, p. 372.

24. Ibid., p. 337.

25. Herold, p. 217.

26. David G. Chandler, *The Campaigns of Napoleon* (New York, 1966), p. 149.

27. Grunne to the Prince de Ligne, 28 September 1809; in Edouard Gachot, *1809 Napoleon en Allemagne* (Paris 1913), appendix J.

28. For a review of this possibility see F.L. Petre, *Napoleon and the Archduke Charles* (London, 1976), pp. 143–144.

29. Personal correspondence from Professor Rothenberg dated 2 May 1988.

30. Delbruck, cited in Gunther Rothenberg, *Napoleon's Great Adversaries* (Bloomington, Ind., 1982), p. 124.

31. For details see G. Peyrusse, *Lettres Inedites* (Paris, 1894), p. 18.

32. *Napoleon's Own Memoirs*, p. 245.

33. General Bonnal, *La Manœvre de Landshut* (Paris, 1905), p. 127.

34. Bonnal, citing Pelet. See Bonnal, p. 358.

35. *Memoirs of Madam Junot, Duchess of Abrantès* (London, 1901), Vol. III., p. 147.

36. See "Premier Bulletin de l'Armée d'Allemagne"; in Saski, II, p. 341.

37. General Koch, *Mémoires de Masséna* (Paris, 1850), Vol. VI, p. 153.

38. Comte Louis Friant, *Vie Militaire* (Paris, 1857), p. 165.

39. Many soldiers did break down and dissolve into bands of marauders during the coming march to Vienna.

40. *Lettres du Commandant Coudreux a son Frère* (Paris, 1908), p. 150.

41. For Savary's complete analysis of this decline see Saski, III, pp. 351–352.

42. Herold, p. 40.

43. Ibid., p. 257.

Appendix I

1. Dorothy Gies McGuigan, *Metternich and the Duchess: The Public and Private Lives at the Congress of Vienna* (New York, 1975), p. 494.
2. McGuigan, p. 461.
3. Binder v. Krieglstein, cited in Petre, *Napoleon and the Archduke Charles,* p. 242.

Bibliographic Note

It must be admitted that the true truths are very difficult to ascertain in history.

Historical fact, which is so often invoked . . . is often a mere word: it cannot be ascertained when events actually occur, in the heat of contrary passions; and if, later on, there is a consensus, this is only because there is no one left to contradict.

In all such things there are two very distinct essential elements—material fact and moral intent. Material facts, one should think, ought to be incontrovertible; and yet, go and see if any two accounts agree. . . . As for moral intent, how is one to find his way, supposing even that the narrators are in good faith? And what if they are promoted by bad faith, self-interest, and bias? Suppose I have given an order: who can read the bottom of my thought, my true intention? And yet everybody will take hold of that order, measure it by his own yardstick, make it bend to conform to his plans. . . . And everybody will be so confident of his own version! The lesser mortals will hear of it from privileged mouths, and they will be so confident in turn! Then the flood of memoirs, diaries, anecdotes, drawing room reminiscences! And yet, my friend, that is history![1]

—Napoleon, 1816

Napoleon viewed history with great suspicion. He referred to it as "agreed-upon fiction." It is a useful warning for the historian.

Crisis on the Danube has two story lines, the diplomatic and the military.

1. J. Christopher Herold (ed.), *The Mind of Napoleon* (New York, 1955), pp. 50–51.

Accurately portraying the diplomatic history has been the more difficult challenge. Two major memoirs, Talleyrand's and Metternich's, were written at a time
when neither felt able to commit the whole truth to paper. They wrote with one
eye toward pleasing the King and Emperor, respectively, and one eye toward
securing their own places in history. Telling their story requires careful compari-
son of their accounts with the statements of their contemporaries. Since both
practiced deception with matchless skill, one can never be certain one has arrived
at the truth. Unlike the military chapters, the diplomatic chapter makes extensive
use of secondary sources, the best of which in this context are Bernard, Cole,
Cooper, and Dard.

Military men write with a view toward history as well. While the historian can
obtain reports written while events were still fresh, these primary sources are
biased. Officers wanted to be promoted and wrote their reports accordingly.
Professional jealousies, honest confusion, and a host of other human characteristics color their accounts. The historian nears the truth by comparing the officers'
assertions contained in their official reports with eyewitness testimony from diaries, letters, amd memoirs. For the military chapters I have based all assertions
upon primary source material. Secondary sources provided technical detail about
weaponry and biographical background.

The correspondence and after-action reports for the French are in volumes I
and II of Saski's wonderful compilation. The Austrian side is best told by Stutterheim, who, although writing in 1811, provides a remarkably honest account.

For all military decisions I have tried to examine events from three perspec-
tives: What information did the participants possess at the time they made a
decision? How did they assess this information? and What was the actual situation? It is easy to criticize a decision with the clarity of hindsight. Only when he
identifies the incomplete and often misleading information that a commander
possessed at the time of decision can the historian arrive at a balanced judgment of
a command performance. Near-exclusive reliance upon primary sources occasionally causes frustrating uncertainties. Yet it seems the only way to avoid writing
a mere "agreed-upon fiction."

The following bibliography only contains citations that contributed to the
book. Sources consulted and then either rejected or not used are not included.

The two best Napoleonic collections I am aware of in the United States are at
the U.S. Army Military History Institute in Carlisle, Pennsylvania, and at the
Library of Congress.

Bibliography

Primary Sources

Abbeel, Jef. *Les Mémoires de Jef Abbeel* in *L'Odyssee d'un Carabinier à Cheval.* Edited by René Willams, Brussels: 1971.

Aubry, Captain. *Souvenirs du 12e Chasseurs.* Paris: 1889.

Berthezène, P. *Souvenirs Militaires,* Vol. III. Paris: 1855.

Bourrienne, Louis de. *Memoirs of Napoleon Bonaparte,* Vol. III. New York: 1891.

Caulaincourt, Armand de. *With Napoleon in Russia.* New York: 1935.

Desmarest, Pierre-Marie. *Quinze ans de haute police sous le consulat et l'empire.* Paris: 1900.

Desmarest, Pierre-Marie. *Temoignages Historiques.* Paris: 1833.

Dienst reglement für die kaiserlich-königliche Cavallerie. Vienna: 1807.

Dupuy, Victor. *Souvenirs Militaires.* Paris: 1892.

Exercier-Reglement für die kaiserlich-königliche Infanterie. Vienna: 1807.

Fouché, Joseph. *Memoirs Relating to Fouché.* New York: 1912.

Friant, Lieutenant-General Compte Louis. *Vie Militaire.* Paris: 1857.

Graham, Thomas. *The History of the Campaign of 1796 in Germany and Italy.* London: 1800.

271

Hewson, Maurice. *Escape from the French: Captain Hewson's Narrative.* Exeter, Great Britain: 1981.

Junot, Madame. *Memoirs of Madam Junot, Duchess of Abrantés,* Vol. III. London: 1901.

Koch, General. *Mémoires de Masséna,* 7 vols. Paris: 1850.

Laborde, *Histoire de la Guerre d'Autriche en 1809.* Paris: 1823.

Larrey, D. J. *Mémoires et Campagnes de Chirugie Militaire.* Paris: 1812.

Lebzeltern, Ludwig Comte de. *Mémoires et Papiers de Lebzeltern, un Collaborateur de Metternich.* Paris: 1949.

Lettres du Commandant Coudreux à son Frère. Paris: 1908.

Lettres Inedites de Guillaume Peyrusse. Paris: 1894.

Marbot, Baron de. *Memoirs of Baron de Marbot,* 2 vols., London: 1892.

Mémoires Militaires du Baron Seruzier. Paris: 1823.

Metternich-Winneburg, Clemens. *Memoirs of Prince Metternich: 1773–1859.* New York: 1881.

Napoleon's Own Memoirs. London: 1823.

Pasquier, Etienne-Denis. *Histoire de mon temps.* Paris: 1894.

Pasquier, Etienne-Denis. *The Memoirs of Chancellor Pasquier.* Cranbury, N.J.: 1968.

Parquin, Charles. *Military Memoirs.* London: 1969.

Pelet, J. J. *Mémoires sur la Guerre de 1809,* Vol. II. Paris: 1824.

Rovigo, Duc de. *Memoires du Duc de Rovigo,* Vol. III. Paris: 1901.

Rouguet, C. M. *L'officeur d'infanterie en campagne.* Paris: 1846.

Ségur, La General Comte de. *Histoire et Mémoires,* Vol. III. Paris: 1873.

Stutterheim, General. *La Guerre de l'An 1809.* Vienna: 1811.

Secondary Sources

Angeli, Moriz Edlin von. *Erzherzog Carl,* 5 vols. Vienna: 1896–1897.

Bernard, Jack F. *Talleyrand: A Biography.* New York: 1973.

Bessières, Albert. *Le Bayard de la Grande Armée.* Paris: 1952.

Bonnal, General H. *La Manœuvre de Landshut.* Paris: 1905.

Boudard, René. "La Conscription Militaire et ses Problemes dans le Départment de la Creuse," in *Revue de L'Institut Napoleonic* 145 (1985–2), Paris.

Bowden, Scott, and Charlie Tarbox. *Armies of the Danube 1809.* Arlington, Texas: 1980.

Brinton, Crane. *The Life of Talleyrand.* New York: 1936.

Chandler, David G. *The Campaigns of Napoleon*. New York: 1966.

Chandler, David G. *Dictionary of the Napoleonic Wars*. New York: 1979.

Cole, Hubert. *Fouché: The Unprincipled Patriot*. New York: 1971.

Cooper, Alfred Duff. *Talleyrand*. Stanford, Calif.: 1967.

Criste, Oskar. *Erzherzog Carl von Osterreich*, 3 vols. Vienna–Leipzig: 1912.

Dard, Emile. *Napoleon and Talleyrand*. New York: 1937.

Doher, Marcel. *Charles de La Bedoyère, Aide-de-Camp de l'Empereur*. Paris: n.d.

Duffy, Christopher. *The Army of Maria Theresa*. New York: 1977.

Duffy, Christopher. *Austerlitz 1805*. London: 1977.

Elmer, Alexandre. *Schulmeister: L'agent secret de Napoleon*. Paris: 1932.

Esposito, General Vincent J. and Colonel John Elting. *Military History and Atlas of the Napoleonic Wars*. New York: 1964.

Gachot, Edouard. *1809 Napoleon en Allemagne*. Paris: 1913.

Gallagher, John G. *The Iron Marshal: A Biography of Louis N. Davout*. London: 1976.

Herold, J. Christopher (ed.). *The Mind of Napoleon: A Selection from His Written and Spoken Words*. New York: 1955.

Holtman, Robert B. *Napoleonic Propaganda*. Baton Rouge, La.: 1950.

Johnson, Ray. "Field Telegraphy in the Austrian Army," *Empires, Eagles, and Lions*, 83 (October 1984).

Kriegsarchiv Wien. *Krieg 1809*, 4 vols. Vienna: 1907–1910.

Lachouque, Henry. *Napoleon's Battles*. New York: 1967.

Langsam, Walter. *The Napoleonic Wars and German Nationalism in Austria*. New York: 1930.

Martinien, Aristide. *Tableaux par Corps et par Batailles des Officiers Tues et Blessés pendant les Guerres de l'Empire*. Paris: 1899.

McGuigan, Dorothy Gies. *Metternich and the Duchess: The Public and Private Lives at the Congress of Vienna*. New York: 1975.

Meynier, Albert. "Levées et Pertes D'Hommes sous le Consulat et l'Empire," *Revue des Études*, 30 (1930) Paris.

Muller, Paul. *L'Espionnage Militaire sous Napoleon I*. Paris: 1896.

Palmer, Alan. *Metternich: Councillor of Europe*. London: 1972.

Petre, F. L. *Napoleon and the Archduke Charles*. London: 1976.

Rothenberg, Gunther. *Napoleon's Great Adversaries*. Bloomington, Ind.: 1982.

Saski, C. G. L. *La campagne de 1809*, 3 vols. Paris: 1899–1900.

Savant, Jean. *Les Espions de Napoleon.* Paris: 1957.

Stearns, Josephine B. *The Role of Metternich in Undermining Napoleon.* Urbana, Ill.: 1948.

Ternaux-Compans, M. (ed.). *Le General Compans.* Paris: 1912.

Thoumas, Charles A. *Les Grand Cavaliers du Premier Empire.* Paris: 1892.

Thoumas, Charles A. *Le Marechal Lannes.* Paris: 1891.

von Pivka, Otto. *Armies of the Napoleonic Era.* New York: 1979.

Wise, Terrance. *Artillery Equipment of the Napoleonic Wars.* London: 1979.

Index

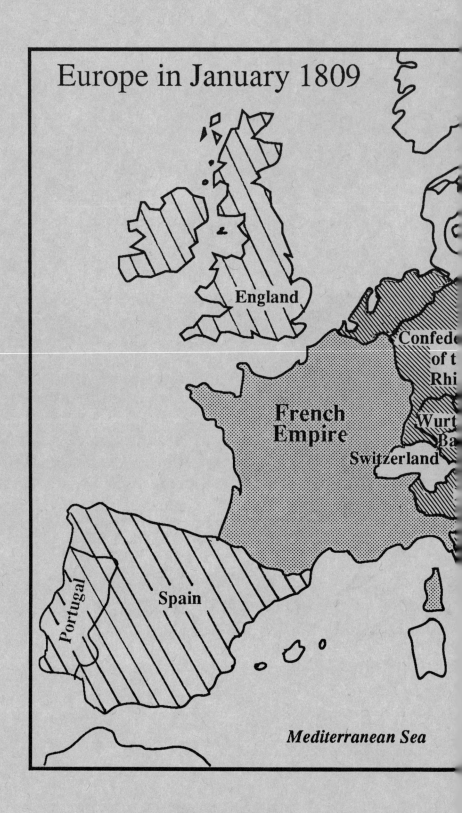

Europe in January 1809

England

Confede
of t
Rhi

French
Empire

Wurt
Ba

Switzerland

Portugal

Spain

Mediterranean Sea